PASTORAL CARE IN WORSHIP

PASTORAL CARE IN WORSHIP

LITURGY AND PSYCHOLOGY
IN DIALOGUE

NEIL PEMBROKE

t&t clark

Published by T&T Clark International

A Continuum Imprint
The Tower Building, 11 York Road, London SE1 7NX
80 Maiden Lane, Suite 704, New York, NY 10038

www.continuumbooks.com

British Library Cataloguing-in-Publication Data
A catalogue record for this book is available from the British Library

ISBN: 978-0-567-26265-3 (Hardback)
978-0-567-33144-1 (Paperback)

Typeset by Newgen Imaging Systems Pvt Ltd, Chennai, India
Printed and bound in Great Britain by CPI Antony Rowe,
Chippenham, Wiltshire

Contents

Contents

Introduction

Personal ministry to individuals and to family units is an important dimension of pastoral care. Over the last 50 years we have seen some very fine works produced that focus on various aspects of pastoral counseling. The pastoral ministry has been greatly enriched by these contributions to theory and practice. However, it is now quite widely acknowledged that we may have accorded this particular dimension a more central role than is warranted. A consequence of this is that other dimensions have received less attention than they deserve. Principal amongst these is the role of the faith community in providing care. The gathered congregation has at its disposal rich resources to share with those who are in need of care, guidance, and nurture. As the members of the congregation minister to each other, they first of all bring their own personal gifts. And second, they participate in the gifts of prayer and worship, preaching, and the sacraments that are offered by the Church. In this book, I make a contribution to the growing movement to expand and enrich the role of the community of faith in pastoral care.[1] In particular, my intention is to reflect in a fresh manner on the way in which the community operates as an expression of care as it gathers for Sunday worship.

As soon as we begin to move into the area of liturgy as pastoral care, however, we need to be careful lest we lose sight of the chief aim and end of worship. Worship is not primarily a therapeutic endeavor. The healing of people who are hurting is not the primary focus in worship; praise of God and an encounter with divine grace sit at the center. Authentic worship is theocentric. God is both the subject and the object of worship.[2] God is the One to whom all our praise, thanksgiving, confession, and supplication are directed. We can therefore speak of God as the object of our worship. However, God is also the motive force behind our prayers, songs, preaching, and ritual actions. Christ perfects our prayer as he represents us before God our Maker. The Spirit prompts our prayer in the first place and then takes our inarticulate expressions and inchoate yearnings and offers them to God on our behalf. God is therefore also the subject of worship. From start to finish, worship is a theocentric event.

Another way of expressing the true nature of worship is to say that it constitutes our response to the gracious initiative of God.[3] The essential nature of God is self-communication. God's deep desire is to communicate Godself in love to humankind. In the Hebrew Scriptures, we read of the way in which God's self-giving love was expressed in the making of a series of gracious covenants. The people of Israel had the great privilege and responsibility of living in and through a covenantal relationship with YHWH. God's self-communication reached its apogee in the covenant established in and through the death, resurrection, and exaltation of Christ. In the old and new covenants, we see the full depth and breadth of God's grace and mercy. The only fitting response is the unreserved offering up of a joyful sacrifice of praise.

God's gracious initiative, then, occupies center stage in the act of worship. Our role is to respond with joy and thanksgiving as we engage again and again with the narratives that celebrate God's unsurpassed loving kindness and mercy. Our attention should be given to opening ourselves to God in order that we might be moved to worship God in spirit and in truth.

Given that this is the true nature of worship, how is it possible to talk about worship as a pastoral act without falling into using worship for our own ends? Does the notion of worship as pastoral care lead us inexorably to a focus on self rather than on God? Ronald Byars has captured the essence of the problem:

> Worship that aims to be therapeutic . . . is anthropocentric by definition. I, the worshiper, stand at the center . . . However much I may be moved or engaged by the novelty of worship that focuses on me, it will in the end leave me spiritually malnourished.[4]

Byars is absolutely right. The only worship that is spiritually nourishing is that which is theocentric in orientation. For this reason, I take the position that the sacrifice of praise is the central act in worship; pastoral care is a support act. Or to change the metaphor, "the pastoral care that occurs as we are meeting and being met by God in worship is a significant by-product . . ."[5] When people come together faithfully and lovingly to worship God, they create a unique space for the operation of divine grace and mercy.

Having declared my position on the relationship between worship and pastoral care, I now want to discuss the scope of the project. The simplest way to do this is to say what this book is not. This is not, first, a book on the pastoral element in "occasional offices" such as baptisms, weddings, and funerals. Others have already covered this topic very well.[6] Nor is it a book that majors on preaching and pastoral care—as important as this is. Again, there are a number of fine treatments of this aspect already available.[7] What this research *is* about is the pastoral dimension in weekly congregational worship. I have selected for treatment four themes that are of crucial importance in this domain—namely, reconciliation, lament, hope, and communion. Clearly this is not an exhaustive list. Grief and loss, guidance, nurture, healing, compassion, justice, and more could be added. In my view, however, the themes that I have selected take us to the heart of the issue of worship as pastoral care and, furthermore, have an association (direct or indirect) with virtually any pastoral concern that one might choose to name.

In developing these four themes, my method is to set up a dialogue between liturgical, biblical, and systematic theology on the one hand, and empirical and psychotherapeutic psychology on the other. The purpose in adopting psychology as a conversation partner is, of course, to move theology out of its well-worn tracks. The four themes that I am working with have been covered extensively by practical, biblical, and systematic theologians. Introducing a psychological perspective has the benefit of casting new light. As I went through the exercise of coming at a theme from both a theological and a psychological angle, I found myself being led down a track that was quite new and interesting—different to the tracks that I had been following through reading the available literature. In following me along these paths, I hope that you will have a similar experience.

Reconciliation with God and neighbor has always been a central pastoral concern. This theme is picked up in Part 1. Within the general area of confession of sin, we will be concentrating on the specific issue of **self-diminishment**. Further, two particular forms of self-diminishment will be discussed. First, there is the diminution of self that is associated with sin in the form of sloth. We have a tendency to do just enough to convince ourselves and others that we are righteous. A first step in overcoming this propensity is coming to a point of self-awareness. Psychologists have demonstrated that the use of a mirror in laboratory experiments makes it much less likely that a person will lapse into moral hypocrisy. Following this lead, an approach to the liturgy of confession that centers on Christ the mirror is offered.

The second form of self-diminishment that is addressed in the first part is that which is associated with shame. Psychologists point out that a propensity for shame typically leads a person to adopt a safe, controlled, and predictable approach to life. Hiding from life is not consonant with our God-given vocation. This tendency, it will be argued, needs to be recognized in our liturgies of confession. Another element is included, however. In order to experience healing, shame-prone people need, more than anything else, acceptance and affirmation. With this in mind, an approach to opening confessants to the affirming gaze of God will be presented.

In Part 2, the theme of lament is discussed. The tradition of protest against God has been largely lost to Western Christianity. This is most regrettable, because there is ample evidence that in the midst of suffering and distress people of faith often experience anger against God. The Church needs to offer an adequate pastoral response to those feeling let down by what they experience as the absence of God. Taking a cue from findings in psychological research, two conclusions are reached. First, a "softer" form of complaint is most appropriate for Christian worshipers in a Western cultural context. We simply do not on the whole share in the passionate, expressive, and explosive temperament associated with biblical and contemporary Middle Eastern expressions of lament. The second conclusion is that for angry feelings to be resolved both ventilation and cognitive reframing are required. This insight was used in constructing the sample "liturgies of anger" that are offered.

Hope is the motif of Part 3. The first theme that is established is witnessing to hope. Following a lead from the psychotherapist Kaethe Weingarten (the phrase is hers), liturgies are presented that offer light in the darkness through communal empathy and trust in Christ.

The second theme that is developed here is the ironic element in the psychology of hope. Observing that many people find hope in the midst of suffering by learning to see their disability or illness as a friend or as a gift, it is argued that worship leaders need to take a lead in stimulating the ironic imagination.

The final part of the book deals with communion. It is argued, first, that Baptism and the Eucharist have the power to "re-Christianize" those of us who have unwittingly fallen into the unhealthy habits and patterns set up by the individualization process. That is, the idea that worship forms us in our identity as Christians will be promoted. In challenging the view of those who argue that the liturgy of the Church has much less power to shape the moral life of worshipers than we would like to think, evidence from both theological and psychological research will be assembled.

In the final chapter, the problem of what the psychologists call unmitigated communion is tackled. Though this problem is not nearly as common as individualism and its associated egoism, it is nevertheless a serious one, and it requires our attention. Some people—and this appears to be an issue for women especially—lose themselves in committing to loving relationships with others. In an adequate love ethic, however, love for others and a proper love for self are balanced. A litany of love shaped by this ethic is offered.

Most of the prayers, rituals, and sermons have been used in worship services around Brisbane over the past 12 months. Since I am a full-time academic, I don't get as many opportunities as I once did to preach and to lead worship. I am therefore very grateful to Sandra Jebb, Alison Cox, and Paul Walton for assisting me in "road-testing" these worship resources. I am also very appreciative of the helpful feedback on early drafts that David Pitman, Douglas Galbraith, and Ray Reddicliffe so generously provided.

Now that we have an overview of where we are heading, it is time to make a start. For a very long time, reconciliation was considered a principal concern of pastoral care. In our recent history, however, we have tended to lose sight of it. It is to this important pastoral issue that we now turn.

PART 1

RECONCILIATION: ADDRESSING SELF-DIMINISHMENT

There will be some who will query the inclusion of confession of sin in the pastoral care domain. In their minds, it should be left to the systematic, moral, and liturgical theologians. I want to begin this first part of the book by indicating why I believe that reconciliation should be accorded a central place in pastoral care.

The biblical witness is clear about the essential problem in human existence. In our unredeemed state, we human beings live in alienation from God and neighbor. Our condition is referred to commonly in the Scriptures as a state of enmity. In our natural state, we are enemies of God and of each other. On our own, there is nothing we can do to change this situation. The movement from enmity into friendship is possible only through receiving Christ's saving gift by faith. In and through the free grace of Christ, our sin is forgiven and we have peace with God and neighbor. With this in mind, Eduard Thurneysen contends that *the* question in pastoral care is this: Are you at peace with God?[1] He goes on to say that "this question is rightly asked and rightly heard only when it coincides with the question: Do you know that all your sins are forgiven you in Jesus Christ?"[2] Forgiveness of sin is the principal concern of pastoral care, according to Thurneysen.

Andrew Purves appreciates the fact that Thurneysen assigns primacy in the ministry of care to the atoning act of Christ, but he contends that to single out forgiveness of sin is to fail to embrace the full message of the gospel. Forgiveness of sin needs to be seen as the means to the end of restoring a broken relationship with God. It is communion with God that is the true aim and destiny of humankind. Pastoral care should therefore be viewed, according to Purves, as a ministry of grace in which people are led into restoration of communion with God.[3]

Other contemporary pastoral theologians have identified reconciliation as a central element in the ministry of pastoral care. Stephen Pattison, for example, defines pastoral care as "that activity . . . directed towards the elimination and relief of sin and sorrow and the presentation of all people perfect in Christ to God."[4] Deborah van Deusen Hunsinger, noting that Christ's redeeming act is at the center of Christian faith and hope, suggests that "we might wish to claim the ministry of reconciliation as the fundamental pastoral task . . ."[5]

These voices, however, represent a minority in the contemporary pastoral theology scene. The ministry of reconciliation is given meager attention by a number of pastoral theologians. There are no doubt a number of reasons for this. Not the least of which is the enormous influence of psychotherapeutic psychology on the pastoral care movement. Counselors and therapists aim to help their clients build a strong sense of self and to develop positive self-regard. A focus on the shadow side, they think, works against this goal. They therefore reject the experience of sin and guilt as neurotic and they see a highlighting of it as abusive. Many pastoral theorists and practitioners have been influenced by this philosophy and as a consequence consciously or unconsciously downplay the issue of forgiveness of sin.

In my view, it is utterly inappropriate and unhelpful to push sin to the margins in discourse on pastoral care. At the heart of the gospel is the conviction that the saving grace of Christ lifts us up out of our pettiness, pride, egoism, and self-deception. In confessing our sin and receiving the grace of forgiveness, we experience freedom and truth. Though there is pain, sorrow, and a temporary drop in self-esteem associated with repentance, there is also the deep joy that comes with knowing that we are forgiven. A facilitation of this encounter with joy and truth, with grace and freedom, is a very important aspect of the ministry of care.

While I can see why Thurneysen and others would want to say that forgiveness of sin is *the* issue for pastoral caregivers, I am not sure that this is the right way to frame the issue. As William Clebsch and Charles Jaekle note, there are other pastoral practices that have also been important historically, namely guiding, sustaining, and healing.[6] Other practices could be named as being of vital importance. Howard Clinebell, for instance, suggests that nurturing—a practice aimed at helping those in our care fulfill their God-given potential—should be added to Clebsch and Jaekle's list.[7] On a more contemporary note, many pastoral theologians also see both care of the natural environment and care of the socio-political system as essential pastoral tasks. Clearly, all these dimensions of pastoral care are very significant ones. Should we say, though, that forgiveness of sin is the most important aspect? Framing the matter this way may not be particularly helpful. It is perhaps better to state that pastoral care is a holistic ministry that is concerned with the intrapsychic, interpersonal, socio-political and ecological domains and that has as its aim elimination of and respite from sin and suffering. It is beyond the scope of this book to bring any kind of resolution to the heavily contested issue of defining the nature and scope of the ministry of care. Perhaps enough has been said, though, to justify the view that forgiveness of sin has a central place in the theory and practice of pastoral care.

Let me now briefly outline the content of the two chapters in this section. I should say at the outset that no attempt is made to develop a comprehensive or systematic approach to the pastoral dimension of public confession. Rather, my aim is simply to pick up on three aspects that have received relatively little attention but which nevertheless present as crucially important. The first of these is an approach to addressing the tendency that some—perhaps most—of us have to use cover stories in an attempt to keep a challenging God and a demanding truth at arm's length. Some theologians refer to this futile and self-defeating tendency as sloth. The second aspect is a strategy for making the affirming gaze of God as real as possible for worshipers who are bound by shame feelings. And last, the sin of hiding from life is identified as one that needs to be given due recognition in prayers of confession. In adopting these pastoral strategies in worship, there is the potential to help people grow past their tendency to self-diminishment. In this way, a common failing and a significant source of personal suffering will have been helpfully addressed.

The focus in Chapter 1, then, is on sin as sloth. Laziness and lack of discipline, combined with self-deception and hypocrisy, lead us into sin. If we fail through overreaching (the sin of pride), we also miss the mark through underachieving. We cheapen ourselves through taking up the lazy option of doing just enough to convince ourselves and others that we are righteous. Helping people to lift the lid on their cover story is no easy task. We are dealing with a psyche that is particularly tricky and very resistant to being exposed. Worship leaders, however, need to do their best in promoting self-awareness and truth. It is suggested in this first chapter that one very helpful way of doing this is to hold up Christ the mirror in the prayers of confession.

In Chapter 2, we concentrate on a quite different, but closely related form of self-diminishment, namely shame. (Shame is related to sloth because awareness of the latter causes us to feel ashamed.) Shame arises when a person judges herself to be inferior, defective, not worth very much. There are three tasks undertaken in this chapter. First, an attempt is made to identify the connection between sin and shame. Second, a proposal is developed for confession of shame-based sin. And last, an approach to opening confessants to the affirming gaze of God is presented.

1

Confessions of a Sly Psyche

There is a tendency in some and probably most people to take short-cuts. Such persons are always on the lookout for an easy way to obtain the benefits that they desire. They are not particularly enamored with hard work and discipline. This tendency to laziness can also be expressed in our spiritual lives. Those who have this problem are content to do just enough to convince themselves and others that they are genuinely living a life of fidelity and service. They fall into running a cover story on their righteousness. It is much less demanding than actually living a Christ-like life. With this particular human failing in mind, some theologians—Karl Barth being at the forefront—suggest that sin can be thought of as sloth. Those who sin in this way settle for the comforting thought that they are actually good people and that all of the biblical and theological talk about a fundamental alienation from God and neighbor is referring to other folk—the less noble ones. Sin as sloth is associated with a *penchant* for finding very good—and usually quite subtle and imaginative—reasons why what may seem like sin is really not.

How to lift the veil on these comfortable cover stories in the liturgy of confession? It is clearly no easy task; worship leaders cannot hope to ever lift it completely. We are working against a stubborn and creative drive to keep it in place. Plantinga and Rozeboom have got it just right:

> To make confession of sin a part of worship is . . . to work against our almost fathomless capacity for self-deception. Confession isn't a perfect antidote to self-deception because our shifty psyche, on its knees to confess sin, will generate only a short list.[1]

The aim in this chapter is to offer suggestions for liturgical practices that will have at least a good chance of penetrating the defenses of the

11

sly psyche. I will take a lead from work on self-awareness by psychological researchers. These researchers have found that the use of a mirror exposes the gap between a people's moral standards and their actions. That is, the mirror seems to bring them face to face with who they are and with what they are doing. It creates a pressure to change their behavior to align with their moral commitments. The metaphorical mirror for the Christian can only be Jesus Christ. The liturgical suggestions that are offered, then, center on Christ the mirror. It is in an encounter with Christ, the perfect model of truth and goodness, that sloth is exposed. Before getting to this, however, it is necessary to set the stage by surveying both the traditional approach to sin—sin as pride—and the complementary approach that we are concentrating on—sin as sloth.

Sin as Pride

In order to set a context for the slightly unusual notion of sin as sloth, a summary of the more familiar concept of sin as pride is offered. The classic statement on the human tendency to *hubris* comes from Augustine. He identifies pride as the root cause of all human failings.[2] Pride is a perverse form of exaltation, observes Augustine, in which the mind is fixed on the standard of the self rather than on the standard of God. Here is found the falsehood that characterizes all sin. Our will is naturally oriented to the promotion of our welfare. Our vulnerability to falsehood, however, leads us into a paradoxical situation. We pursue a course contrary to God's will and purpose believing that it will actually contribute to our welfare. Instead, we end up in misfortune. Adam and Eve, notes Augustine, were caught in this trap of falsehood as they attempted to snatch from God the knowledge of good and evil. We all inherit a legacy of sin and death from Adam (original sin). Not only do we imitate Adam's tendency to self-assertion and disobedience, we are actually "infected" with it from birth. We share in Adam's sin by generation as well as by imitation. We add our personal sins to the original sin that we inherit.

This notion of pride as the source of sin is also important in the reflections of Reinhold Niebuhr[3] and Paul Tillich,[4] although it takes quite a different turn with them. Though there are important differences in emphasis in the two treatments, the central message is much the same. Human beings are caught in a tension between nature and spirit, between finitude and freedom. Living with this

12

tension produces an anxiety which pervades our whole existence. In a misguided attempt to overcome our *angst*, we seek to elevate ourselves to the sphere of the divine. This will-to-power, Niebuhr contends, expresses itself in the pride of power, knowledge, and virtue. In a vain attempt to overcome our lack of power, our poverty of understanding, and our moral weakness we seek to raise ourselves to that divine level which is beyond limitations and bounds.

Karl Barth also includes a major treatment of sin as pride in his systematic theology.[5] For Barth, there is in us a "mad desire to be as God" which takes the form of thinking that we can be our own source and standard.[6] This mad desire involves a fundamental paradox. Barth's paradox is different, though, to Augustine's. The absolute irony of the situation for Barth is that the God of majesty and glory freely and lovingly chooses to humble himself for our sake by assuming human form, but instead of humbly and gratefully accepting this great gift we make a vain and silly attempt at exaltation by reaching for divinity.

Sin as pride, however, does not fully capture the human tendency to destructive living. Along with a drive to self-inflation and arrogant self-assertion, there is also a tendency to self-compression that manifests in laziness, complacency, and self-deception.

Sin as Sloth

Sloth in the context of sin means that we are too indolent, too undisciplined, and too silly to reach out and embrace our freedom and dignity in Christ. The slothful dimension of sin points to our smallness and pettiness. If describing our dark side as pride highlights our drive to self-inflation and overreaching, referring to it as sloth is indicative of our tendency to self-compression and underachieving. Barth captures this particularly well:

> The sin of [the human] is not merely heroic in its perversion. It is also . . . ordinary, trivial and mediocre. The sinner is not merely Prometheus or Lucifer. He is also—and for the sake of clarity, and to match the grossness of the matter, we will use rather popular expressions—a lazybones, a sluggard, a good-for-nothing, a slow-coach, a loafer. He does not exist only in an exalted world of evil; he exists also in a very mean and petty world of evil.[7]

13

We will develop Barth's treatment later. First, it will be useful to consider the way in which sin as sloth is presented in the Scriptures. Mark Biddle is a helpful guide here. He finds an Old Testament expression of the slothful aspect of sin in the writings of the teachers of wisdom.[8] A central belief in the Wisdom tradition is that God has incorporated a principle of order and justice into God's creation. Humans have the capacity to know this principle and to live in harmony with it. While the first step is always learning the wise ways of God, it is equally important, according to the Wisdom tradition, to engage the will in enacting them in one's life.

Biddle points out that if God's will for humankind has been captured by the principle of wisdom embedded in the created order, to refuse to embrace this principle is to sin. To live in and through the wisdom of God is to flourish. To ignore it, or to flaunt it, or to only half-heartedly embrace it, is to cause harm to oneself and to others. Biddle avers that this rejection of God's wisdom should be interpreted as the sin of giving up our authentic humanity:

> A great proportion of human suffering proceeds not from the evil hearts of fallen humanity, but from the avoidable ignorance and unnecessary incompetence of human beings who have failed to actualize the potential of their humanity. Willful ignorance and immaturity is the abdication of one's authentic humanity. It is sin.[9]

Biddle goes on to observe that in the New Testament, abdication of our humanity is captured in the notion of falling short of the glory of God (Rom. 3.23).[10] This is not immediately obvious. The first step in making this connection is to note the link between Christ our goal and the glory of God. Biddle points out that the glory of God is expressed in and through the life, death, resurrection, and exaltation of Christ. In Christ's faithful enacting of the event of salvation, his status as the perfect image of God is revealed. To look on the face of Christ is to see the glory of God. Christ is for us the example *par excellence* of life in, through, and for God. The proper goal for all human beings, then, is to conform to Christ, the ultimate image of God. It goes without saying that attaining the image—or at least a reasonable approximation of it—is something that we do in degrees. The image of God is not an inherent state of being, but rather a process of maturation. The person who is mature is the one who is expressing to a high degree the loving, giving, and faithful nature of Christ. Sin as sloth is failing to find the energy, will, faith, and wisdom to robustly engage with the process of growing into authentic personhood. It is the sin of complacently settling for only a dim reflection of the image of God.

Karl Barth's treatment of sin as sloth is important because he takes these notions of folly and inauthentic humanity and develops them in all their depth and complexity.[11] Here we can cover only the broad outlines of his analysis. In essence, Barth sees this form of sin as revealed in the fact that we are too lazy, too silly, and too ill-disciplined to embrace God's gift in Christ of freedom and life. Rather than take the wise option of a genuine existence lived in loving relationship with God and neighbor, we stupidly opt for an empty and isolated existence. We shut ourselves up in a tight space and lock God and fellow humans out. Or to use Barth's metaphor: "[The human] turns his back on God, rolling himself into a ball like a hedgehog with prickly spikes."[12]

It is not necessarily that slothful people reject God altogether. It is rather that they reject the true God—the God who calls them into the freedom and discipline of a life lived in the grace of Christ and the power of the Holy Spirit. The sin of the slothful person is an "escape to religion."[13] In this escape, God is rendered innocuous; the election of God is drained of its power, strength, and urgency. What is left is a comfortable, predictable, and easy piety. It is simply stupid of us to turn our backs on the joy and freedom of an authentic life in Christ. Stupidity is for Barth one of the essential marks of sin as sloth. It is interesting to note here that there is a clear link with sin in the Wisdom tradition. For the teachers of wisdom, to turn one's back on the principle of order and justice established by God is the ultimate folly. It can only lead to an inauthentic existence. Barth forcefully captures the nature of this folly in declaring that we stupidly let ourselves fall away from God and into emptiness:

[H]uman stupidity at its root consists in the fact that God is revealed to man but that man will not accept the fact in practice; that in the knowledge of God, in the clear light of His reality, presence, and action, he is radically known by God but refuses and fails to know God in return and to exist in this knowledge; that he lets himself fall as one who is already lifted up by God and to God. It is this letting oneself fall—a process in which we are all implicated—that is the really stupid element in our stupidity.[14]

Obviously the fact that we are in fact taking a stupid option is something that we have very little awareness of. It would be a stupid person indeed who knew exactly what he or she was doing in rejecting God's gracious outreach and yet continued on his or her merry way into emptiness. Our folly always comes disguised, says Barth.[15] The disguise does not fool us completely, however. The foolish person—on one level at least—thinks that all is relatively well; but on another level, he or she senses that something is quite amiss.

We live under a "great concealment"[16] that is very difficult to penetrate. Our cover story tells us that to withdraw into self is more enhancing of our personhood than a loving engagement with God and neighbor. In our depths, we know that this is not true. We know on a deep level that falling away from God and our fellow humans constitutes a denial of our authentic humanity. That we conceal this truth from ourselves constitutes for Barth the sin of hypocrisy:

> [W]e deny our humanity when we think that we can and should
> exercise it apart from our fellow-men. And when we try to con-
> ceal this, to deny this denial of our humanity, we are not justified,
> but accused and condemned, by the sound positive reason for
> our reluctance. In our denial and concealment of that which we
> are and do we can and will only make it worse and really be and
> do it. Hypocrisy is the supreme repetition of what we seek to
> deny with its help.[17]

In Barth's mind, the "quite respectable word" philanthropy shows up this concealment and hypocrisy.[18] The attempt to meet the needs of those who are disadvantaged is of course a good and noble endeavor. What troubles Barth is the fact that so often when we engage in philanthropy we are doing not much more than soothing our conscience. We create for ourselves and for others an illusion of really caring for those in need. It is an illusion because our commitment is not to the other-as-concrete person but rather to the anonymous person. Our love is for humanity, not for this or that particular individual. It costs us very little to serve the anonymous person. There is, then, a fundamental act of self-deception at work here. In turning our faces in care and concern to humanity in general—an entity that asks very little of us—we successfully hide from ourselves the fact that we have hardly even begun on the journey into genuine giving.

The sin of withdrawing into ourselves, of isolating ourselves from God and neighbor, is for Barth a form of dissipation.[19] Slothful persons let their lives slip through their fingers. Barth refers to them as "vagabonds" who will not accept discipline.[20] The whole history of morality is shot through with exhortations to find the will and self-discipline to live the good life. That the advocates of moral living have had only limited success is for Barth due to the fact that "the vagabond in us can always merrily escape the discipline which is brought to bear . . ."[21] Time and again we subvert any and all attempts to inculcate a spirit of discipline. We do this, observes Barth, by spinning a clever and convenient cover story. Discipline, we tell ourselves, is really just another name for a foreign rule. It constitutes an attack on our freedom and autonomy. The sin, we protest, is not in our rejection of discipline, but rather in the fact that others are so intent on stifling our freedom of spirit. The sin of sloth is so dangerous because it is associated with this self-deception. Referring to the dissipation at the core of the slothful life, Barth draws out this fact very clearly:

> We cannot recognize what we have here called the dissipation of man until we have fully heard the ways in which it tries to conceal and vindicate and even glorify itself. We cannot know it until we have considered the show of holiness with which it knows how to invest itself . . . The vagabond in us is not prepared to be depicted as the rogue he really is. He prefers to portray himself as a nobleman, knight, and hero.[22]

The Psychology of the Vagabond

The self-deception that is the stock-in-trade of the vagabond is illustrated quite beautifully in a series of psychological experiments conducted by Daniel Batson and his associates.[23] The findings of these studies indicate that moral hypocrisy is a common human failing. It is defined by the researchers as "seeking to maximize personal gain by appearing moral while, if possible, not incurring the costs associated with a moral outcome."[24] It is, in a word, sloth. Slothful persons want the benefits of appearing moral, but they don't want to pay a price for them. Moreover, it only works if they can spin a cover story that they are genuinely good people. They pride themselves on moral action, but in fact they haven't actually acted morally.

In using these studies as illustrative material, it is not suggested that Barth's analysis of sin operates primarily at the level of morality; clearly it does not. Barth is seeking to identify one of the root causes of our alienation from God and neighbor. He finds it in a tendency to sluggishness and complacency that prevents us from fully embracing the free grace of God. Moral failure and hypocrisy are two symptoms of the malady, and self-deception is the strategy for putting off going to the doctor. It is the basic sickness that Barth is primarily interested in. I find the psychological studies by Batson et al interesting because they highlight so clearly the pettiness and hypocrisy that are associated with the slothful orientation.

The moral dilemma that is set up in the studies is a trivial one. Research participants were given the opportunity to assign themselves and another participant (actually fictitious) to certain tasks. At the start, it was made clear that the other participant would not be told how the tasks were assigned. There were two tasks to be assigned: a "positive consequences task" in which participants had a chance to earn raffle tickets; and a "neutral consequences task" which was described as quite dull and uninteresting. The experimenters chose this mundane moral dilemma because, first, they wanted "to get less scripted responses," and, second, they wanted a situation in which there would be a broad consensus on the morally right approach.[25] The final element in the design is that participants completed a moral responsibility questionnaire prior to the laboratory session.

In order to test for moral hypocrisy, two features were included. First, the experimenters provided an explicit statement on the moral nature of the dilemma, indicating that most people think that the fairest way to assign the tasks is to give both participants an equal chance of being assigned the positive consequences task by, for example, flipping a coin. Including the coin, second, introduced a degree of ambiguity. If all participants use the coin in an honest manner, 50% of participants would assign the other participant to the positive consequences task. If there is significant deviation from the 50% result in the direction of assigning oneself to the positive consequences task, it would be evident that there is a motivation to appear moral ("I did the right thing; I flipped the coin") while still serving self-interest ("It's nice that I still ended up with the positive task"). That is, it will have been shown that moral hypocrisy is operating.

Of the 20 participants in the study, 10 flipped the coin and 10 did not. When asked about the most moral way to assign tasks, flipping the coin was the most frequent response from both those who flipped and those who did not. Of the 10 who flipped the coin, 8 said flipping was the most moral action. Of the 10 who did not flip the coin, 6 said flipping was the most moral action.

Of the 10 participants who did not flip the coin, only 1 assigned the other participant to the positive consequences task. What is more revealing is that of the 10 participants who flipped the coin, only 1 assigned the other participant to the positive consequences task. This proportion (.10) is significantly lower than the .50 associated with chance alone. The researchers have this to say about this finding:

> Apparently, either ours was a very charitable coin, or with self-interest an issue, flipping the coin introduced enough ambiguity into the decision process that participants could feel moral while still favoring themselves. ("It's heads. Let's see, that means . . . I get the positive task." "It's tails. Let's see, that means . . . the other participant gets the neutral task.") Apparently, some of those flipping the coin took advantage of this ambiguity to hide self-interest in the guise of morality. Aggregating responses across participants, we were able to unmask this moral hypocrisy.[26]

It is evident that self-deception is operating here. A number of the participants wanted the good feeling associated with moral action, but they did not want to pay a price for it. The only way they could convince themselves that they had acted morally even though they pursued self-interest was to hide their true motivation from themselves.

In a subsequent study, the experimenters chose to label the coin in order to make it impossible, or at least very difficult, for the participants to deceive themselves.[27] About two-thirds of the 40 participants chose to flip the labeled coin. Of the 12 who chose not to flip the coin, 10 assigned themselves to the positive consequences task, leaving the dull and boring task for the other participant. What is quite remarkable, though, is that of the 28 who chose to flip the coin, only 4 (.14) assigned the other person to the positive consequences task. Remember that if chance is the only factor operating, the proportion would be .50.

A final manipulation used by the researchers is very revealing.[28] In this study, the coin provided was not labeled. The new feature is the addition of a mirror. For some participants, the mirror was set up facing them; for others, it was set up with its back to them. Its use was designed to test the impact, if any, of self-awareness on the morality of the behavior. Self-awareness manipulations have been associated with increased awareness of discrepancies between behavior and personal standards, prodding a person to act in accordance with standards.

Approximately half (23) of the 52 participants chose to flip the coin. In the case of those participants not exposed to a mirror, of the 13 who chose not to flip the coin, 11 (.85) assigned themselves to the positive consequences task. More significantly, of the 13 who chose to flip the coin, only 2 (.15) assigned the other person to the positive consequences task. The findings in the earlier study are confirmed here.

What is really interesting is that when the participants were faced with a mirror, the coin was used in a scrupulously fair manner. Ten of the 26 participants chose to flip the coin, and of these, 5 assigned the other participant and 5 assigned themselves to the positive consequences task. Six of the 16 who chose not to flip the coin (.38) assigned the other participant to the positive consequences task.

Formulating a Pastoral Response

It seems that when I look at myself in the mirror, the sly side of my psyche is decommissioned. A mirror brings me face to face with who I am and with what I am doing. This empirical fact points to our pastoral task in relation to the self-deceptive tendencies of the slothful self. Our job is to hold up a mirror for others and for ourselves. The mirror is necessary because most of us have—to varying degrees—a tendency toward game-playing; we can hide the truth from ourselves. We are usually unaware that our shifty psyche is at work. We live through a cover story. The cover story is that we are living true religion, when in fact the truth is that mostly we are seeking to escape from it. Often we convince ourselves that our lives are bound to the true God, when in fact too often we opt for a cozy relationship with a congenial deity. The pastoral task is quite simply to blow the cover. This is of course easier said than done. The tricky psyche is particularly resourceful and persistent in resisting all attempts to bring it into the light.

One useful strategy, however, is to hold up a metaphorical mirror. Here again Barth's theology is a helpful guide. The traditional approach to the doctrine of sin and grace is to first construct a picture of the dark side of humanity, and then to describe God's saving action in Christ. Barth reverses the procedure. He avers that the sinful nature of humankind can only be properly understood in the light of the event of reconciliation.[29] Simply studying the experience of humankind will not provide us with a true and full picture of sin. Nor will studying the sad and long history of injustice and oppression. Nor, finally, will collating and integrating the various biblical statements on sin. It is only when we look into the mirror that is Christ, Barth contends, that we see the truth about ourselves. "We see Him, and in this mirror we see ourselves, ourselves as those who commit sin and are sinners."[30]

The notion of Christ as mirror is behind Zwingli's pattern of placing the prayer of confession after the sermon.[31] He seems to have had in mind the notion that we can only truly confess our sins after our true nature has been illumined by the Word. An effective proclamation of the Word has the power to open eyes and ears, hearts and minds. Hiding is more difficult when the spotlight of truth shines in one's direction. Game-playing and pettiness is shown up in the light of the Gospel. There is a chance, a good chance, that the tricky maneuvers of the psyche will be exposed in an encounter with the living Word. Clearly, there is a strong rationale for following the Zwingli order. That being said, it is not suggested that this should replace the usual pattern of putting it at the front end of the service. However, the suggestion that we find in a number of worship books of placing the confession of sin after the sermon during the festival of Lent is a useful one.

What does it mean to hold up Christ as a mirror in our preaching? There are at least three ways in which preachers attempt to fuse the horizon of the Gospel with that of the contemporary person. First, there are those preachers who seek to establish a mutually critical dialogue between the theology of the text and the important insights offered by the leading lights in the intellectual scene. That is to say, a conversation is set up between biblical theology and gleanings from relevant psychological, sociological, or philosophical discourses. Despite their blind spots, it is recognized that thinkers such as Jung and Rogers, Buber and Heidegger, Weber and Habermas have much to contribute to our understanding of what constitutes authentic personal and social life. Further, quite a few of their insights are judged to have a basic affinity with central biblical perspectives. Of course, the wise preacher does not attempt to give her congregation a philosophy or psychology lecture. However, it is possible to drop in salient reflections from these great thinkers in an accessible way and in the process make a strong connection between the text and relevant psychological and social dynamics.

In the second category are those preachers who concentrate on the social justice dimension in the Bible. God is viewed first and foremost as the One who has a fundamental option for the poor and the oppressed. From the pulpit, a range of pressing socio-political issues is discussed in the light of Christ's message of peace, reconciliation, and justice. The prophetic word is proclaimed; social sin and forms of oppression are exposed and people are challenged to renew their commitment to work with God in the power of the Spirit in the fight for equality and freedom.

Finally, there are those preachers who are both keen observers of everyday life and gifted storytellers. They offer stories from life in the everyday world—some mundane and humorous, and some profound and poignant—that connect with the good news of God's saving love in Christ. One pastor put it this way in a recent conversation: "When I step into the pulpit, I talk about real people in the real world. Too many preachers get lost in theological flights of fancy. Let's keep it real." The connection between the text and the everyday world is strongly established.

Here are three styles of preaching, then, that are very familiar to us. It is not suggested, though, that these are pure types. Many preachers cross boundaries. Though their primary commitment is to justice, some preachers also include therapeutic or philosophical insights when it is appropriate. And there are preachers who regularly draw from leading secular thinkers to make their point about Christ's call to promote peace and justice. A focus on everyday life, finally, is a feature in a variety of preaching approaches.

Preachers all have their particular gifts, interests, and theological commitments. The point that is being made is that there is a variety of ways to hold up the mirror that is Christ in order that worshipers may begin to see themselves as they truly are. The Word can be effectively and faithfully proclaimed using a number of different styles and covering a range of content. It is my contention, though, that whatever container the sermon comes in, a real illumination of our hearts and minds—the kind that is necessary if there is to be a genuine confession of sin—requires that sin and grace be placed very definitely in the center. Psychology, sociology, philosophy, justice theory, and stories from the everyday world play support roles; they are not the principal players. I consider that Paul Scott Wilson is right. Preaching should always be grounded in the encounter between our darkness and the light that God brings into the world. It needs to have four primary foci: sin in the text, grace in the text, sin in the contemporary world, and grace in the contemporary world.[32] It is in the interplay between sin and grace, on the one hand, and between text and today's world, on the other, that Christ's liberating Word is lifted up. It is in this interplay that Christ becomes for us a powerful mirror.

The other way in which Christ the mirror can be held up is through the prayer of confession. Commonly, the focus in this prayer is exclusively on our failures and shortcomings. It is suggested here that shining the light on Christ will help significantly in exposing our slothful tendencies, and especially our tendency to conceal the truth of who we really are. Some examples of how this might be done are offered below.

Christ the Mirror in Confession

Prayer of Confession A

(The congregation is divided into two sides for this prayer.)

Leader: For Jesus, there was no need to project an image of righteousness.
People (*Side A*): O God, open our eyes.
People (*Side B*): O Lord, have mercy.
Leader: In Christ we see absolute authenticity in personhood and in action.
People (*Side A*): O God, show us the truth about ourselves.
People (*Side B*): O Lord, have mercy.
Leader: In Jesus, there was no hint of self-deception, no reason to pretend to be good.
People (*Side A*): O God, illumine our inner being.
People (*Side B*): O Lord, have mercy.
Leader: In Christ there is truth and authenticity. In him there is healing and freedom. Sisters and brothers, I declare to you that your sins are forgiven. Be at peace.
All: Amen.

Prayer of Confession B

Leader: We settle for a domesticated deity and a comfortable religion.

Voice 2: Christ is the glory of God, the perfect image of goodness and truth.

People: *Kyrie eleison* (Lord have mercy)—sung three times

Leader: We like to appear to be good, but we don't want to pay the price of actually being good.

Voice 2: Christ is the glory of God, the perfect image of goodness and truth.

People: *Kyrie eleison* (Lord have mercy)—sung three times

Leader: We use euphemisms and sanitized language to mask our sin.

Voice 2: Christ is the glory of God, the perfect image of goodness and truth.

People: *Kyrie eleison* (Lord have mercy)—sung three times

Leader: The way of Christ is the way of truth and authenticity. In him there is healing and freedom. Sisters and brothers, I declare to you that your sins are forgiven. Be at peace.

All: Amen.

2

Shame, Confession, and God's Affirming Gaze

In the last chapter, we concentrated on the self-diminishment that is associated with sloth. We discussed the fact that we have a tendency to cheapen ourselves through pettiness, hypocrisy, and laziness. Here we will address a quite different, but at the same time closely related, form of self-diminishment—namely, that which is associated with shame (the relationship consists in the fact that awareness of sloth leads to feeling ashamed). Shame is essentially the feeling that one is inferior, inadequate, and defective. In a word, it is feeling small. Some consider it to be the preeminent cause of emotional distress in the modern industrialized world.[1]

It will be argued that there is a particular form of sin associated with shame. There is a strong tendency in those who are prone to shame to hide, to seek a secluded existence. The fear of being shamed leads such persons to avoid challenging situations; in the routine and relatively predictable world they construct for themselves the risk of being exposed as inferior and inadequate is reasonably low. This decision to choose comfort and predictability over self-realization and an authentic existence, it will be argued, is sinful.

It is further contended that while it is important that worship leaders are cognizant of this particular form of sin and include it in the prayer of confession from time to time, it is even more important that they also make provision for a liturgy of affirmation. Persons suffering from shame feelings desperately need to feel accepted and confirmed in their personhood. In the context of worship, it is the confirmation of God that is primary. With this in mind, a proposal for facilitating an encounter with God's affirming gaze is offered.

Shame is a complex and subtle affect. It is closely related to guilt, but it is also distinct from it. Most people are not aware of the distinctions;

they simply bundle the two affects together. It is obviously important to be relatively clear about what shame is. It is to this task that we now turn.

A Map of Shame

As I have just mentioned, feelings of shame arise when the self evaluates itself as flawed, defective, and inferior. It involves, then, a negative self-assessment. When a person makes the judgment that she has fallen short of an ideal, she feels shame. She wants to look or be a certain way, but cannot manage it. As Silvan Tomkins so neatly expresses it, "desire has outrun fulfillment."[2] It is possible to feel shame about almost anything. Some people condemn themselves as socially awkward, clumsy, and gauche. Others feel dull, incompetent, and ignorant. Cowardice and betrayal are especially potent sources of shame. It is possible to feel ashamed of one's appearance, height (or lack of it), weight, disability, or disfigurement. Shame, to give one last example, can be associated with familial or national identity.

It is apparent that shame takes on a variety of forms. Shame is not a unitary entity; it is an umbrella term for a variety of traits and tendencies associated with feeling inferior or defective. Stephen Pattison is right to suggest that the best way to approach shame is to adopt "a kind of family resemblance theory."[3] In mapping the territory of shame, the members of the shame family will first be introduced. This will be followed by a description of the characteristics that the members all share.

Introducing the Shame Family

There are a number of different typologies for shame. Included in the one I offer are these five types: *situational shame, aesthetic shame, inherited identity shame, inferiority shame, and moral shame.*[4] This mapping of the varieties of shame, I believe, provides a comprehensive picture. As the last two categories are the most significant for our discussion, they will receive a more extended treatment.

Situational shame

The term "situational shame" comes from Robert Karen.[5] It describes those embarrassing moments—slurping one's soup in polite company, tripping over one's shoe-laces at an inopportune moment, a joke falling flat—which come to us all at some time. "Situational shame keeps us bathing regularly, dressing appropriately, eating with utensils, and able to work in close proximity to others without acting on every aggressive or sexual impulse."[6] Clearly, we are dealing here with the low toxicity end of the shame spectrum.

Babcock and Sabini helpfully define embarrassment as that emotion which is evoked by a perceived discrepancy between one's behavior and one's conception of one's "persona."[7] A persona is "a self-imposed standard or model for action."[8] Embarrassment is an unavoidable part of life. Our human fallibility, together with the importance we place on social mores, means that inevitably we all end up at some time or other "red-faced" and feeling silly.

Aesthetic shame

In a culture which places such a high value on physical beauty, there is a great potential for those who fall short of the ideal to feel shame. Whereas the ideal in other forms of shame may relate to intelligence, social skill, or moral strength, here we are dealing with an aesthetic ideal. When one perceives a gap between the real self and the desired physical ideal, shame is the painful result.

Aesthetic shame can vary from relatively slight discomfort over one's appearance to a sense of horror and self-loathing. In every other way a person may feel a sense of healthy pride, and yet disfigurement of the body has the potential to all but destroy emotional well-being.

Inherited identity shame

We are all born into a particular family, class, and culture. Our inherited identity may be a source of pride. Sometimes, though, it carries with it a burden of shame. Members of ethnic minority groups may internalize the prejudicial stereotypes of the dominant culture. They may come to condemn themselves as "dirty," "ignorant," or "lazy." Even when a person begins to be successful according to the standards of the dominant majority, a lingering feeling of inferiority may plague her. James Fowler calls this "ascribed shame."[9]

It may seem irrational to feel shame simply because one happens to be born into a particular class or culture. After all, everyone is an individual with her own unique set of gifts, abilities, and personal qualities. It is not possible, though, to define personal identity in terms of an "atomistic" self.[10] I am who I am, in part, because I was born into *this* particular family, into *this* social class, in *this* country. The identity ascribed to a person by class and culture may generate pride, or it may result in feelings of defectiveness and inferiority.

Inferiority shame

Cultural identity is sometimes a source of shame. In the literature, however, shame is more commonly related to feelings of inadequacy arising purely out of personal experience. In broad terms, a sense of inferiority may be related either to talents and abilities or to personal qualities. A person may feel shame because she judges herself to be incompetent. She may also feel shame because she considers she is boring, timid, socially inept, lacks a sense of humor, to list just a few of the possibilities. Or she may feel ashamed on both counts.

It is common for people to feel that something is lacking in their personality. Most of us have a desire to enhance our personal qualities. We would like to be more assertive, more in control, more engaging and lively in relationships, more articulate—the list could go on and on. The problem is not necessarily a lack of intelligence or ability. A person may judge herself to be very successful in her chosen vocation and be quite comfortable in that setting. In a social situation, however, she feels out of place and silly. She thinks that others find her "stiff" and uninteresting. Another person, who is very creative and works largely on his own (e.g. writer, artist, software designer) may feel small mainly because when he engages with others he allows them to dominate and control him.

A sense of shame may, on the other hand, be related to feelings of incompetence. Almost everything a person does, from cooking lasagne to giving an important business presentation, turns out less well than she would like. Another person would like to have the ability to even *get into* a position of having to give such a presentation.

The reflection on shame by the psychotherapist Donald Nathanson[11] takes into account both lack of achievement and personality failures. He concentrates, though, on the former. Nathanson works with the relationship of shame to its counterpart, pride. Shame and pride are tracked through a series of developmental stages defined in terms of size and strength, dexterity and physical skill, dependence vs. independence, cognitive ability, communication, the sense of self, gender identity and sexuality, and, finally, interpersonal skills. The issues raised in this discussion rotate around one pole defined by skills, abilities, competence, and success, and another described by failure, a sense of inferiority, and assaults on self-esteem. When one has moved through a stage relatively successfully, one accrues a sense of personal competence, self-worth, and healthy pride. Failures along the way, on the other hand, may coalesce to shape an identity defined by a sense of inferiority and shame.

Increasingly, people in modern industrialized societies, dominated as we are by a preoccupation with success, concentrate almost exclusively on incompetence and failure as the locus of shame. With this in mind, Agnes Heller refers to a "one-dimensionality" in the Western (or as we tend to say now, Northern) experience of shame.[12] In the competitive, highly structured workaday world, we never really confront others with our global personalities. Other persons only see the particular roles we are called on to play. "We wear our 'roles' outside and our shabby incognito inside."[13] In this context, shame is evoked by an evaluation by the self and by others that a role has been performed incompetently. Interestingly, Heller observes that it is only at war that a person is known as a total personality.[14] Here the real self, in all its many facets, is put to the test. In the firing line, skill, competence, and success are no longer the only channels for approval or disapproval. One is judged in terms of courage, ingenuity, goodness of heart, and solidarity with fellow soldiers.

Moral shame

This last observation points to the fact that shame and pride have a moral reference. Moral lapses produce a sense of shame.

Following Kant, Gary Thrane contends that a sense of honor derived from sensitivity to shame is the only truly moral motivation.[15] The link between the moral personality and shame is established in terms of autonomy and identity. An important dimension in autonomy is the capacity for embracing the ideals and standards that are truly one's own. Autonomy is a personal good because it requires "freedom, courage and self-command."[16] When a person follows externally determined standards, he or she feels a sense of shame. The loss of autonomy produces a loss of dignity and sense of worth.

Thrane argues that shame rather than guilt is the truly moral feeling. "Those who merely dread the punishing voice of conscience (guilt) are not moral. Only those who love their virtue and dread its loss (shame) are moral."[17] If the only motivation one has for moral behavior is the fear of guilty feelings, one's performance of good actions will be marred by the grudging spirit behind them. A person influenced by shame feelings, on the other hand, derives satisfaction from fulfilling his or her duty. The sense of freedom and of self-worth associated with having nothing to be ashamed of motivates moral behavior. Further, the capacity to live according to principles is evidence of a firm character. One needs self-command and willpower to act in accord with high ideals.

A sense of honor and responsibility drives moral behavior, but shame is always lurking in the shadows. As soon as one establishes high standards, moral failure and the associated shame reaction are ever-present possibilities. The idea of liability to shame as a motivation for moral behavior is closely associated with Carl Schneider's notion of "discretion-shame."[18] Discretion-shame is contrasted with "disgrace-shame." When a person has done something that she considers unworthy of her best character, there is a feeling of disgrace. She judges that she has acted badly and this is followed by a shame reaction. There is also an experience, observes Schneider, of "shame felt before." If discretion-shame is to have ethical value it must be something more than mere emotion. After all, an emotion hardly qualifies as a virtue. Feelings are changeable and unpredictable; the virtues are settled dispositions, character traits. Since discretion-shame, observes Schneider, is closely linked to modesty, there is some suggestion that a sense of shame is more than an emotion. Modesty is usually considered to be a virtue. A highly developed sensitivity to shame may be thought of as an enduring attitude or character trait. "Shame, then, is not 'just a feeling,' but reflects an *order of things*. Furthermore, discretion-shame not only reflects, but sustains, our personal and social ordering of the world" [emphasis in the original].[19] Moral failure represents a transgression against the personal and social orders. Awareness of the harm that is done to these orders makes us ashamed.

We have covered quite a bit of ground: from slurping one's soup in a restaurant to acts of moral failure. Though the members of the shame family bear a clear resemblance to each other, there are also some striking differences. The reason that we talk about a shame family is because there are a number of characteristics that are shared by the members. It is to a discussion of these characteristics that we now turn.

The Main Characteristics of Shame

Shame is a very complex phenomenon. Taking all of the major writings on shame together, there is quite a wide range of characteristics that is covered. It is perhaps enough for us to concentrate on only the main ones.

Exposure

Shame occurs when particularly sensitive and vulnerable aspects of the self are exposed.[20] Exposure may be to others, or to oneself, or to both. Shame is registered as a painful emotional jolt when aspects of the self that are considered unworthy and inferior are suddenly opened to the disapproving gaze of others. When this happens, we want to disappear, to "sink through the floor." The dysphoria is so strong that avoidance of situations that have a potential for shame—such as help-seeking, socializing, sex, public speaking, and competition—becomes a strong temptation.[21]

This public exposure is so commonly observed and so vivid that it seems that the attention of some researchers has been drawn away from the private dimension. The fact that a shame reaction is some-times a very personal affair is overlooked. David Ausubel, in line with the anthropologists Margaret Mead and Ruth Benedict, argues that shame always demands an audience, real or presumed.[22] Helen Merrell Lynd, however, rightly points out that "[e]xposure to oneself is at the heart of shame."[23] The shame one feels in deceiving others into believing something about oneself that is untrue is particularly intense and painful.

The psychoanalytic scholar, Léon Wurmser, suggests that there are intimate links between shame and exposure on the one hand, and shame and perception on the other.[24] "Moments of self-exposure" and "acts of perception" play important roles in the shaping of identity. Seeing/being seen and hearing/being heard are the modalities which facilitate a comparison of one's self-concept with the concept others have of one. "The modes of attentive, curious grasping and of express-ing oneself in nonverbal as well as verbal *communication* are the arena where in love and hatred, in mastery and defeat our self is forged and molded" [emphasis in the original].[25] When the interchange is defective, the core of the self-concept is disturbed and becomes shame-laden.

Hiddenness

Given that shame is acutely painful and is associated with the exposure of sensitive and vulnerable aspects of the self, we would expect that there would be a tendency to block the feeling from conscious awareness.

W.H. Auden, in reviewing Stendahl's *Diaries*, expressed surprise that the latter found it so difficult to admit certain facts to himself: "How can admitting anything to oneself be daring?"[26] This comment indicates an ignorance of shame dynamics. Our first reaction to shameful realities about ourselves is to hide from them.

In her ground-breaking phenomenological study of shame, Helen Block Lewis observes two distinct ways in which patients repress shame. First, there is the defense of "by-passing" shame feeling.[27] The shame events are recognized, but shame feelings are blocked from entering consciousness. This is achieved by what she calls a "distancing" maneuver. The self views itself through the eyes of the other, but without much affect. That is, the shame affect is bypassed and replaced by an impassive viewing of the self from a variety of perspectives. For example, a patient may speculate, in a quite dispassionate way, about what the therapist is thinking about him at the moment.

The second form of hidden shame Lewis labels "overt, undifferentiated shame."[28] Some patients in Lewis' study who manifested a high level of shame affect were unable to identify their feeling state as shame. Rather, they used words such as "depressed," "tense," "lousy," or "blank" to describe their psychological state.

Incongruence

A shame reaction occurs when a person is suddenly aware that her behavior is incongruous with, inappropriate to, the situation she is in.[29] It is not that she has done something wrong; no sin has been committed. Rather, there is a painful awareness of a gap between her actions and the expectations of the environment. The person is acting on the assumption that a particular behavior is appropriate, but in a moment of painful awareness she discovers that the assumption was false. It is the experience of suddenly finding oneself out of tune with one's environment. To illustrate this, let me refer to an experience from my time in parish ministry. The committee of the Men's Breakfast group invited a local Roman Catholic man to speak at their next gathering. He was a very humorous man and he "spiced up" his stories with "colorful" language. I really enjoyed him. But I seemed to be in the minority. The majority of the men were from strict evangelical backgrounds and were quite offended by his bad language. Looking at his audience, he was expecting to see happy, laughing faces, but instead he was greeted with frowns of disapproval. His face suddenly went quite red and he lost his poise.

Threat to trust

Lynd observes that this sudden awareness that one is out of key with one's environment results in a threat to trust.[30] One is led to question one's own adequacy and/or the reliability of the values of the world of reality. In order to supplement the illustration above, I will use a familiar domestic scenario. It also depicts the link between misplaced confidence and shame. A child has labored long and hard in the kitchen preparing a feast for her mother. Where the child sees a labor of love and a delectable offering, her mother sees only a very messy kitchen and a waste of ingredients. Instead of the expected smile of appreciation, the would-be chef receives a glare of anger and reproach. Lynd sums up the situation in relation to misplaced confidence nicely:

> The rejected gift, the joke or the phrase that does not come off, the misunderstood gesture, the falling short of our own ideals, the expectation of response violated—such experiences mean that we have trusted ourselves to a situation that is not there.[31]

The jolt of shame is triggered by this sudden awareness that what one thought could be relied on has betrayed the confidence one had in it.

Contempt for self

The jolt of shame carries with it a particular set of cognitions. These are cognitions that orbit around scorn and contempt. They run along these lines: "How stupid you are!" "What a foolish thing to do!" "You are such a loser!" What is especially painful about this form of self-victimization is that it convinces the person that she is basically unlovable. She feels only scorn for herself, and she is certain that others must be feeling exactly the same way. Here we are close to the core of the agony that is shame. Indeed, Wurmser contends that the "*basic shame is the pain of essential unlovability*"[32] [emphasis in the original]. With this in mind, Pattison suggests that the metaphors of dirt, stain, and pollution capture the shame experience most adequately. "To see chronically shamed persons," he writes, "as people who essentially experience a sense of themselves as excluded, inferior, defiled, polluted and polluting, indeed as toxic dirt, is not far-fetched."[33]

Wurmser goes a step further and asks where unlovability is located on the map of human interaction. Here he links the experiences of lovability and being loved together. Wurmser suggests—and this will be important for us later—that the location is the face:

> *Love resides in the face*—in its beauty, in the music of the voice and the warmth of the eye. Love is proved by the face, and so is unlovability—proved by seeing and hearing, by being seen and heard. A child can be loved without being given the nipple; but love cannot exist without face and music.[34] [emphasis in the original]

Involvement of the whole self

Moving to our final characteristic, shame researchers consistently use the global aspect of the shame experience to differentiate it from its cousin, guilt. A person feels guilty over actions (or omissions) which have caused harm to others. Guilt can be localized in a certain aspect of the self, namely, that which is associated with a particular moral transgression. A person with a gambling problem, for example, may say, "I am basically a good person. I just get carried away when I go down to the racetrack." Shame, though, cannot be located in a discrete act which can be separated off from the self. The difference may be expressed this way: "I am guilty of this bad act; but I *am* my shame."

As Wurmser accurately observes, shame has a global quality because it is evoked by a discrepancy between a tested self and an ideal image.[35] This image is not simply constructed out of a delimited reality such as actions, but out of all the components which define a self. It is through shameful events that the self is revealed. Personal identity is shaped in this way. The shame events throw up the contours of one's selfhood and of the world of reality one inhabits. Guilt may be assuaged by confession or restitution, but the experience of shame may be transcended only by a re-shaping of identity.

Shame and Sin

In the description of the shame family above, we noted that moral shame is one of its members. Given this fact, it is to be expected that shame and guilt often go together. Having acted against the moral order, a person feels guilt over the harm she has caused, but she is also ashamed of herself for acting so badly. The two affects sit so closely together that it is quite difficult for most people to untangle them.

Thus, in the experience of sinning, shame and guilt are both very prominent. Shame and sin have been traditionally linked, though guilt has been the emotion that has been most often highlighted.

Don Capps has argued that in today's world we need to reverse the order if we are to accurately reflect what most people are experiencing.[36] Shame, he contends, is generally more prominent than guilt in the experience of sin. There would be nothing especially bold or novel about this suggestion if it were not for the fact that Capps is thinking of inferiority shame rather than the moral version. He contends that in a narcissistic age, a "sense of wrongfulness" is more likely to be experienced in terms of shame than guilt.[37] The narcissist senses the distortion in her way of being in the world and it causes her pain. She connects this distortion and pain, however, not with moral failure but rather with personal inferiority and inadequacy. I appreciate very much the fact that Capps has highlighted the important role shame plays in the experience of sin. His writing has stimulated me to think hard about the linkages between the two.[38] I have come to the view that it is not the negative evaluation of self and the consequent sense of self-depletion that constitute sin; the sin associated with shame is found in the evasive tactics, in the attempt to live a secluded, safe life, in hiding from life—in a word, in the failure to live an authentic life. *It is not the sense of self-diminishment but rather the compression of one's engagement with the challenges and opportunities that life presents that is sinful.* In using this expression "the compression of one's engagement," I am referring to a tendency to hide from others, from God, from life. I identify this shame-related experience rather than the experience of feeling inferior because I am committed to the view that sin is primarily offense against God. Cornelius Plantinga puts it nicely when he says that sin has "first and finally a Godward force."[39] This statement requires some development. In God's creative work, God established a right and good order for all the relationships that constitute life on the planet. The relationships we have with self, with other humans, with animals, and with the earth are in accord with the divine will and purpose when they are enacted in an ethos of love, compassion, respect, and justice. When we engage in these relationships in a destructive way, when the primary motive forces are greed and self-interest, we insult God. God, in an act of love and justice, has established a right order for life in the cosmos. Yet we willfully abuse this order in a petty, short-sighted attempt to further self-interest. Our egoism is driven by a number of forces. Prominent here are pride, sloth, and a lack of trust in God. Whatever is driving the egoistic attitudes and behavior, the end result is always the same: damage is done to the relationships that are constitutive of our life in the world. We were made for wholesome, loving relationships; egoism, tragically, results in a state of alienation. Sin is alienation from self, others, animals, and the earth, but it is first and foremost alienation from God.

When a shame-prone person suffers the pain that is associated with feelings of inferiority, inadequacy, and defectiveness, the heart of God is grieved, but God is not offended. God feels deep compassion for the shame-bound person when she suffers under the attacks of her internal critic, but there is nothing in this experience that offends against the holiness and justice of God. The situation is no different in relation to other common forms of emotional distress such as anxiety, depression, phobic behavior, and obsessive-compulsive behavior. The tragedy of mental dysfunction is that those who suffer from it torture themselves. The fact that a person who is mentally unwell engages in self-victimization does not in itself alienate her from God. The dysphoria and self-injury associated with mental illness should not be labeled sin. To do so is to distort the meaning of the term.

Above it was indicated that one of the relational vectors in God's good ordering for life in the world is relationship to self. If the torture of the self associated with shame and other forms of mental dysfunction cannot be legitimately included in this category, what *does* sin against self refer to? One prominent approach comes from feminist theologians who define sin as self-loss. Valerie Saiving suggests that the sinful tendency in women is best described as:

> triviality, distractibility, and diffuseness; lack of an organizing center or focus, dependence on others for one's self-definition; tolerance at the expense of standards of excellence . . . In short, underdevelopment or negation of the self.[40]

Judith Plaskow has also identified self-loss as a common form of sin in women (although she recognizes, as does Saiving, that it is not confined to women).[41] Plaskow uses Doris Lessing's heroine in the *Children of Violence* series, Martha Quest, as a case study. She concludes that Martha's besetting sin is "her failure to make choices, to take responsibility for her own life."[42] Women tend to lose themselves in others. They too readily cede responsibility to those around them, thereby losing direction and focus. It is in these terms, some feminist theologians have argued, that a contemporary understanding of sin should be constructed.

It is no doubt true that behind this self-loss a propensity for shame is sometimes to be found. Persons who feel inferior and lack self-confidence will very often gladly have others take responsibility for their lives. It is not necessarily the case, though, that shame is a factor in this process. The way in which male and female identities and relations have been traditionally appropriated is a product of socialization. There are still plenty of women who possess a healthy sense of pride but who nevertheless sacrifice their needs and goals in serving others. They have simply accepted that this is what is required of a good wife and mother.

The failure to live an authentic life can be tied directly, however, to a central dynamic in the shame experience. Shame-bound persons, as we saw above, desperately want to avoid situations of uncontrolled exposure. They are afraid that stepping out into the open, so to speak, will put them at considerable risk of being shown up as inferior and defective. Their defense against this frightening possibility is hiding. Shame-prone people attempt to keep life as controlled and manageable as possible. The secluded life, the life lived in a contained, familiar, relatively predictable zone is very attractive to them. Shame experiences are much less likely when one is traversing well-known territory surrounded by familiar faces.

The tactic of hiding oneself away in a carefully delimited zone makes for a relatively comfortable life. In this way, the pain of shame is managed. What is destructive in this approach is that it prevents one from living an authentic life. What drives this hiding from life is the judgment that underestimation of self and self-diminishment are acceptable losses in securing an existence in which shame experiences are much less likely. From a faith perspective, these are not acceptable losses. God's intention is that we live life fully, adventurously, and genuinely. This means that we need to be prepared to stretch ourselves, to take on challenges, to risk failure and feelings of inadequacy. We are called to be imitators of Christ. Christ is the glory of God. He is the glory of God because he lived absolutely faithfully, following God's lead into deeply challenging and often hostile territory. Jesus never allowed himself the luxury of hiding. His escape into seclusion was an "escape" into the grace of the Father/Mother that gave him the strength and courage to live his mission. There is no suggestion of evasion here. Christ is the exemplar of the authentic life. Paul tells us that sin is falling short of the glory of God (Rom. 3.23). One important aspect of a life reflecting the glory of God is the embrace of freedom and taking up options for personal development, creative self-expression, and service. To run away from these possibilities through a fear of falling short of the mark and thereby feeling ashamed is sin.[43]

Shame is not sin. Burdening oneself with the judgment that one is inferior and defective is not sinful. Running away from a full and free engagement with life and its challenges is. God's intention for human life is not self-diminishment but rather self-realization. In taking up options and possibilities that promote creativity and personal development, one experiences joy, freedom, and a sense of fulfillment. This is what God intends for us. A self-actualized person also has more to offer God in God's project of extending the divine reign of love, peace, and justice. God is not dependent on us to advance the realm of God, but God calls on us to give of ourselves as fully as we can in this work. Living well within ourselves means that we rob the realm of God of useful resources for ministry and mission. When we choose to wall ourselves off in our zones of comfort and predictability, there is a negative impact both on the self and on our relationship with God. As we have noted before, sin is traditionally thought of as self-assertion and self-exaltation. But the Bible also points to weakness and avoidance as expressions of sin. In reflecting on the evasion tactics that shame makes a person vulnerable to, Niels Gregersen makes this apt comment: "[I]n the biblical traditions, both over and underestimation of self are uncovered as sin . . . The sin of weakness . . . the taking of evasive action, is shown to be the form of escape it fundamentally is."[44]

Shame, Confession, and Affirmation

So what does all of this discussion on the proper relationship between shame and sin mean for the prayer of confession? From what has been said, one obvious implication is that included in corporate confession should be an acknowledgment of the tendency that some people have to escape, to hide from life, to avoid the challenges of living an authentic existence. There will be healing, release, and possibly growth as a result of bringing this particular failing before God. Those of us who are taking a comfortable, safe route and refusing the challenge of self-realization will recognize the infidelity in this and accept that it must be confessed and changed. There is, however, a deeper source of suffering and bondage in shame-prone persons that needs to also be addressed in the liturgy of confession. The sin of evasion is grounded in a negative global self-evaluation. This denigrating approach to self does not need to be confessed—it is not sin—but it does need to be addressed. The pain associated with the feeling that one is inferior and flawed cannot be healed through confession and an assurance of pardon. What the shame-bound person needs is not only forgiveness but especially acceptance and affirmation. In his empirical study of confession in the Finnish Lutheran Church, Paavo Kettunen refers to this as mercy.

> To absolve a person from shame would mean forgiving something that is focused on a person's whole self. On the other hand, with guilt the absolution is directed at the human act—be it psychological or concrete—from which the guilt has arisen. Being "surrounded" by mercy is more holistic than receiving absolution. In this state people as a whole are the object of mercy and love at a moment when they do not have the strength to regard themselves worthy of receiving love and mercy, when they only want to cover their faces, hide, and flee.[45]

Because shame is such an isolating experience, the love and acceptance of others is crucial. In the context of faith and in the setting of worship, the affirmation of God is especially important. What is needed is to communicate to confessants in a full and compelling way the "mercy"—the affirmation and acceptance—of God. Shame-proneness has deep roots and is very resistant to being weeded out. It is clearly not possible in a liturgical setting to achieve anything like full healing. Even a partial release from the bondage of shame is a significant gift, however.

Some might argue that a liturgy of affirmation could be placed anywhere in the service. It does not need to be associated with the prayer of confession. Anyone who takes this line fails to appreciate the indissoluble link between sinning and the shame dynamic. For the shame-bound person, an awareness of sin feeds into her global negative evaluation. It strengthens her conviction that she is defective, flawed, and unworthy. Confession of sin will bring release at one level, but the deeper sense of wrongfulness will remain untouched. With this in mind, Harold Ellens proposes a reformulation of the traditional approach to forgiveness and healing. The usual under-standing, based as it is on a juridical model, recognizes only justice, justification, forgiveness, and restoration. In a therapeutic approach, affirmation and healing are included. His formula is this: "(Pain / shame / guilt / anxiety) + (passion / compassion / mercy / grace) = (Forgiveness [and other therapies] / affirmation / healing / actualiza-tion)."[46] Forgiveness alone will not help the person bound by shame. An experience of God's affirmation and acceptance is also required to support a movement into a feeling of being whole, right, and worthy.

God's Affirming Gaze

We saw above that the critical gaze of others has the potential to evoke shame feelings. It is part of human nature to evaluate and to judge. It is God's nature to look upon God's children with mercy and acceptance. The power and beauty in divine grace is that it gives us the encouragement and confidence that we need to fully embrace the challenges of life. Along this line, Elisabeth Moltmann-Wendel reminds us that grace is the power that allows us to affirm ourselves in our selfhood, and to live in freedom and authenticity. The uncondi-tional acceptance of God, she says, is like that of a mother who loves her newborn child regardless of whether it is beautiful or ugly.[47] Sitting under the validation of God's grace, we are able to say: "I am right, good, full of quality."[48] This "being good," I hasten to point out, should not be construed as a moral quality. Rather, it refers to the self, to one's personhood. The affirmation "I am good" means that the self is right, justified, full of quality. None of this represents a denial of the sinful nature that we all share in. What is affirmed is that knowing a loving and gracious God who, in and through Christ, sees us as right and good, means that we can see ourselves that way too.

The human gaze sometimes shames; the divine gaze always affirms and heals. "God's gaze is the *gaze of reinstatement*, which contrasts with the stares of others, intent on sizing up"[49] [emphasis in the original]. Recall Wurmser's observation that both love and unlovability are tied into the face. The face is also central in Paul Goodliff's work on the healing of shame. Goodliff makes the helpful suggestion that the affirming gaze of God can be experienced in worship through medi-tation on the face of Christ.[50] He contends that the use of a Christ icon has the potential to open a window into the acceptance and healing love of God. Contemplation on the image draws us into the embrace of divine grace and gives us the courage to face our shame.

There has always been, of course, a strong aversion in the Protestant church to the use of icons. Fear of idolatry is prominent here. To many Protestants, it appears that worshipers who make use of icons are devoted to the image rather than to God alone. Related to this is the concern that the icon functions as a magic object. In the theology of the Eastern Orthodox tradition, however, the icon is construed as a portal into the mystery of God's love and grace. As Jean-Luc Marion puts it, "[T]he iconic gaze never rests or settles on the icon, but instead rebounds upon the visible into a gaze of the infinite."[51] An icon reminds worshipers of central theological truths and heightens awareness of the divine presence.[52]

Short of a mystical encounter, we need some vehicle to draw us into an experience of the grace and mercy of God. God is not accessible via the senses; we need concrete entities that will serve a mediating function. Words, especially those of the Scriptures, work in this way. Music also directs our hearts and minds to the divine presence. The same is true of the material elements that we use in the sacraments. Images are simply one more way—a very powerful way—in which a connection with God's love is established. In the presence of an icon, "you become aware that you are present to God and that God is working on you by his grace . . ."[53]

The use of a Christ icon in the liturgy of confession offers an alternative to a verbal communication of God's unconditional acceptance. Its use opens up a space for deep contemplation. Incorporating a Christ image is potentially very powerful because of the significance of the gaze in the shame experience. The gaze of affirmation and acceptance is a strong antidote to the self-victimization that is on the one hand such a tragic, and on the other, such an intransigent aspect of the shame experience.

Applications

There are at least three practices that are suggested by our discussion on shame, sin, and confession. First, prayers of confession focusing on hiding from the opportunities and challenges of life need to be included. An awareness of the inhibiting force of shame suggests that not only moral failures but also failures in self-realization should be confessed. Or put differently, the sin of personal diminishment needs to be confessed along with the sin of overreaching. The following prayer of confession was written for a service of worship by my friend, Sandra Jebb, after reading a draft of this chapter.

> God of grace and goodness,
> your mercy comes to us is ways that continually surprise us.
> You offer your mercy with no strings attached
> when we come to you with hearts ready and open.
>
> Forgive us those times when we focus on ourselves,
> and lack faith in your strength, love, and willingness to help us.
>
> Forgive us when we block out your call
> to take up new challenges,
> because we believe we're not able or equipped to do them.
>
> Forgive us when fear makes us small,
> and doubt invades our hopefulness;
> when we make all sorts of excuses,
> and try to hide from your loving gaze.
>
> Loving God,
> In our busy daily schedules from sunrise to sunset
> remind us again of your loving presence hovering near us and
>   in us.
> Free us from the shame, self-doubt, and lack of faith
> that hinder us in the moment by moment possibilities
> that you set before us.
> Breathe your Spirit afresh on us
> so that we may be empowered to live in freedom,
> to act courageously,
> and to be active and fearless bearers of healing and mercy.
> We ask this through your Son Jesus,
> who touched and healed all who came to him. Amen.

Second, we need to be mindful that the need for an experience of God's affirming love is extremely strong in shame-prone personalities. This indicates that the word of grace that is spoken in the liturgy of confession needs to have two aspects to it. The first dimension—very familiar to us—is that through the grace of the God in Christ we are forgiven; the second is that in the eyes of grace we are whole and beautiful. After the prayers of confession, the worship leader would address the congregation in a manner such as this:

Leader

There are two words of grace I am privileged to declare. God graciously forgives our sin. And God accepts us unconditionally and lovingly affirms us.

Hear the first word of grace:
If we confess our sins,
God is faithful and just, and will forgive our sins
And cleanse us from all unrighteousness.

Hear the second word of grace:
God's acceptance of us is unconditional.
In God's eyes, we are beautiful, full of quality.[54]

The third application works in the same way as the second, except that it uses an image to facilitate an encounter with the affirmation of God. That is to say, it picks up on the beauty of the affirming gaze of God. The location for this meditation is after the prayer of confession. Choose an appropriate image of Christ for electronic projection. These are available in plentiful supply on the internet. As the image is projected, the worship leader makes a brief statement. It would be something like this: "I invite you to spend a minute or two reflecting on the image on the screen. As you look into the face of Christ, allow yourself to be drawn into the grace that unconditionally accepts and affirms you." Meditative instrumental music (music with words can be distracting) should be played for two or three minutes as people are reflecting. When the music concludes, the worship leader concludes the segment with a declaration such as this: "God is full of grace and mercy. In God's eyes, we are beautiful, full of quality. Amen."

PART 2

LAMENT: THE THERAPEUTICS
OF COMPLAINT

For virtually all of us, life is from time to time shot through with intense pain and suffering. The sources are many. People bear heavy burdens such as physical and mental illness, accidents, loss of loved ones, relationship breakdowns, job loss, and much more. Living with a vivid awareness of the deep suffering, despair, and horror that others not personally known to us experience is also a source of anguish—though of course it is not felt nearly as acutely as personal pain. It is deeply troubling to switch on the television and to witness the horrible plight of those suffering through the ravages of war, hunger, and illness. For people of faith, it is sometimes the case that anger and frustration are felt not only in relation to the situation, but also in relation to God. There is for many of us a strong feeling that God has abandoned us in our time of greatest need.

The biblical tradition of lament offers suffering people a communal space in which to express the emotions that are so real and intrusive for them and, at the same time, so scary and uncomfortable. In the laments, feelings of anger, anguish, frustration, and disappointment are vented. The lament tradition demands that we rethink our usual presuppositions concerning the nature of prayer. The spirituality of lament and the common approach to prayer stand in stark contrast.

Prayer is usually passive; the lament is an aggressive form. It is a spirituality "that is prepared to break through passive conventional piety and, so to speak, go on the attack."[1] Prayer is typically viewed as acceptance of the divine will; the lament is a cry of complaint and protest. Most think, finally, that prayer should be peaceful and controlled; lament is fired by anger and raw emotion.

It is not surprising, therefore, that most of our congregations fail to offer people an opportunity to lament. The psalms of lament hardly ever see the light of day.[2] There is an unrelenting positive tonality in virtually all of our worship services. It doesn't seem to occur to many worship leaders that complaining to God and expressing anger have a central place in Christian liturgy. If we fail, however, to provide people who are experiencing rage, confusion, and anguish with a liturgical expression of what they are feeling, we isolate and alienate them. They feel cut off and disenfranchised because the message that they get is that their feelings are not acceptable—or at least not acceptable in this place.[3]

In this second part of the book, I offer two proposals for rectifying this pastoral failure. In Chapter 3, it is recognized that there are "hard" and "soft" forms of complaint in the biblical tradition. We find, first, angry, almost violent, outbursts against God. But at the same time there are prayers of protest with the hard edges taken off. The argument in Chapter 3 is that while there should be some liturgical opportunities for expression of anger and rage, the usual pattern for lament should be the milder form. This milder approach has two forms. First, there is prayer in which the complaint is hidden within a petition. Second, the protest is covered over with an affirmation of trust. It is suggested that to regularly give an opportunity for worshipers to make their complaint against God using these soft forms will meet the needs of most of them most of the time.

It is also acknowledged, however, that it is necessary to offer a pastoral and liturgical response to those persons whose anguish is deep and whose anger against God is strong. In Chapter 4, liturgies of anger are developed. Psychological research indicates that simply venting anger does not usually lead to a significant reduction in the angry feelings. In order to bring at least partial resolution, the emotional ventilation needs to be accompanied by a cognitive reinterpretation of the relevant event or events and of the attitudes and behavior of those involved. With this in mind, it is suggested that our liturgies of anger need not only to give vent to our annoyance with God, but they also need to include theological affirmations that point in the direction of resolution.

3

Asserting Ourselves before God

The world that God has created is both beautiful and terrifying. Accordingly, our experience of it is shaped both by a joyful and comforting sense of the presence of God and a bewildering and disorienting feeling of divine absence. While worship leaders have been more or less successful in facilitating a joyful celebration of God's presence with us, they have generally struggled in their liturgical response to the hiddenness of God. Worshipers who are carrying a heavy burden of pain and distress bring to the sanctuary intense feelings of confusion and abandonment by God, and too often they receive little or no pastoral support from the liturgy. The theology of most of our worship leaders is centered on the absolute sovereignty and perfect goodness of God. What this means is that the only appropriate response in worship to human suffering is thought to be humble submission and joyful acceptance. For those who have a high view of the sovereignty and providence of God, there is no place for anything but praise and patient bearing of suffering. God is supremely gracious, wise, and good; therefore in all things we should come before God with praise on our lips and obedience in our hearts.[1] There is another option, however. In the lament tradition, there is a refusal to docilely accept the seeming absence of God. In a bold and risky move, the People of God assert themselves before the throne of God. They insistently ask the question, why? Why have you abandoned us, O God? Why do you hide your face from us? They argue with God and seek to persuade God to come quickly to their aid. It seems to them that their covenant partner is falling down on the job and they want to shake God up and get God moving again.

Now when it comes to asserting ourselves in our relationships with others, we can take either a hard or a soft line. We can be very direct and forthright, or we can take the hard edge off by being

47

understanding and flexible. It is interesting to observe that in the lament tradition we find both hard and soft versions. Sometimes the poet or biblical character launches an all-out assault on the throne; at other times the complaint against God is indirect or covered over with an affirmation of trust. In what follows, the argument will be put that while there is certainly a place in our worship for strongly asserting ourselves before God, the personal and spiritual needs of most worshipers will be met by a softer form of protest. In this softer form, negative petition and gentle protest are both employed. The first form hides complaint under petition. The second form hides complaint under an affirmation of trust.

As I have indicated, there is certainly a place for strong complaint in our worship services. For some persons, having their rage against God acknowledged will be very significant in a process of renewing their relationship with God. Most, though, will not feel a need for this strong form of protest. We Westerners simply have a different temperament to our Middle Eastern sisters and brothers. A full-blooded, angry protest to God is on the whole not something that comes naturally to us. Therefore, it is my contention that an appropriate pastoral approach is to use the softer version of lament regularly and to include the stronger protest only occasionally.

The Dominant Tradition: Submission and Praise in All Things

As I have just said, lament is an important but neglected tradition. The dominant trend in theology and in liturgy has been to focus on the sovereignty, goodness, and providence of God. There is a strong and influential line in our theological heritage that shuts lament out. Human suffering is viewed through the lens of God's absolute sovereignty and perfect goodness. The only appropriate responses are seen to be joyful praise and patient acceptance—or occasionally, repentance. I want to begin our discussion by tracing this line from Augustine, through Calvin, and ending up with Barth. There are, of course, a number of other important voices that could have been included here. I am not intending to provide anything like an exhaustive treatment; I simply want to point up one important reason why lament has all but dropped out of our theological thinking and liturgical practice.

Augustine on Suffering and Confession

In his *Confessions*, Augustine describes two episodes of intense personal grief. The first refers to his mourning the loss of a dear friend from Tagaste; the second to his grief over the death of his mother. In these descriptions that are at once beautifully poetic and deeply insightful, Augustine breaks open for his readers the depth of suffering that he has experienced. Such was the intensity of the grief that he felt over the death of his friend that a pall of darkness and gloom settled on him. In this state of acute sorrow and anguish, he felt alienated not only from all the things that he formally loved, but also from himself:

> Everything on which I set my gaze was death. My home town became a torture to me; my father's house a strange world of unhappiness; all that I had shared with him was without him transformed into a cruel torment. My eyes looked for him everywhere, and he was not there. I hated everything because they did not have him, nor could they now tell me "look, he is on the way," as used to be the case when he was alive and absent from me. I had become to myself a vast problem.[2]

Tears of grief and sorrow flooded out. It was only in his weeping that he found solace: "Only tears were sweet to me, and in my 'soul's delights' weeping had replaced my friend."[3] At this point, the modern reader will no doubt feel a strong point of connection with Augustine. His poignant description of the stabbing, disorienting pain of grief, together with his account of the healing effect of tears, resonates with the contemporary understanding of mourning. But what follows will surely knock the modern person completely off balance. Augustine informs his readers that the reason that he has offered this personal account of grief is to make a confession of sin: "Why do I speak of these matters? Now is the time not to be putting questions but to be making confession to you."[4] But why is grieving a sin? Surely it is simply a natural human reaction to the loss of a loved one. Where is the offense against God in this? Grief, for Augustine, is not in and of itself sinful; rather, it is an indication that there is disorder in one's relational value system.[5] The relational life of the Christian person has both a horizontal and a vertical dimension. Grief is an indication that one has tied oneself too strongly to the horizontal axis. Immediately after making his confession, Augustine reflects that: "I was in misery, and misery is the state of every soul overcome by friendship with mortal things and lacerated when lost."[6] It is sinful to become overly attached to the things of this world. It is appropriate to enjoy temporal things and to praise the Creator for gifting us with them. But Augustine warns against becoming "stuck in them and glued to them with love through the physical senses."[7] Temporal things are a threat to the soul because "it loves to be in them and take its repose among the objects of its love."[8] But lasting peace can be found only in the One who transcends time and suffering.

By the time Augustine lost his mother, he had converted to Christianity. As a consequence, his approach to his grief was markedly different. This time he attempted to dam up the flow of his tears:

> I closed her eyes and an overwhelming grief welled into my heart and was about to flow forth in floods of tears. But at the same time under a powerful act of mental control my eyes held back the flood and dried it up. The inward struggle put me into great agony. Then when she breathed her last, the boy Adeodatus cried out in sorrow and was pressed by all of us to be silent. In this way too something of the child in me, which had slipped towards weeping, was checked and silenced by the youthful voice, the voice of my heart.[9]

Augustine mustered all of his formidable will to hold back the tears. But grief is such an overwhelming force that even he could not control it. After Monica's burial, as he lay in bed contemplating his mother's love and devotion, the floodgates opened. As in the case of his weeping over his friend, he makes his confession over his outward expression of grief: "And now, Lord, I make my confession to you in writing. Let anyone who wishes read and interpret as he pleases. If he finds fault that I wept for my mother for a fraction of an hour . . . let him not mock me but rather, if a person of much charity, let him weep himself before you for my sins . . ."[10] Augustine is asking a person of charity to weep before God for his sin of being too attached to a mortal person. It is not the weeping *per se*, but rather what it is a sign of that is the problem.[11] That he should break down and cry over the loss of his mother is a clear indication that he had bound himself too closely to her. Augustine ponders on why it is that he suffered such a sharp stab of inward grief. "It must have been the fresh wound caused by the break in the habit formed by our living together, a very affectionate and precious bond . . ."[12] Each and every person that we form close attachments with must at some time depart, and when he or she goes so does our peace. It is only in God that we find complete repose. The bonds that tie us to God can never be broken, unless one chooses this side of heaven to do so. "The Word himself cries to you to return. There is the place of undisturbed quietness where love is not deserted if it does not itself depart."[13] Though the things of this world are given to us by the Creator for our enjoyment, we are not to cling to them. It is in God and God alone that we find lasting peace and happiness. Augustine contends that if a person is overcome with grief it is evidence of the fact that she is guilty of too much worldly affection. He would not think for a minute that one should raise a protest against God for what seems to be a hiding of the divine face in a time of deep suffering. Confession, not lament, is the appropriate response.

Calvin on Patience in Suffering

If Augustine asks us to confess our suffering (or at least what it signifies), John Calvin requires us to bear it patiently. God knows us through and through, notes Calvin. God knows our frail and sinful human nature. And God knows that we need the firm hand of discipline if we are to conform ourselves ever more closely to Christ. This is Calvin's starting point in his approach to human suffering. In times of prosperity, health, and general flourishing, we become over-confident in our capacities and inner resources.[14] When we are indulged by God's kindness and goodness, we are corrupted by pride and complacency.

> Thus, lest we become emboldened by an over-abundance of wealth; lest elated with honor, we grow proud; lest inflated with other advantages of the body, or mind, or fortune, we grow insolent, the Lord himself interferes as he sees to be expedient by means of the cross, subduing and curbing the arrogance of our flesh.[15]

Suffering comes from the hand of God and is an expression of divine providence. God lovingly chastises us for the furtherance of our salvation. For Calvin, the world is "a vast reformatory."[16]

According to Calvin, Christians are aware—or at least we should be—that the Lord wills the suffering that we experience. The truth is, we deserve the discipline that we receive; all divine actions—including works of chastisement—are shaped by divine justice and equity.[17] We therefore have no reason to complain. The appropriate response from Christians is to bear our sufferings patiently, comforted by the knowledge that God has our eternal good in mind.

> [W]hatever be the kind of cross to which we are subjected, we shall in the greatest straits firmly maintain our patience. Adversity will have its bitterness, and sting us . . . but our conclusion will always be, The Lord so willed it, therefore let us follow his will.[18]

Calvin does not expect Christians to be superhuman, however. He does not expect us to bear the burden of life's pain and distress with a smile on our faces. With this in mind, Calvin protests against the new version of Stoicism that some Christians of the time were embracing. Convinced of the virtue in the Stoic principle of *apatheia*, these misguided persons claimed that the expression of emotion in the face of trial and tribulation constitutes a moral failure. According to Calvin, the new Stoics "convert patience into stupor, and a brave and firm [person] into a block."[19] It is natural to shun and dread suffering. It is only human to feel resentment, anxiety, and depression in the face of tribulation. But, Calvin contends, Christians in the end recognize that the suffering they are experiencing is ultimately an expression of God's love and mercy, and they are therefore able to bear it patiently. Since this suffering has come upon us as an expression of divine discipline, impatience constitutes rebellion against divine justice. If we are able to patiently endure suffering, God uses it to help us overcome our sinful tendencies and to conform ourselves more completely to Christ. The knowledge that bearing our burdens unites us more closely to our Savior is a great comfort. Calvin writes as follows:

> How powerful should it soften the bitterness of the cross, to think that the more we are afflicted with adversity, the surer we are made of our fellowship with Christ; by communion with whom our sufferings are not only blessed to us, but tend greatly to the furtherance of our salvation.[20]

In sum, God uses suffering for our salvation, so we should bear it patiently.

Barth on Joy in Suffering

The central term in Karl Barth's approach to suffering is joy. For Barth, to be joyful means essentially that one expects that life will show itself as God's gift of grace.[21] God has given us life, and more importantly all of life is caught up in the covenant of grace. God is present in and through Christ in everything that takes place in the sphere of life as Lord, Savior, and Victor. There is no aspect of life that does not come under divine sovereignty and grace. Those things that we assign a positive value to—health, prosperity, achievement, a happy family life, etc.—and those things that we judge to be negatives—sickness, poverty, failure, and family breakdown, etc.—together sit under the divine overrule. Even that which is totally alien to God, utterly opposed to God, what Barth refers to as *das Nichtige* (nothingness or the nihil), comes under God's rule.[22]

It is because everything belongs to God and is ours only as gift, because the divine will and purpose is being worked out in every aspect of the operation of the cosmos, that God alone decides what it is that is the true goal of all human activity, and therefore what is our true joy.

> But this means that our will for joy, our preparedness for it, must be wide open in this direction, in the direction of His unknown and even obscure disposing, if it is to be the right and good preparedness commanded in this matter. It should not be limited by the suffering of life, because even life's suffering . . . comes from God, the very One who summons us to rejoice.[23]

All of human life and history falls under the "shadow of the cross,"[24] the cross that is the judgment and the salvation of the world. It is here that we encounter with absolute clarity the height, depth, and breadth of God's love and grace. We should not therefore "be surprised and angry that we live in this shadow." Everything that we believe is a source of our joy and fulfillment "breaks forth from this shadow."[25]

> But this means in practice that the real test of our joy of life as a commanded and therefore a true and good joy is that we do not evade the shadow of the cross of Jesus Christ and are not unwilling to be genuinely joyful even as we bear the sorrows laid upon us.[26]

Barth's argument, then, is that because God has made everything in the created order God's own through the Son, everything—bright and dark, day and night, success and failure, joy and sorrow, birth and death—is good. There is no reason for disquiet, for discontent, for complaint when we find ourselves in the deep abyss, when light turns into shadow. The shadow, every bit as much as the light, comes from God and is comprehended by God. In a word, everything is embraced by providence. That Barth is able to posit joy as the appropriate response in the face of the suffering is a natural outcome of the way he constructs the doctrine of providence.

Barth defines providence as "the superior dealings of the Creator with His creation, the wisdom, omnipotence and goodness with which He maintains and governs in time this distinct reality according to the counsel of His own will."[27] This governance or divine overrule, Barth insists, is absolute. There is no area, no aspect, no creaturely occurrence in the life of the cosmos that does not come under God's rule, and, moreover, God's will and purpose is expressed in all these things. That this is the case is something that Barth asserts time and again in his treatment of providence.

God's lordship is not just any kind of lordship, observes Barth, but is instead a "fatherly lordship."[28] It is therefore a kind, loving, and friendly lordship. Much more significantly, it is governance that is expressed in and through the life, death, and resurrection of the Son. The rule of God has a very definite *telos*. This *telos* is union with God in Christ.[29] God is at work in all things and in all people establishing a covenant of grace. In preserving us in being and companioning us in all our activities the ultimate aim of God is to draw all people into this saving covenant.

That it is a covenant founded on grace means that the gift is freely given. God is present in all our activity; God rules in all our activity; but God does this in such a way that we are granted a genuinely free sphere of operation.[30] The gift of God's presence would not be a gift if the human was constrained, controlled, and humiliated by that presence. Yet Barth is quick to point out that this does not mean, cannot mean, that human activity is in some respects independent of God. God's rule covers all aspects and areas of creaturely occurrence. God's project of drawing all people into the covenant of grace is worked out in and through human activity. What this means is that the activity of God and the activity of the human is ultimately a unity. The companioning of human persons means that God is "so present in the activity of the creature, and present with such sovereignty and almighty power, that [God's] own action takes place in and with and over the activity of the creature."[31]

The logic of Barth's theology is clear. God's lordship means that everything that exists belongs to God and is filled with the divine presence. Every human activity is foreordained by God and used by God for the purpose of communicating the divine love expressed in the cross of Christ and spread abroad in the power of the Holy Spirit. If the covenant of grace is at the center of everything that happens—the light as well as the shadow—the appropriate response at all times and in all situations is praise and joy. Even in suffering we can be joyful. Indeed, the real test of our joy in Christ is whether or not it is still to be found in times of sorrow.

The Road Less Traveled: Complaint and Protest

Conditioned as we are by the kind of theological thinking that I have outlined above, it is no surprise that lament has all but been dropped from our worship. Ellen Charry puts it very well:

> On the view that God's goodness, knowledge, and power are absolute, shock and anger in the face of tragedy are unseemly because they appear to doubt God. On a very strong belief in God's powerful goodness, what happens must be for our good, and we should rejoice gratefully, even if we are being punished. For such persons, lament is also precluded because it conveys a questioning of divine goodness.[32]

The rejection of lament and the promotion of a response to suffering shaped around humble submission and joyful praise in all things can be traced to the Bible. We need to recognize, though, that there are also other notes that are played in the Scriptures—those of complaint and protest. The People of God do not always show a readiness to quietly and patiently accept the fate that has befallen them. In times of distress and misfortune, they complain to God about what they see as God's inconsistency. God has blessed them in the past for their fidelity. Now, as far as they can tell, they are no less faithful in honoring their covenant commitments, but God seems to have abandoned them. If they were guilty of grave sins, they would expect to be heavily chastised. But they consider that the pain that has been visited on them is out of all proportion to any offense they may have committed against God. They are not prepared to docilely accept their suffering as part of God's perfect will. Instead, they launch an assault on the throne of God, asking the question, why? Why, God? Why have you abandoned us to this horrible fate? It seems as if God has become an enemy. But ultimately lament is an affirmation of faith. Though those making the complaint are filled with anger and confusion, still they desperately hang on to God. "The sufferers continue to cling to God, whom they can no longer understand. Their despair can almost exhaust their patience . . . But they can go no further than this; accusation never turns to condemnation."[33] There is strong protest, but it is virtually always joined to an affirmation of hope.

Israel's Assertiveness in the Face of Suffering

This tradition of protest needs to be set in the context of the contractual theology that is absolutely central in the belief and practice of Israel. The Sinai covenant sets the life of Israel and its relationship with YHWH in the framework of a tight system of sanctions. If the People honor their covenant commitments, they can expect to be blessed by their God. But if they fall away from these commitments, they will come under divine curse. Contractual theology establishes personal and communal life as an ordered experience governed by a clearly defined moral rationality. There is a predictable pattern to all of life; the pattern is set by the covenant laws and sanctions.

In the frame of contractual theology, there is a particular approach to suffering. Both the reason and the remedy are plain for all to see. People are afflicted by pain and distress because they have sinned against God. If they expect to be delivered out of their suffering, they should turn to God in repentance and plead for mercy and healing. Job's friends articulate this frame for suffering very clearly. For example, Bildad offers this piece of pastoral counsel to Job:

> Does God pervert justice?
> Or does the Almighty pervert the right?
> If your children sinned against him,
> he delivered them into the power of their transgression.
> If you will seek God
> and make supplication to the almighty,
> if you are pure and upright,

surely then he will rouse himself for you
and restore to you your rightful place (Job 8.3-6).

Though this kind of thinking is prominent in the Hebrew Scriptures, we also find opposing voices. There are those who cannot accept
it because it simply does not match their experience. They have done
nothing so wrong that they deserve the horrible fate that has befallen
them. This system governing divine–human relations seems to them
to be too hard and uncompromising. It needs to be strongly challenged. "The reason . . . is that *it lacks a human face* . . . It is a system of
reality that allows no slippage, no graciousness, no room for failure"
(emphasis in the original).[34]

The lament tradition is grounded in the sense that God is acting
inconsistently. Often there is a protestation of innocence. It is obviously not the case that the sufferers think that they are completely free
of guilt. Rather, they assert that any wrongdoing on their part does
not merit the harsh punishment that has been meted out. The poets of
the lament want some answers. They can no longer understand God
and God's ways. The divine *modus operandi* has become a puzzle. It is
not an intellectual exercise that we are talking about here, but rather
something that is experienced in the inner depths. The psalmist feels
the tension and confusion so acutely that it is tearing him apart. Out
of this inner turmoil comes a desperate need to understand. The poet
wants to know why God has allowed him to fall into this awful
situation:

My God, my God, why have you forsaken me?
Why are you so far from helping me, from the words of my
    groaning?
O my God, I cry by day, but you do not answer;
and by night, but find no rest (Ps. 22.1, 2).

Why, Lord? This is the question that burns within the hearts of the
lament poets. "The why is at the core of the lament against God
throughout the entire OT. The one who laments can no longer understand God."[35] The other question that the psalmists commonly put
with some urgency is how long. How long, O God, will you hide
your face from us? How long must we endure your absence? How
long must we wait to see your justice done?

What seems to be God's slowness in enacting divine justice is also at the center of Jeremiah's confessions. The townspeople are deeply offended by Jeremiah's proclamation of their guilt and of the awful punishment that is coming their way. The prophet urgently presses his message; he is constantly warning the people; but nothing happens. It is life as usual for them. Jeremiah has become a laughingstock. Not only that, but his life is being constantly threatened. Jeremiah impatiently pleads for the Lord to bring retribution against these evildoers. That God is so slow with his justice is cause for complaint:

> You will be in the right, O Lord,
> when I lay charges against you;
> but let me put my case to you.
> Why does the way of the guilty prosper?
> Why do all who are treacherous survive? (Jer. 12.1)

As the pressure builds and builds on the prophet, he reaches breaking point. Jeremiah begins to lament his whole life (Jer. 20.14–18). In his desperation and turmoil he takes aim squarely at God. He protests that God has seduced and deceived him (Jer. 15.18, 20.7). It is not absolutely clear what Jeremiah means by this accusation of divine deception.[36] It could be that he is expressing his frustration over his public humiliation and accusing God of misleading him by not bringing about the doom that he has been commissioned to announce. Or it could be that Jeremiah is disappointed over the fact that despite his urgent and persistent warnings there has been no response from the people. Be that as it may, the main point is that in the face of public shame and violent threats Jeremiah is not prepared to humbly accept that God's will is being done. The prophet asserts himself before the God whom he considers has failed him.

The manner in which Jeremiah found the nerve to assault the throne of God very likely had a significant effect on the writer(s) of the book of Job.[37] Job's protest against the unfair treatment meted out by God is particularly harsh. The start of the book, however, gives absolutely no indication of this. Job humbly and quietly submits to the sovereignty of God. The Lord has the right to bless him with prosperity, health, and family; and the Lord has the right to take it all away (Job 1.21). How can we account for this docile stance that is so out of kilter with Job's approach in the rest of the book? Perhaps he was initially in a state of shock; feeling totally overwhelmed by the force of the blows he received. In this shaken state, he numbly and meekly accepts his fate at the hand of God. But with distance from the painful reversals and the time for reflection that this provides, he decides that he is not ready to quietly accept his fate after all.[38] In fact, he wants to call contractual theology into question. That he could be afflicted in this way despite his innocence means that it simply does not work:

> Though I am innocent, my own mouth would condemn me;
> though I am blameless; I do not know myself;
> I loathe my life.
> It is all one; therefore I say,
> he destroys both the blameless and the wicked.
> When disaster brings sudden death,
> he mocks at the calamity of the innocent.
> The earth is given into the hand of the wicked;
> he covers the eyes of his judges. (Job 9.20–24)

Job's challenge to God is a bold one; it took a lot of nerve. He took the risk that God might not receive it, that God might react to his assertiveness by crushing him. At the end of the book (Job 42.7), however, we read of God's validation of Job's approach. Brueggemann paraphrases it nicely: "Tell your three friends to clam up because they are so boring. I am not going to listen to them anymore. But you, Job, if you speak for them I will listen because you're my kind of guy."[39]

It is clear, then, that there were those amongst the people of Israel who in the face of deep pain and distress tested contractual theology and found it wanting. The ones who lament are those who are so fed up with suffering that they can no longer suppress their anger and disappointment with God. They have had enough of being docile and submissive. On this Brueggemann is eloquent:

> The moment when Israel found the nerve and the faith to risk an assault on the throne of God with complaint was a decisive moment . . . The lament is a dramatic, rhetorical, liturgical act of speech which is irreversible . . . It makes clear that Israel will no longer be submissive, subservient recipients of decrees from the throne. There is a bold movement and voice from Israel's side which does not blindly and docilely accept, but means to have its dangerous say, even in the face of God.[40]

In having "its dangerous say," Israel "pushes the relationship to the boundaries of unacceptability."[41] I find here an interesting correlation with the results of psychological research on assertiveness. Assertiveness is variously defined in the literature, but for our purposes it is sufficient to construe it as a tendency in a person "to actively defend, pursue, and speak out for his or her interests."[42] Researchers on assertion are agreed that speaking up and pursuing one's interests most often has a negative social impact. Persons engaging in assertive behavior are generally viewed by others as less friendly and likeable than those who adopt a non-assertive stance.[43] Taking an assertive approach puts a strain on the relationship. Now the dynamics in the YHWH–Israel relation on the one hand, and in purely human relations on the other, are quite different. The issue of whether or not Israel presents as "friendly and likeable" is presumably not a major concern for God! But God does have primacy in the relationship and for Israel to rise up and state its case was risky. It was not clear to the People ahead of time that YHWH would find their assertiveness acceptable.

With the fact that assertion puts a strain on a relationship in mind, a number of psychologists prefer to train clients in an empathic rather than a direct approach. In empathic assertion, the feelings or the position of the other person is acknowledged. For example, a person changing an appointment may say, "I'm sorry to inconvenience you, but I really do need to reschedule my Friday session." The use of empathy is but one possibility in relation to taking the hard edge off assertive speech. It is part of a cluster of behaviors that together constitute an "obligation component."[44] Other options in this group include extra consideration, flexibility and compromise, and expressions of affection, appreciation, and gratitude. The point in referring to the obligation component in assertion is not to suggest that Israel could have been a little more empathic in its protest. I have drawn attention to the fact that there are "hard" and "soft" versions of assertiveness because we find a parallel in the lament literature. In having its say, Israel does not always launch a full scale assault. Some of the laments are statements of protest with the hard edges taken off.

Hard and Soft Forms of Lament

I will first lay out some representative strong versions of complaint. Here reference will be made to laments in the Psalms, in Jeremiah, and in Job. The soft versions are drawn only from the Psalms. It is evident that some of the psalmists did not feel comfortable directly challenging God.

Amongst the hard versions of protest we find the following:

> You have made us like sheep for slaughter,
> and have scattered us among the nations.
> You have sold your people for a trifle,
> demanding no high price for them . . .
> Rouse yourself! Why do you sleep, O Lord?
> Awake, do not cast us off forever! (Ps. 44.11–12, 23)

> Why is my pain unceasing,
> my wound incurable, refusing to be healed?
> Truly, you are to me like a deceitful brook, like waters that fail.
>   (Jer. 15.18)

> Why are times not kept by the almighty, and why do those who
>   know him never see his days?
> The wicked remove landmarks;
> they seize flocks and pasture them.
> They drive away the donkey of the orphan;
> they take the widow's ox for a pledge.
> They thrust the needy off the road;
> the poor of the earth all hide themselves . . .
> [The poor] go about naked, without clothing;
> though hungry, they carry the sheaves;
> between their terraces they press out oil;
> they tread the wine presses, but suffer thirst.
> From the city the dying groan,
> and the throat of the wounded cries for help;
> yet God pays no attention to their prayer. (Job 24.1–4, 10–12)

Along with these direct, forthright assaults on the throne of God we find indirect ones. Westermann has identified what he calls the "negative petition" in the psalms of lament.[45] Here the complaint is hidden within the petition. In order to communicate his sense of abandonment by God, the poet uses verbs such as to hide, drive out, cast off, forsake, and be silent. Psalm 27 is a good example of the negative petition:

> Do not hide your face from me.
> Do not turn your servant away in anger . . .
> Do not cast me off, do not forsake me,
> O God of my salvation! (Ps. 27.9)

There are other lament psalms in which this same reluctance to directly confront God is in evidence. The question of why—why do you hide yourself?—is asked, but it is covered with an affirmation of trust.[46] The hard edge of the complaint is taken off by coupling it with a declaration of faith. Consider these examples:

> I say to God, my rock,
> "why have you forgotten me?" (Ps. 42.9)

> For you are the God in whom I take refuge;
> why have you cast me off? (Ps. 43.2)

Lament in Contemporary Worship

The practice of lament is hardly ever part of our worship. Within our congregations there are people who are experiencing deep pain and distress. They pray fervently for God to come to their aid, but God seems a long way off. These are people who are frustrated, angry, and disappointed. In our liturgies, we need to provide an opportunity for these suffering and alienated folk to come before God with their sense of abandonment.

Having noted above that there are strong and mild forms of complaint in the lament tradition, my suggestion is that it is the latter style that should be used most frequently in our worship services. Some will interpret this as a failure of nerve. It will be seen as a capitulation to the pervasive liturgical culture of niceness and politeness. The first point that I would make in response to this anticipated criticism is that I do in fact believe that there is a place for offering "liturgies of anger." In the next chapter, a proposal for such liturgies is offered.

The second response that I would like to make is that the psychological research, as we have seen, shows quite clearly that most people do not appreciate direct, forthright assertive behavior. They just do not like it; they find people who engage in it less likeable and friendly than those who do not. The feeling of discomfort will very likely be intensified when the assertiveness is set in the context of prayer. For some, to chastise the Sovereign One, the creator and governor of the universe seems like the ultimate act of arrogance and disrespect.

Against my proposal, it could also be argued that there is little point in trying to soften the impact of incorporating lament through using less confronting forms because there will be those worshipers who will be opposed to the idea of prayers of protest no matter what. It may well be the case that there will be a cohort in the congregation who will never accept that complaint is a legitimate form of prayer. However, a thorough program of congregational education on the place of lament in Jewish and Christian worship life should serve to bring a significant number of the skeptics on board. Such a program will highlight the fact that there may actually be more love and faith contained in a protest against what seems to be God's absence than there is in docile submission and quiet resignation. It will point to the truth that there is more authenticity associated with bringing our total experience of life—peacefulness *and* anger, a sense of order *and* disorientation, God's presence *and* God's absence—than with offering up an edited version in which only the nice, "acceptable" bits are included. My contention is that amongst those who have come to appreciate the place of lament in worship, the majority will engage more naturally with the soft version than the hard one. Moreover, in their wrestling with the hiddenness of God, to have the opportunity simply to put the questions why and how long will be healing and renewing. This will be enough for most worshipers.

Nancy Duff suggests that just as we call people to repentance every Sunday, we should also establish a weekly practice of calling people to lament.[47] This may be overdoing it. I am not convinced that we need to lament every time we gather for worship. Perhaps the pastoral needs of worshipers will be adequately met by monthly expressions of complaint and protest. The reader will make up her or his own mind on this. The point is that the practice of lament needs to be a regular feature of our Sunday worship. Further, most often our prayers of protest should be clear and firm, but without the sharp and ragged edges that we find in some forms of Old Testament lament. This softer form of assertion before God, I contend, will adequately meet the pastoral needs of most worshipers. In my pastoral experience, most do not feel a need to rage against God. But many do experience disappointment and confusion over what seems to them to be the absence of God. The opportunity to bring these feelings and concerns before God has the potential to heal the inner wounds and to reinvigorate faith.

There are a number of worship books available that include examples of the style of lament that I have been advocating.[48] By way of supplementing these fine offerings, the following liturgies are provided.

Liturgy A

This liturgy is inspired by the medieval Jewish worship practice of inserting poems of protest or *piyyutim* into the statutory liturgy.[49] The traditional Jewish liturgy contains not only standard prayers taken from the Talmud and the ritual codes, but also various kinds of poetic embellishments. These poetic additions take the form of hymns to be sung either prior to, or after, the standard prayers, and of poetic inserts in the standard prayers themselves. The particular practice informing the liturgy below is the juxtaposition of the poem of protest with prayers of adoration and praise. The poem is sandwiched between the pious prayers. The special power of the protest is derived from its setting in a dialectical structure.

The first step in this liturgy is to choose an appropriate hymn of praise. Then a number of laments need to be written to match the number of verses. In the service, the congregation is instructed to pause after each verse, or after each time the refrain is sung, in order to offer the prayers of protest. I've chosen the hymn, "How Great Thou Art." The refrain of this hymn is as follows:

Then sings my soul, my Savior God, to thee,
How great thou art, how great thou art!
Then sings my soul, my Savior God, to thee,
How great thou art, how great thou art!

Lament 1
(recited by the congregation after the refrain is sung for the first
time)
Great you are, O God.
Why have you forgotten us in our suffering?

Lament 2
(recited after the refrain is sung for the second time)
We are hurting, Savior God.
How long must we endure the pain?

Lament 3
You are the rock of our salvation.
Why do you hide your face from us?

Lament 4
Christ has won the victory over sin and death. Alleluia!
When will you lift the heavy burden from us?

Liturgy B

In this responsive prayer, a refrain (based on Ps. 27.9) is recited after each prayer offered by the leader:

Leader:
Fear and hatred are everywhere.
Bombs are blasting; guns are spitting death;
And communities are being shattered.
The violence is like a forest fire out of control.

People:
Do not hide your face from us.
Do not cast us off, do not forsake us,
O God of our salvation.

Leader:
Disease preys on us mercilessly.
No one knows when or where it will strike next.
There are bodies that are wracked and ruined.
The afflicted live with constant worry and distress.

People:
Do not hide your face from us.
Do not cast us off, do not forsake us,
O God of our salvation.

Leader:
The end of an unemployment line is an unhappy place.
Economic jargon offered as an explanation is cold comfort.
It's so difficult to cope with feelings of worthlessness, anxiety,
   and despair.

People:
Do not hide your face from us.
Do not cast us off, do not forsake us,
O God of our salvation.

Leader:
This is pain like no other.
To lose someone you love is to lose too much.
Everything seems so empty; the joy is all but gone.
Those who mourn cry out: When will it get better?

People:
Do not hide your face from us.
Do not cast us off, do not forsake us,
O God of our salvation.

Leader:
Life sometimes seems to ask too much of us.
Our chests get tight and our heads begin to hurt.
The pressures are constant.
Life was not meant to be this hard.

People:
Do not hide your face from us.
Do not cast us off, do not forsake us,
O God of our salvation.

Leader:
God of grace and mercy, we give you thanks for hearing our
cries of distress. We praise you for your love and fidelity. Amen.

In these liturgies that I have offered, there is complaint and protest,
but the hard edges have been taken off. On occasions, however, there

are people in worship for whom it was a real struggle just to get themselves into the sanctuary. They feel deep disappointment and disillusionment with God; there is anger in their bellies. There is a strong strand within the tradition of lament that speaks to their experience. We now turn our attention to the shape and function of "liturgies of anger."[50]

4

Praying Our Anger

Judy is a leader in her church. Normally, she is in church every Sunday, and she loves it. Recently, however, she has been feeling that she simply cannot bring herself to join in worship. Today she is back in church after an absence of four weeks. During the regular "Joys and Concerns" segment in the service she stands to address the congregation:

> I guess many of you are wondering why I haven't been in church for a while. You all know how much this congregation means to me, and how I love to share in worship with you. Over the last few months I've been going through a really difficult time in my relationship with the Lord. For some reason, all the harsh realities in the world—the things I mostly seem to be able to keep at arm's length—have been really hitting me. Two of my close friends have been diagnosed with cancer and things look pretty bad for them. I find myself thinking a lot about all the crazy violence, hatred, and killing that's going on day in, day out in places like Iraq, Afghanistan, and the Dafur region. I can't make sense of it. It's been really getting to me. I'm normally pretty upbeat, but I've been real depressed lately. And for the first time I've found myself getting angry at God. We believe that God is unsurpassed goodness. We believe that God is a God of power and might. But I've been thinking to myself, "Things just don't add up. If all that's true, I expect God to being doing a heck of a lot more than he is." So I say to him, "It's not good enough, Lord. I need some answers." But so far . . . nothing!
>
> You know why I haven't been coming to worship? Because I just couldn't face you folk. All your bright, happy faces and joyful praise to the Lord comin' right at me. Ya know, I don't feel much like praising God at the moment. Worship here with you

is not a place I want to be right now. It really hurts me to say this, but there it is. It's the truth. I'm sorry.

Judy's congregation is not an isolated case. It is only rarely that a worshiping community will make space for the expression of feelings of anger against God. As we saw in the last chapter, the psalms of lament provide an opportunity for an honest and forthright outpouring of frustration, disappointment, and anger. It is part of our heritage, but it is a part that we have let slip away. It is not difficult to see why. The expression of anger in any context is for most of us uncomfortable and for some of us frightening. In the context of the divine–human relationship we may go past these negatives into feelings of profound disrespect or even blasphemy. For the psalmists, however, rage against YHWH, far from constituting infidelity, was a deep act of faith. As we shall see, they took YHWH's covenantal promises very seriously. They had an unshakable faith that what God pledges, God will do. If God seemed to be falling down on the job, so to speak, they felt entitled to be angry and to make their protest in the strongest possible terms. When one reads the psalms of lament one has the strong sense that this is real, raw, honest faith at work. This is what Judy desperately wanted in her crisis of faith, but sadly she couldn't come to worship because she knew that all she would get was polite, dignified prayers and happy, smiling praise.

To make a space for feelings of anger in worship is to take worshipers into a tumultuous, disturbing, and uncomfortable place. It is not a place that we should go to too often. We don't need to. Let the worship of the Lord be mostly joyful and celebratory. God's boundless grace and love should indeed warm our hearts and fill our mouths with praise. But the experience of Judy serves as a salutary reminder that in our Sunday congregations there are people who are experiencing spiritual vertigo, who have been knocked off-balance by an encounter with the dark and ugly side of life, who are feeling acutely the fact that life isn't fair. They are angry about all this, and they are angry with God. Reclaiming the lament tradition for contemporary worship validates these kinds of feelings and allows for their expression. Such expression, in turn, opens up the possibility of at least partial resolution.

Others have also argued for a renewal of liturgies of anger. They point out that just as the people of Israel felt quite at liberty to vent their anger, so too should we moderns. What I have discovered in my research on the psychology of anger, however, is that reduction of angry feelings requires not only expression or ventilation but also some cognitive reinterpretation. That is, the situation that caused the anger needs to be mentally reframed if the anger is to be dissipated. With this in mind, what I will be arguing in this chapter is that our liturgies of anger need to do more than simply give vent to our annoyance with God; they also need to include theological pointers in the direction of resolution. In both the psalms of lament themselves and in other places in the Christian heritage we find helpful theologies for grappling with what seems to be God's failure to act in the midst of evil and suffering. These theological interpretations can be distilled into a short liturgical affirmation and included after the expression of anger. The theological distillates provide an opportunity for the cognitive reinterpretation that psychological research identifies as significant in the resolution of anger.

Before we get to this end-point in our discussion, it is necessary to set the scene. In order to do this, we will need to discuss the place of anger in Israel's worship poetry.

Anger in the Psalms

Our Sunday worship tends to be characterized by restrained emotion, polite petition, and reverent praise. It is a confronting experience to read some of the psalms of lament and encounter unabashed expression of anger and rage. How could they do that, we wonder? Did it not enter their heads that their prayer could be construed as irreverent, disrespectful, or even blasphemous? That they did not think of their poems of complaint in this way is due to their understanding of the covenant and of the rights and duties of the parties to it. This was alluded to in the previous chapter; here it will be developed more fully.

The covenant that YHWH established with Israel is grounded in, on the one hand, YHWH's promise to bless and protect Israel, and on the other, Israel's pledge to be faithful to the divine will as articulated in the *Torah*. Integral to this covenant relationship is a blessing and curse structure. YHWH can be relied upon to reign down blessings upon the People, but only on the condition that they are faithful. There are sanctions embedded in YHWH's relationship with Israel. If Israel falls into rebellion and infidelity it can expect to have YHWH's wrath visited upon it.

70

The curse of the covenant, however, is not the major note struck in the relationship. Israel saw itself as living under the blessing of a loving and gracious God. The appropriate response is wholehearted praise and devotion. Further, as Brueggemann has shown, there is an indissoluble link between Israel's praise and its obedience.[1] "Praise," he observes, "is a mood and practice of liturgical activity that provides the glad and generative context for obedience."[2] Praise, in the deepest sense, is the act of unreservedly handing over one's life to God; it is therefore the guarantor that obedience is not something given grudgingly, but freely and in a spirit of gratitude.

When the covenant is viewed by Israel as operating as it should— YHWH is at work blessing it with prosperity, peace, and security— praise comes readily and is offered fulsomely. In a climate of blessing, the heart overflows with wonder, amazement, and gratitude. But of course life for Israel did not always run along smoothly and happily; there were times when YHWH's hand of blessing seemed to be tightly shut. There were times when the joy and peace of life were shattered. In the psalms of lament we read of such times—times in which the poet feels torn apart by sickness, or by threats from enemies, or by shame and humiliation. This shattering of the poet's life led to a "shattering of meaning."[3] We find the poets struggling to make sense of the fate that has befallen them:

My God, my God, why have you forsaken me? Why are you so far from helping me, from the words of my groaning? (Ps. 22.1)

Rouse yourself! Why do you sleep, O Lord?
Awake, do not cast us off forever!
Why do you hide your face?
Why do you forget our affliction and oppression? (Ps. 44.23–24)

Personal and communal meaning is shattered because YHWH the Faithful One seems to have fallen down on his covenantal responsibilities. God has pledged to come quickly and mightily to the aid of the People when they are troubled or threatened. In the dark times, the power, goodness, and majesty of YHWH are expected to be fully present. That is what YHWH promised in establishing the covenant with Israel. But it is not what is being experienced now. The poets struggle with the experience of a strange absence, with the hiddenness of God.

How should the People of God react in this situation? One option is found in contractual theology. On this view, if things are awry then someone has failed in their covenant commitments and it sure isn't God. The counsel of those advocating a strict version of this theology is to respond to the crisis by confessing sin and renewing the pledge to faithful living. But this is not Israel's characteristic liturgical and pastoral option.[4] As we saw in the last chapter, the primary response for Israel when its life is unraveling is one of lament and complaint. Israel is usually not prepared to roll over and take the blame for the problems: "Complaint and lament subvert the thin claim of obedience by a practice that is genuinely dialogical so that Yahweh's primacy and preeminence in the relationship are provisionally overcome."[5] Two very important aspects of the covenant relationship are alluded to in this provocative statement. First, the covenant is a genuinely dialogical relationship. The God of the covenant is experienced by the People as a "You," and this means that God can be addressed by them in a spirit of reciprocity.[6] That there is reciprocity in the covenant relationship means—and this is the second important aspect—that when YHWH seems to have defaulted on his commitment, Israel has a right to reverse the roles and forcefully make its moral claim on him. This temporary turning of the tables is captured well by Jewish theologian, David Blumenthal, when he observes as follows:

> As God is a jealous God demanding loyalty from us in covenant, so we, in our searing humiliation, demand. We transform our anger, through the covenant, into our moral claim against God. As God is angry with us in covenant, so we are angry with God in covenant. We experience a true anger, which becomes a true moral claim, rooted in our mutual covenantal debt.[7]

This kind of approach to the divine–human relationship cuts right across the grain of the theological scholasticism that shapes the understanding most of us have of the nature of this relationship. According to this theology, God is wholly other, absolutely sovereign, inscrutable, immutable, and impassible—in a word, "above the fray."[8] God is therefore the one making all the demands and issuing all the challenges; the human partner has no moral claim on God. This one-sided style of relating is totally foreign to Israel's thinking. Israel locates God *in* the fray. It is more than ready, when the circumstances seem to warrant it, to voice its strong protest. This is a daring theology and a risky practice; it pushes the relationship to the absolute limit.[9] The psalmists dare to rage against God; they are bold enough to go on the attack. They know that if they have been rebellious, they have no right to complain about their misfortune. That is why in launching a "prosecutorial argument against/with God,"[10] they must at the same time be able to declare their innocence. The last stanza of the following lament is a good example of this.

In God we have boasted continually,
and we will give thanks to your name forever.

Yet you have rejected us and abased us,
and have not gone out with our armies.
You made us turn back from the foe,
and our enemies have gotten spoil.
You have made us like sheep for slaughter,
and have scattered us among the nations.
You have sold your people for a trifle,
demanding no high price for them.

You have made us the taunt of our neighbors,
the derision and scorn of those around us.
You have made us a byword among the nations,
a laughingstock among the peoples.
all day long my disgrace is before me,
and shame has covered my face
at the words of the taunters and revilers,
at the sight of the enemy and the avenger.

All this has come upon us,
yet we have not forgotten you,
or been false to your covenant.
Our heart has not turned back,
nor have our steps departed from your way,
yet you have broken us in the haunt of jackals,
and covered us with deep darkness. (Ps. 44.8–19)

Here we see very clearly demonstrated the People's conviction that they have the right to sometimes reverse the roles in the covenant relationship. If they judge that they have been faithful to the covenant and are therefore undeserving of the pain and suffering that has been visited on them, they are more than ready to launch a withering attack on their God. This is a very genuine and honest way of relating. We do not see here any hiding behind polite and subtle rhetoric. The anger and rage are bubbling over; restraints are shed and the poet goes on the attack. The lament psalms confront us with a vigorous, deeply honest and edgy way of relating to God that is quite foreign to many of us.

Praying Our Anger: Holding on to the Relationship

It is true to say, in general, that anger has a bad reputation. Most of us are only too aware of its destructive potential. When we are angry, we are very susceptible to the damaging option of words and/or actions designed to inflict hurt and humiliation. Through passive and active aggression, through verbal and physical abuse, we visit pain and distress on the targets of our anger. It is not in the least bit surprising that psychologists have assiduously engaged with the task of researching the dark side of anger. As a result, we now have a huge body of literature devoted to the topic; a comprehensive picture is available of the destructive power in anger and of the way it is characteristically expressed.

Anger is commonly viewed as "a beast within" that usually needs robust management if it is to be restrained and valued relationships maintained. The anger management literature is immense and a variety of cognitive–behavioral strategies have been offered. Therapists generally recognize that these strategies have proven helpful for a large number of people.[11]

What psychologists and psychotherapists have not given nearly as much attention to is the *positive* role that anger plays.[12] A notable exception is the psychotherapist, Andrew Roffman. Roffman argues for the salubrious effect of helping a client move her understanding of anger from an "inside-the-person" to an "in-relationship-to-others" phenomenon.[13] In doing this, she finds that her construal of anger changes from enemy to resource. According to Roffman, anger should be viewed as a signal that alerts a person to the importance of a particular issue or aspect of a relationship.[14] The client can then choose to develop an alternative pathway—a more constructive one—for a response to the angry feelings. This is especially important in the context of maintaining valued relationships.

Other psychologists have identified the nexus between constructive anger and keeping relationships on a positive footing. After conducting extensive empirical research, James Averill concluded that anger can and usually does have a positive outcome for parties in conflict. Seventy-five percent of his research subjects reported that they responded to feelings of anger not with aggression but rather with talking the incident over in an attempt to come to a point of resolution.[15] The stated aim was to express anger constructively in order to restore the relationship.

Taking his cue from clinical experience rather than empirical research, the psychotherapist, Robert Holt, also reports that people in a conflict situation often choose to express their anger constructively.[16] There is an implicit assumption here, suggests Holt, that it is possible to have more than one winner. What motivates those clients who have this view is a desire to maintain a positive relationship with the other. In order to achieve this goal, a person endeavors to give direct and genuine expression to her feelings of displeasure and resentment, while maintaining enough control that the intensity of the expression reflects the true quality of those feelings. That is, she does not allow herself to be carried away by the anger. She does not try to dampen down her angry expression, but neither does she allow it to ramp up to a level that is out of proportion to the level of hurt and disappointment that she feels.

Holt reports that clinical experience shows that incompletely or poorly expressed anger has deleterious effects on the relationship. Typically, the result is withdrawal, a decreased desire to communicate, and a feeling of alienation. "Love dies in such a chilly climate and is replaced by forced, empty attempts to enact an unfelt role, or by pseudo-mutuality."[17]

Some have argued that the same dynamics apply in the context of the divine–human relationship. Carol Christ avers that when a person is feeling that God has failed to act or has acted unfairly, the only way to maintain a loving relationship is through venting anger. Indeed, it may actually bring new vigor and life to the relationship: "[T]he expression of anger at God may precede a renewed relation. Anger is a form of relation."[18]

There can be no genuine relation to God unless we are prepared to be honest. To bring our raw, tumultuous, and dark feelings before God is to relate in depth, on the level of reality and truth. Suppressing these feelings consigns the relationship to superficiality and ultimately leads to a feeling of alienation from God.[19]

Blumenthal affirms that the psalms of lament have a special role to play here. We have learned well that in order to find some peace in times of suffering and disorientation a level of acceptance is needed. But this is not the complete picture. In order to express our full humanity, we also need to come before God in anger and protest:

> When bad things happen to good people, I know that accep-
> tance is only half the answer. The other half is acknowledging
> anger and rage—learning to think them, to feel them, and even
> to pray them. That is what the angry psalms are for. That is what
> the liturgy of protest is for. To help us bring our anger and rage
> to God, even if it is God we are angry at.[20]

In times of darkness and disequilibrium, it feels to some of us at least that God has failed us. We feel abandoned by the One who has covenanted to be with us always, ministering help and care.

With this in mind, Sheila Carney contends that "[w]ays must be sought to express our anger, our frustration, our experience of injustice in the presence of God and with the support of the community."[21] She goes on to affirm Carol Christ's suggestion that women and men keep a record of their grievances against God and use them from time to time in a litany of anger.

While I affirm this recognition of the importance of bringing not just our praise and thanksgiving before God, but also our disappointment and frustration, I also want to raise the question of whether or not the act of expressing anger at God liturgically will, in and of itself, resolve the angry feelings. It is quite possible that for some it might. For others, however, it might simply leave them feeling more aggrieved, more confused, and therefore more angry. Indeed, there is a significant body of empirical and clinical psychological research that indicates that this is likely. This research reports that the expression of anger against the target of that anger most often does not lead to a reduction of anger, but rather to an increase. It is a combination of ventilation of angry feelings and cognitive reinterpretation that leads to a mitigation of anger. This has clear implications for the way in which we design our liturgies of anger. I contend that we should provide both an opportunity for expression of anger against God, and a stimulus to personal insight, in our liturgical formulations. Before moving to a discussion of how this might be enacted, let us take a look at this psychological research.

Anger Reduction: Both Expression and
Insight Required

There is a relatively widespread view amongst the general populace that venting pent up feelings of rage gets rid of them. The message of pop psychology is that one should not hold it in, but rather "let it all hang out." Expression of anger is not something to be ashamed of, neither is it something to be afraid of. That a person is able to vent her angry feelings is seen by most to be evidence of the fact that she is honest, has a high level of self-esteem, and is emotionally healthy. Suppression of anger is generally considered to be damaging both to self and to the relationship one shares with the target of one's anger. It is this kind of thinking that seems to be behind the suggestion by Christ, Carney, and others that it is healthy and honest to offer a place in the liturgy for ventilation of anger against God. The psychological research that we are about to survey, however, suggests that this is only half the answer. Two recent survey articles make a case for the view that a reduction in the level of anger requires not only expression but also cognitive processing and insight.[22] Kennedy-Moore and Watson draw the following conclusions after conducting a very thorough review of the available literature on emotional expression:

[Research] suggests that anger expression is not helpful in and of itself but that it can be adaptive when it leads to or is accompanied by cognitive changes ...

[T]he combination of emotional expression and insight is more helpful than simply venting of emotion ... [A]nger expression is helpful only if it leads to positive cognitive or interpersonal changes such as compromise, reinterpretation, or restoration of self-esteem.[23]

There are two interesting published studies that offer support for this view that both emotional expression and insight are required for the reduction of anger. Green and Murray[24] devised a research procedure in which subjects (all male college students) were first provoked by being subjected to personal criticism. Then the researchers employed three different methods to attempt to reduce the hostile feelings in their subjects. In group 1, the subjects were allowed to express their feelings toward the instigator. The subjects in group 2 were not afforded an opportunity to express their angry feelings; they simply heard the instigator reinterpret his behavior and withdraw his critical personal evaluation. The subjects in the last group were allowed to express their feelings and then witnessed the instigator reinterpret and retract his criticism.

Three of the groups in the research were given an anger reduction procedure; the fourth was a control group. The subject–confederate pair was instructed to get to know each other better by writing a short and quite personal biographical letter. The biographical letters were exchanged, and each person was asked to express his honest response in a written "critique." The subject's reply was most often mildly positive. The confederate, on the other hand, responded with a standardized insulting appraisal.

In the *expression* procedure, the researcher encouraged the subject to express negative feelings about the confederate. The typical response involved resentment and a challenge to the confederate's evaluation. The confederate simply stated that he had followed the directions; there was therefore no retraction of the critique.

In the *reinterpretation* procedure, the confederate began by asking why the subject had not offered a critical assessment. In an ensuing discussion between the researcher and the confederate, it was made clear that the confederate had misunderstood the word "critique" and had thought that he was expected to make some nasty comments. He then attributed his critical comments to the misunderstanding and indicated that he actually felt quite positive about the subject. The subject was not given the opportunity to express his feelings.

The *expression/reinterpretation* procedure combined the first two. The subject was encouraged to express his feelings; this was followed by the confederate going through his routine of stating that a misunderstanding was involved, followed by a retraction of his critique.

The *hostility induction/no reduction* control procedure, finally, consisted of discussing a one-page report of a student's opinion on learning. The subjects had been part of the hostility induction procedure, but were not taken through the hostility reduction procedure.

After the procedures, the subjects were evaluated as to their level of aggression. It is not necessary for our purposes to discuss the two instruments used in the measurement procedure. What is important is that Green and Murray found that both ventilation and reinterpretation are necessary in order to reduce anger. They summarize their findings as follows:

The only experimental procedure that clearly reduced hostile aggression was the expression/reinterpretation condition . . . Reinterpretation by itself appears to be an inadequate means of reducing hostile aggression . . . When used alone, expression was also unsuccessful.[25]

The second experiment that I find illuminating was conducted by Arthur Bohart,[26] and involved role playing. Role playing is employed by Gestalt therapists, along with therapists using other approaches, to open up fresh insights and perspectives in a situation of conflict. The client is asked to construct a dialogue between herself and the other person. First the client plays herself, and then switches roles and plays the other person. In attempting to think and feel like the person whom one is in conflict with, access is gained to a level of understanding and empathy that would not be available if the client stayed focused only on her perspectives and feelings. Empathic attunement with the other person reduces anger, generates new insights, and opens the way to more constructive dialogue.

Bohart worked with a group of all-female college students. His experimental method involved asking each subject to think of two recent and unresolved incidents involving another person or persons (referred to by Bohart as the "provocateur") in which anger was produced. She was then asked to select the more significant of the two incidents and to visualize it for two minutes. Each subject was randomly assigned to a control, intellectual-analysis, discharge, or role-playing condition. The role-play condition involved both emotional expression and cognitive reinterpretation.

Bohart found that role playing is the most effective means of reducing anger and resolving conflict:

The results support the hypothesis that role playing can be effective in modifying feelings, attitudes, and behaviors associated with interpersonal conflict. In addition, role play consistently appeared to be better for this than either discharge, intellectual analysis, or no treatment . . .

The greater effectiveness of role play is in accord with the position that *insight and emotion must go hand in hand for change to occur.* Discharge alone did not seem to be effective [emphasis added].[27]

Both these research projects involved students rather than therapy clients; however, similar findings were obtained in a clinical study of the processes and outcomes in encounter groups.[28] The 17 groups in the study used a variety of therapeutic approaches and each one met for 30 hours. For quite a few of the groups, venting strong emotion, including anger, was seen to be therapeutically important. The researchers found, though, that the discharge of emotion alone was not therapeutic. What was efficacious was the emotional ventilation combined with cognitive reappraisal.

It is evident that these research findings have strong significance for the way in which the liturgical expression of anger against God is facilitated. The reduction of angry feelings and a renewal of the relationship with God require not only the provision of an avenue for emotional ventilation, but also the offering of theological and pastoral insight. It is my contention that the expression of anger should be accompanied by a cognitive reframing of the experience. Two obvious foci for this reframing are saving grace and divine solidarity with suffering. In using the term "divine solidarity" my intention is to communicate the fact that God does not stand aloof from our pain and suffering. God has chosen not to insulate Godself from the dark side of our existence, but rather to fully immerse the divine self in it through the life, passion, and death of Christ. These theological themes are the central elements in two liturgical patterns—one ancient and one contemporary—that I believe point the way for us in constructing healing liturgies of anger.

Liturgies of Anger

The first pattern is found in the lament psalms themselves. In concord with the formula indicated by the psychological research cited above, we find in these psalms both anger and insight. When one reads a psalm of lament, one cannot help but be struck by what is a very abrupt change in mood. The poet takes us very quickly from angry protest into praise and hope. Though there are some exceptions (see, e.g., Psalm 88), virtually all the laments have this form. Psalm 13 demonstrates it very clearly:

How long, O Lord? Will you forget me forever?
How long will you hide your face from me?

How long must I bear pain in my soul,
and have sorrow in my heart all day long?
How long shall my enemy be exalted over me?

Consider and answer me, O Lord my God!
Give light to my eyes, or I will sleep the sleep of death,
and my enemy will say, "I have prevailed";
my foes will rejoice because I am shaken.

But I trusted in your steadfast love;
my heart shall rejoice in your salvation.
I will sing to the Lord,
because he has dealt bountifully with me.

Something must have happened between the "How long, O Lord?" and the "My heart shall rejoice." Brueggemann suggests that it could either be an inner, spiritual experience or an external act by an elder, priest, or other authorized person.[29] He opts for the latter and comments that it "must have had a profound emotional, as well as theological, impact on the complainer, for a whole new world of trust and gratitude is entered into in that moment."[30] The most popular hypothesis concerning the liturgical intervention is that proposed by Begrich.[31] He suggests that a liturgical leader answered the complaint and plea in a standard "salvation oracle." Though we have no record of these speeches, the suggestion is that they were originally situated in between the complaint and the song of praise. It is further postulated they were preserved in texts such as Jer. 30.10–11; Isa. 41.8-13; 43.1–7. The salvation oracle is God's promise to come to the aid of those in distress to effect healing and deliverance. In proclaiming the word of assurance—"Fear not, for I am with you"—the speaker responds to the deep fear and anger of the suffering person, facilitating a movement into praise and hope.

Begrich's proposal is, of course, speculative. It is not surprising that there are those biblical scholars who, while acknowledging its appeal and the creativity behind it, simply reject it. That this is the case is not a matter of concern for us. What is significant about the hypothesis for our purposes is the reason why so many biblical scholars are attracted to it. And that is that it provides a plausible explanation for the fact that the poet feels able to shift gears quickly from lament to praise.

There must have been a speech event in the liturgy that smoothes out, so to speak, this shift. Hearing the "fear not" of YHWH directs the thoughts of those who are worshiping to God's incomparable grace and mighty power. It is quite natural, then, to make the move from angry complaint to hopeful praise. In the psalms of lament, we find both expression of anger *and* cognitive reinterpretation. The salvation oracle is the catalyst for a reframing of the relationship between the situation of distress and YHWH's covenantal promises. The angry complaint is sparked by the thought that YHWH is absent in the time of greatest need. Hearing the oracle, however, brings to mind the thought that while YHWH is currently "hiding his face," this is really just an aberration. The dominant themes in the divine–human relationship are abundant grace and strong deliverance. The people are reminded that YHWH has worked mightily for their salvation many times before, and YHWH will do so again. This cognitive shift enables the resolution of lament into praise.

The second liturgical pattern that I think is reflective of the psychological principle that both expression and insight are required for reduction of anger is offered by Marilyn McCord Adams in her wonderful book of sermons entitled, *Wrestling for Blessing*.[32] Adams introduces her sermons by informing the reader that she has attempted to address the polarized experience of life which involves an encounter with both unsurpassed goodness and life-shattering evil. The way that she seeks to deal homiletically with this polarization in lived reality is, first, to give honest and full expression to the hurt and anger that is an undeniable part of our human experience, and, second, to proclaim the comforting message that God has identified in Christ with the worst that we can suffer. That is, on the one hand she is determined to tell the truth about human pain and disorientation. But on the other hand, she is determined to remind us that the fact that God is in solidarity with our suffering really means something.

A good example of Adams' approach can be found in her sermon entitled, "Crucified God: Abuser or Redeemer?" In reflecting on the horrible abuse that we see everywhere in the world, she raises the uncomfortable question of why God permits it, along with the even more uncomfortable thought that perhaps God shares in it. Adams recognizes that when we are faced with these deeply unsettling questions, there is a tendency to suppress our confusion and our anger. She then offers a more salubrious alternative:

The cross of Christ is a symbol of the way human lives are counted for nothing—not only in Serbia and Rwanda, in Afghanistan and Iraq, but everywhere and always, right here and now. The cross of Christ is an exposé of how people are battered, tortured and disposed of; of how life and creativity are crushed out of us, on a mere whim, out of meanness, out of sheer greed . . .

Elevating Christ crucified to a religious symbol, making the cross the centerpiece of our liturgical decoration seems to award such scandal the Divine seal of approval. For many it raises the fear and superstition that God is a child-abuser: after all, did he not *make* his Son Jesus suffer? Can we not identify with Jesus in the Garden with loud cries and tears, only to submit like an adaptive child to the Father's hostile will? Does not the cross, with its commission to imitate discipleship, send the message that God is determined to let life and the world batter and bend us until we are unfit for his presence, and then cast us off as vile worthless things? . . .

Taking such messages really to heart would drive us to rebel against God, symbolically to kill him by embracing atheism. Instead, many of us become polarized, maintaining our religious alliances on the surface, burying our wounds and anger ever more deeply within.

Truth to tell, we do not know why God permits abuse . . . But I invite you to an exercise of deep spiritual intimacy: take this question directly to God, and watch what she shows you! . . .

God determined to be one of us, take to himself our whole nature—a body that could be tortured, a mind that could be blown by unbearable pain; a psyche that could be gripped by fear, tear and rip with desertions and betrayals; a physique that could break and die. God did it out of love, to identify with us in the worst that befalls us.[33]

Adams clearly does not seek to suppress the dark, ugly side of human experience. Nor does she pretend that God can be sprung from the dock with a neat, facile piece of theology. She knows that some of us are angry and confused, and that we find it extremely difficult to deal with these feelings. But she is not content to simply acknowledge the pain and the rage. She moves past this to offer a compelling theodicy: We are not alone in our suffering; God has fully immersed Godself in the worst pain and torment that human life can throw at us. The anger is acknowledged; but the problem of God's absence is reframed by pointing to God's solidarity with suffering humanity.

Having outlined these two worship patterns that contain both an expression of the anger that some of us feel and a theological reframing that opens the way to insight, healing, and hope, I want now to offer some concrete examples of a liturgy of anger reflecting this pattern. Before moving to this task, it is important to acknowledge that this is risky and uncomfortable territory for worship leaders. The terrain is likely to be equally, if not more, threatening for most worshipers. If lament has not been part of the congregational culture, many will find the act of expressing anger at God unpleasant and uncomfortable; some may find it shocking and even blasphemous. It goes without saying that it would be pastorally irresponsible to simply drop in a liturgy of anger one Sunday morning. As mentioned in the last chapter, the pastor needs to prepare the congregation by first preaching on the psalms of lament and on the way Israel felt comfortable with prayers of anger. In particular, the preacher needs to highlight the fact that the covenant relationship was understood by Israel as genuinely dialogical. That is, it is important for worshipers to understand that the covenant involved mutuality and reciprocity; when it seemed that YHWH had fallen down in his covenantal responsibilities, the People felt free to reverse the roles and take a prosecutorial stance. We are also partners in a covenant with God—a covenant established in and through the life, death, and resurrection of Christ. Ours is also a dialogical relationship, and it is right, when the occasion warrants it, that we make our complaint before God.

Prayer of Anger A
(Note: *The complaint part of the prayer should be read with an angry tonality. This is not the time for a polite pulpit voice.*)

Leader: The prayer that you are about to hear is for those of us who at this time are hurting and angry with God. It is also for those of us who may at this moment be feeling good about life and their relationship with God, but who remember times of disorientation and disappointment in that relationship. It may be that you have never felt free enough to bring your true self before God. Whatever place you are in at this moment, I invite you to engage with this prayer.

Voice 1:

O God,

We are hurting.
We are hurting and we are afraid.
Life shouldn't be this hard!
There is too much pain, too much distress; it's too much.

Night and day we pray.
We pray with all the faith we can muster.
Are you sick of hearing the same old prayers, O God?
We are certainly sick of praying them!

Where are you, God of grace and mercy?
How long will you hide your face from us?
You promised to come to our aid in times of distress.
We trusted in you and you have let us down!

Do you know how hard it is to keep the faith?
Just a little relief would be good enough.
But things are getting worse, not better.
It really is so unfair, O God!

Voice 2:

Reading from Romans 8.31–35; 37–39.

What then are we to say about these things?
If God is for us, who is against us?
He who did not withhold his own Son,
but gave him up for all of us,
will he not with him also give us everything else?

Who will bring any charge against God's elect?
It is God who justifies.
Who is to condemn?

It is Christ Jesus, who died, yes, who was raised,
who is at the right hand of God, who indeed intercedes for us.

Who will separate us from the love of Christ?
Will hardship, or distress, or persecution,
or famine, or nakedness, or peril, or sword?

No, in all these things we are more than conquerors
through him who loved us.
For I am convinced that neither death, nor life,
nor angels, nor rulers,
nor things present, nor things to come, nor powers,
nor anything else in all creation,
will be able to separate us
from the love of God in Christ Jesus our Lord.

Amen.

Prayer of Anger B

O God,
Life is beautiful:
Pretty places that delight our senses and brighten our souls.
Wonderful people filled with life, love, and light.
Blooming health, strength and vitality.
Satisfying achievements that fill us with pride and purpose.

And life is ugly:
Twisted, distorted landscapes hewn out of hate and violence.
Dark and dangerous people who hurt and abuse.
Bodies that are failing and filled with sickness.
Failure that shatters confidence and wounds the soul.

Where are you, Strong Deliverer, when we are hurting?
Why do you hide your face when we most need to see it?
Do you feel our pain? Does it touch you deep within?
Or are you sitting pretty in your comfortable heavenly abode?

But you are not sitting pretty, are you, God?
You, too, have encountered ugliness and horror.

You immersed yourself in our human condition.
Your body was torn apart by fear and hatred.
Torn apart for us.

Amen.

Prayer of Anger C

Have someone read one of the strong lament psalms, introducing it with this statement:

Sometimes we feel like God has let us down. We find ourselves in pain and distress and God is nowhere to be found. Our prayers seem to get no further than the ceiling. The people of Israel had this same experience. Because they believed that they shared in a relationship of mutuality with God, they felt justified in addressing God with their anger and disappointment. But their prayers did not stop with complaint. The psalms of lament begin in angry protest, and end in hopeful praise.

As you listen to this lament, I invite you to identify with its mood and its themes. Some of you will have no trouble doing this. You are hurting and you are angry with God. It will be easy for you to connect with the sentiments of the psalmist. Others may not be experiencing any significant pain at the moment. And you may not be feeling any anger against God. If this is the case, perhaps you would like to imaginatively situate yourself in a time and a place when you were in the mood for lament. If it is your need and your desire, connect with the anger and the protest. And then open yourself to be touched by the message of praise and hope.

NB: *The reader should be instructed prior to the service to read the psalm with the angry tonality that it is meant to have.*

PART 3

HOPE: LIGHT IN THE DARKNESS

Nurturing hope is widely acknowledged to be a central pastoral activity.[1] This is so because walking out of the shadows into the light through the power of the resurrection is at the very heart of the Gospel. Ministers of the Gospel offer care by holding up the possibility of a new beginning in and through the grace of Christ. The final word in any situation belongs to God and it is always one of hope. David Lyall expresses quite beautifully the way in which this dynamic plays out in the pastoral ministry:

> We sit with the depressed, believing that there is no human darkness into which a glimmer of light cannot break through, that the last word is not of despair but of hope. We stand by the remorseful in the conviction that there is no human folly that cannot be forgiven, that the final word is not of judgment but of grace. We support the bereaved, believing that there is no human grief that cannot in some measure be consoled, that the last word is not of death but of life.[2]

In describing this ministry, Don Capps coined the phrase "agents of hope."[3] In Chapter 5, I refer to pastoral caregivers as witnesses to hope. It is not actually my phrase, though. It comes from the psychotherapist, Kaethe Weingarten. Through her clinical experience, Weingarten has come to the conclusion that hoping is not something that one should attempt to do on one's own. What is required is a community of witnesses that supports and encourages a person in her confusion and distress as she reaches for the light. With this in mind, liturgies of hope are developed. The aim in these liturgies is twofold. First, an attempt is made to establish a ritual pattern for expressing communal empathy and understanding. Second, a concluding gesture is included that joins the suffering person with Christ the light.

In Chapter 6, the ironic imagination is the central focus. At the center of the theology of William Lynch is the notion of the "ironic Christic imagination." In Christ, weakness is strength, the last are first, and the poor in spirit are called blessed. This central theological insight is correlated with a psychological one—namely, that people who are suffering often find new meaning and hope when they begin to see their illness or disability as a gift or as a friend. It seems that an ironic imagination is an important asset when confronted by life's darker side. In light of this, strategies for stimulating it through worship are offered.

5

Hope Needs Witnesses

When we find ourselves in a situation that is unsatisfactory and distressing, we need hope to sustain us. In the most general sense, our hope is for release and relief. We look forward to a time when life will be more comfortable and agreeable. Both the present and the future feature in hope. Hope has the power to enhance our sense of well-being now through an imaginative projection into the future. Further, hope is also intimately connected with the past.[1] It is the memory of positive outcomes after trying circumstances that funds the hopeful imagination. For people of faith, these turnarounds are associated with God's gracious action in personal and corporate histories.

Much of the current psychological thinking on hope has an individualistic orientation. High-hope people, according to this thinking, are those who have, first, the resourcefulness to find ways around blockages to their goals, and second, the mental strength to persist until they have reached the end-point. Hope is something that the individual does. There is another view on hope, however—one that fits much better with the Christian tradition. On this view, hope is something that we do together. Those who are caught in difficult circumstances need witnesses to their pain and distress who can help them find hope.

In one sense, virtually everything that takes place in a service of worship is a witness to hope. The prayers, the hymns, the Bible readings, the preaching, and the sacramental liturgics all point us to the source of our hope: the grace our Lord Jesus Christ, the love of God, and the communion of the Holy Spirit. In what follows, however, the expression "witnessing to hope" is used in a particular way. Taking a lead from the psychotherapist, Kaethe Weingarten,[2] it indicates a loving and empathic communal presence, often involving ritual, aimed at making meaning of personal distress. With this in mind, I offer ritual practices for worship that I trust will make a useful contribution to a liturgical witness to hope. In order to lay the groundwork for this, it is necessary to discuss both the psychology and the theology of hope.

A Psychology of Hope

Hoping is one of those experiences that we think we know exactly what it is until we attempt to spell it out. When we try to say exactly what constitutes it, we very quickly come to realize that hope is an elusive phenomenon. Describing it will be a difficult task, but let us make a start. To put it in general terms, hope is an expectancy of good in the future.[3] Or to be more specific, it is the expectation that future positive feelings will outweigh future negative feelings.[4]

Hope becomes important to us when we find ourselves in a difficult and trying situation. It is a very uncomfortable place to be; we feel distressed and worried. We feel trapped by our circumstances. When this is the case, it is easy to fall into apathy and despair. Hope pushes against the forces dragging us down into the depths. What sustains us is the knowledge and the feeling that there is a way out.[5]

Psychological Definitions of Hope

Speaking generally about hope provides an entry point into the experience. It is important, though, to make our understanding of it as sharp as possible. Definitions are helpful in this regard. Let us consider some representative attempts to capture the psychology of hoping.

Hoping is the perception that what one wants to happen will happen, a perception that is fueled by desire and in response to felt deprivation.[6]

To hope is to believe that something positive, which does not presently apply to one's life, could still materialize, and so we yearn for it.[7]

Hope is . . . a predominance of expected future positive feelings over future expected negative feelings. Hope, comprised of both desire and expectation, involves the interaction of affect and cognition.[8]

These definitions suggest that there are at least three central elements in hoping. First, as has already been indicated, hope is associated with an experience of deprivation. When the situation that we find ourselves in is disagreeable and trying, we naturally hope for something better in the future. The philosopher, Gabriel Marcel, uses the metaphors of darkness and captivity to capture this felt sense of deprivation.[9] Living in the shadow land of illness, loss, depression, or failure has the emotional tonality of captivity. The captive suffers through a deep sense of alienation—an alienation of the self from itself. This loss of the integrity of one's selfhood Marcel vividly describes as "tearing me out of myself."[10]

The second essential element associated with these definitions is desire. When we feel trapped in an unpleasant and distressing situation, our yearning is for relief and release. William Lynch, a theologian who has engaged in depth with the psychology of hope, refers to this desire as wishing: "We must take [the human] as essentially a wishing, desiring being who, in this exalted sense, must at all costs be in contact with his own wishes. Where there is no wishing there can be no hope."[11] His point is an important one. In the absence of yearning for positive outcomes, there is only apathy and hopelessness. However, his choice of the term "wishing" is unfortunate as it has the potential to create confusion. Psychologists tend to distinguish wishing from hoping. This is so because the former does not involve the same level of personal investment as the latter.[12] Most often, we are not overly serious about the things we wish for. We make statements like, "I wish I could play tennis like Roger Federer." Or, "I wish I could win a million bucks and retire to the good life." It would be very nice if our wishful thinking became a reality, but if it doesn't we tend not to be overly distressed. This is because our wishes are not tied up with those things that really matter to us. It is true that we sometimes use the word "wish" in relation to something that we do care a great deal about. For example, I might say, "I wish that Aunt Mary would get better." This is not genuine wishful thinking; but rather a case of using the word "wish" to express the experience of hoping. Hoping is associated with those areas of our lives that are intimately associated with our well-being. Included here are such things as our cherished relationships (including our relationship with God), our health and that of those we love, and our financial security. When something is amiss in one or more of these areas, we find ourselves hoping for a positive turnaround. Because these aspects of our existence are so vitally important to us, we naturally invest a great deal of ourselves in them.

If our hopes fail, it comes as a great blow. It would be *nice* for our wishes to materialize; we *desperately want* the things we hope for to become a reality.

The problem with Lynch's formulation is in the area of terminology rather than content. The thinking behind Lynch's approach is certainly right. He refers, for example, to wishing as the source of an "interior motion" in people.[13] He goes on to state that the "whole vocation" of the wishing faculty is "to move forward into reality with interest and desire."[14] This is exactly what the psychologists mean when they identify yearning or desire as fundamental in hoping. It is unfortunate that Lynch chooses to use wishing rather than either of these terms to convey his ideas; by doing so he introduces an unnecessary element of confusion.

The final aspect of hope that is highlighted by our definitions is that both affect and cognition are involved. The affective element is usually associated with the desire that we have just been discussing.[15] The person who hopes is gripped by a deep yearning for positive outcomes in the future. Lazarus suggests that the emotional aspect is also evident in the increase in the level of intensity of one's mental state.[16] Hope elevates one's mood. Korner contends that the affective component is best described by the terms "clinging, holding on to hope."[17] It is very close, he suggests, to the feeling of faith. When assaulted by fear and doubt, the person who hopes is sustained by the feeling that the light will eventually break in. One wonders, though, whether it is right to assign this type of "feeling" to the category of affect. Capps seems right to suggest that it is an intuition or a perception rather than an emotion.[18] He refers to the fact that one can have an intuition or a felt sense that what one desires will eventuate that is so strong that feelings of doubt are overcome.

Hope, according to the psychologists, also has a cognitive dimension. For the one who hopes, there is an *expectation* that the current unsatisfactory situation will be superseded by a more agreeable one.[19] One is sustained by the belief that the present distress will eventually pass. The thinking element can be thought of as a "rationalizing chain" that "represents a dike against uncertainty, the cognitive support against external doubts, the antidote for the anxiety generated by the possibility of a negative outcome."[20]

It is worth noting at this point that for Christians—and this is something that will be discussed more fully below—the affective and cognitive components of hoping are rooted in God. In relation to the affective element, first, it is clearly the case that because of our faith conviction that God is working in us and for us through the grace of Christ and in the power of the Spirit, we are able to hold on to hope. Because we trust in God's loving kindness, we are confident that our yearning for a more positive situation will be satisfied. We recognize, however, that finding ourselves in a more positive situation may not necessarily mean that our affliction has been lifted. The knowledge that God is acting to help us make sense of what we are experiencing and to bring peace and strength is also a significant source of hope for us. In terms of the cognitive element, second, when our belief that God is acting lovingly and powerfully for our good is strong, we have a corresponding strong expectation that things will improve.

Many psychologists, after reviewing what has been presented so far, would be struck by the failure to include what they take to be of the very essence of hope, namely, the pursuit of goals.[21] At the forefront of the goal-based approach to the psychology of hope we find C.R. Snyder and his associates.[22] In their early work, they defined hope as "a cognitive set that is based on a reciprocally-derived sense of successful agency (goal-directed determination) and pathways (planning to meet goals)."[23] Here the three essential components in the theory—goals, pathways, and agency—are identified. Now of course one might say that the definitions of hope presented above also suggest that goal-directed behavior is central. The goal of the person in a situation of deprivation is clear enough: it is to get out of it. She feels trapped in the darkness; her aim is to escape into the light. This approach will not satisfy Snyder and his associates, however. They contend that the goals referred to must be quite specific in order to develop an adequate psychology of hope. "If you recall the historical skepticism aimed at hope," they write, "it often appeared to result because it was vague and lacked an anchor. Goals provide the end-points or anchors of the mental action sequences; they are the anchors of hope theory."[24] Two different types of goals are identified.[25] First, there are positive "approach" goals. Examples include a writer wanting to get a publisher for a book, and a dieter desiring to maintain her newly acquired slim figure. In the second category, we find "avoidance" goals. The defining feature of this type of goal is a desire to avert a negative outcome. For instance, a regular beachgoer may use sun screen in an attempt to avoid skin cancer.

Goals cannot be achieved without a strategic approach. In order to attain the end-points that we desire, we need to plan. That is, we need to map the path that we are going to follow. "Pathways thinking taps the perceived ability to produce plausible routes to goals."[26]

Agency, lastly, is the motivational component; it drives people along the routes to their goals. It requires mental willpower to engage in a sustained approach to achieving a desired end-point. Agentic thinking "provides the spark for a person's goal pursuits."[27]

Experience indicates that it is not that often that we find a trouble-free, easy, or direct route to our cherished goals. Along the journey we usually encounter some obstacles. The high-hope person, Snyder et al. point out, has both the capacity to envision pathways around a block-age, and the requisite mental strength to keep pushing forward.

One question that immediately presents itself upon reviewing the Snyder et al. approach is whether or not the experience they describe is really hope. It seems more like optimism to me.[28] Optimism is usu-ally construed as a feeling or conviction that one will prevail in one's quest, despite the obstacles in one's path. In his survey of the psychol-ogy of optimism, Christopher Pearson has this to say:

> Optimism enters into self-regulation when people ask them-selves about impediments to achieving the goals they have adopted. In the face of difficulties, do people nonetheless believe that goals can be achieved? If so, they are optimistic; if not, they are pessimistic.[29]

Given this interpretation of optimism, it is not surprising that Pearson includes the work of Snyder and associates in his survey. In reviewing their goals–pathways–agency approach, it seems clear that what they are describing is more an optimistic outlook than the experience of hoping. It is important that we do not confuse the two terms. They are closely related, but they can also be distinguished. Gabriel Marcel makes a distinction between hope and optimism that is germane to our area of interest. The differentiation that he posits revolves around the I–We axis. Optimism operates in "the province of the 'I myself'."[30] *I* make the judgment that *I* have the personal resources to overcome the roadblocks on the path to my goal. Hope, on the other hand, is sustained in a relational context. Marcel avers that the most adequate expression for hoping is "I hope in thee for us."[31] For him, the fact that hope is indissolubly bound up with com-munion is so true that he wonders "if despair and solitude are not at bottom necessarily identical."[32] Marcel views the despairing person as a neighbor, as one who addresses him with a particular appeal for help. He puts it this way:

> Assume that [the despairing person] asks the question: "Do you pretend that it is in my power to hope, although all the exits seem to me closed?" Doubtless I will reply: "The simple fact that you ask me the question already constitutes a sort of first breach in your prison. In reality it is not simply a question you ask me; it is an appeal you address to me, and to which I can only respond by urging you not only to depend on me but also not to give up, not to let go, and, if only very humbly and feebly, to act as if this Hope lived in you; and that means more than anything else to turn toward another—I will say, whoever he is—and thus to escape from the obsession which is destroying you."[33]

Optimism and hope are distinct (though closely related) phenomena. I am optimistic because I trust in myself and in the resources at my disposal. I am hopeful because the other has heard my appeal and entered into a loving solidarity with me.

Hope and Witnessing

The one who enters into a loving solidarity with a friend who is feeling trapped in her circumstances is referred to by the psychotherapist, Kaethe Weingarten, as a witness.[34] Weingarten draws attention to the shortcomings in the individualistic view of hope sponsored by C.R. Snyder and associates.[35] In making her case, she refers to these two items on the Adult Trait Hope Scale they have developed:

I meet the goals I set for myself.
I can think of many ways to get out of a jam.

The items in the Adult Trait Hope Scale are designed to measure the person's conviction concerning her ability to reach her desired end-points relying on her personal resources alone. For Weingarten, as for Marcel, hope is the responsibility of the community. It is something that people do together. She asks us to imagine a Hope Scale that is predicated on the conviction that hope is the work of the community. The items listed above would be revised as follows:

> I can count on the support of others to help me meet my goals.
> Together, my friends, family, colleagues and I can always find ways
> to get out of a jam.[36]

Weingarten makes the point, as we also have, that optimism and hope are not the same thing.[37] For her, following Václav Havel, optimism refers to a conviction that something will turn out well, whereas hope is the confident feeling that something is meaningful, regardless of how it turns out. Witnessing to the one who feels trapped in an unsatisfactory and distressing situation is first and foremost aimed at helping her to make sense of it. Weingarten illustrates the work of the witness through an account of an experience she shared with her daughter, Miranda.[38] Miranda was born with a rare genetic disorder. There are unusual symptoms associated with it. The result is that her bodily functioning is unpredictable and unreliable. It goes without saying that she must cope with considerable physical and emotional pain. Weingarten tells the story of witnessing to Miranda this way:

> In March 1995, Miranda dislocated one hip and both her shoulders. Her friends found her situation disturbing and upsetting. They asked, "Why did it happen when you were just sitting on the couch?" Miranda had no explanation.
>
> People who study narratives talk about whether they are coherent or not: that is, do they make sense to most people . . . Miranda's stories about her disorder rarely make sense. They lack coherence. I couldn't bear that this particular feature of her disorder should contribute to the isolation she already felt. I determined to create a context in which the fact that Miranda's narrative of her condition was often incoherent would not matter. I suggested to her that she and I design a ceremony and invite a group of friends and helpers whom she would trust to share the history of her living with her disorder. Open to anything, Miranda agreed.
>
> The ceremony made vivid for us that our family needed to create forms of being with others that more accurately reflected how we conceptualized our experience. Fervently believing

that it was "unjust" for Miranda to bear her pain alone, and disavowing the idea that pain is inherently an individual and personal matter, we expanded the boundaries of our support beyond our family to a community of caring persons . . ."[39]

Biblical Witnesses to Hope

Hope is something that we do together. At the center of the community of hope that Christians and Jews form is God. Hope joins us one to another; God is "the guarantee of the union which holds us together."[40] The central theme in the grand narrative of the Bible is the self-communication of God. Witnessing can be a passive activity. A person may witness an event and do little or nothing in response to it. God, however, is an active witness. God is *agape* and it is the nature of *agape* to desire the best for others and to actively give of self in securing this desideratum. In the Scriptures we find story after story of God's healing and liberating engagement with individuals and communities.

It is because God is an active witness that the people learn to trust and to hope. All of the major events recorded in the Bible can be construed as narratives of hope. The Genesis narratives revolving around Abraham, Isaac, and Jacob, first, should be read as testimonies to hope.[41] What these stories attest to is that the identity and the future of the People of God are intimately bound up with the promises of God. The people are invited to imaginatively project into a future in which God will insure a long line of descendents, greatness as a nation, a new land, and, through them, a blessing to the nations. They come to know YHWH as the God who is faithful in keeping promises. Their hope, then, is something that builds over time. It is constructed on the foundation of memory. The stories that fund the communal memory are stories of the mighty acts of a God for whom no barrier is too high, no obstacle too large.

That paradigmatic story of hope, the Exodus, began with a cry of pain.[42] After a long period of containment and control, oppressed persons come to a point of simply accepting that what they experience is the way life is. They allow themselves to be molded by the order that has been constructed by their overlords. But something happened to change the situation for the Hebrew slaves in Egypt. They were no longer content to passively embrace the world that had been shaped for them by those in control. In finding a voice for their grievance and distress, they made a start on the road of defiance and protest. There is hope in protest.

The situation for the Hebrew slaves was radically changed because they dared to cry out. Their cries reached the heavens and the heavens responded. The cry of distress was not addressed to YHWH, but YHWH nevertheless heard it and acted decisively to set this people free.

The prophetic texts of the eighth to the sixth century B.C.E. also center on the themes of promise, hope, and trust. The poems that we find there take us into the future God has prepared for the people. It is true that many in the community of the time could not see past the order of things that they were caught in. Whether the order was established around injustice and idolatry in the community, or around the oppressive practices and controlling interests of aggressive nations, what is currently in place is what many accepted as the norm—or at least as simply the way things are and will always be. There is nevertheless a shaft of hope that penetrates into the darkness as the prophets declare, "Behold, the days are coming." A new order is on the way. The drive into a new and better world, the prophets declare, comes from nowhere else but the mystery of God.

In the New Testament, God-with-us is given an ultimate expression in the person and work of Jesus Christ. The hope of Jesus, our hope, is centered on the coming reign of God. "Jesus came to Galilee, proclaiming the good news of God, and saying, 'The time is fulfilled, and the kingdom of God has come near; repent, and believe in the good news'" (Mk 1.14–15). We have seen that captivity is a central image for the deprivation that necessitates the sustaining power of hope. The reign of God is characterized by the release from all forms of bondage:

> The Spirit of the Lord is upon me,
> because he has anointed me to bring good news to the poor.
> He has sent me to proclaim release to the captives
> and recovery of sight to the blind,
> to let the oppressed go free,
> to proclaim the year of the Lord's favor. (Lk 4.18–19)

In his healings and exorcisms, in his words of affirmation and forgiveness, in his befriending of the outcasts, in his challenge to unjust and oppressive practices, Jesus inaugurates a reign of love, freedom, and righteousness. The hopeless feel trapped; everywhere they look, all they see is "No Exit" signs. Jesus embodied the *agape* of God. Love takes as its mission showing trapped people the way out. Love takes those who are trapped in sin, suffering, and injustice through the door that opens on to a new and brighter future—one characterized by peace, healing, and freedom. The resurrection is the definitive statement on this future. It is a foretaste of the glorious existence that awaits us. We hope for a measure of freedom now, but our ultimate hope is for the end time when God "will wipe away every tear" (Rev. 21.4).

Hope, Witnessing, and Liturgy

Witnessing in the context of worship is first and foremost oriented to the hope we have in Christ. The faithful witness is the one who supports the suffering person in turning to her best hope.

Witnessing on the human level is of course also very significant in building hope. It is not something, however, that can simply be injected into any and every worshiping fellowship. It is not possible to find witnesses where there is no genuine experience of community. If we are to tell each other our stories of pain and confusion, we need a relatively high level of trust. Unless we judge that there is a strong bond of love in the body of worshipers, we simply will not have the confidence to tell the truth about ourselves. The tasks of helping each other to nurture hope and of building community are indissolubly linked.

In those places of worship where the cords of love are relatively strong, where people do on the whole trust each other, there are two significant ways in which witnessing typically takes place. First, those who are experiencing suffering are invited to bring it before the community in order that others can pray with them and for them. In this way, the prayers of intercession are personalized. The second form that witnessing commonly takes involves the use of a "joys and concerns" segment. People have the opportunity, first, to share those events and experiences that have brightened their lives. And related to our interest here, they are also invited to bring to the community the struggles and worries that are burdening them. Often these concerns are picked up later in the service through intercessory prayer.

The engagement with Kaethe Weingarten's approach to witnessing to hope has helped me to develop a different approach to the ones outlined above. This contact sparked two important thoughts in relation to a transfer into the liturgical domain. First, a central element in Weingarten's method is the empathic response from the witnesses who support a person in pain and distress. A service of worship is not group therapy; there is no legitimate channel available for personalized therapeutic responses to an expression of suffering. That is to say, it is not appropriate for a worship leader to offer empathic responses to a person after she has shared her story of pain with the congregation. What the leader *is* able to do is to offer a liturgical expression of empathy. In the context of prayer it is quite appropriate, on the one hand, and potentially very supportive, on the other, to acknowledge the pain and distress that those who have shared their story are feeling. What I have in mind is a general expression of understanding and support set in the context of prayer.

Second, Weingarten's use of ritual in the witness to hope prompted me to include this element in the liturgies I set out below. While it is true that we don't need Kaethe Weingarten to show us the value of ritual in pastoral care—we have known about this for a very long time—engagement with her experiences was a useful prime to my thinking on the matter.

With these thoughts in mind I developed a worship segment which I believe offers a strong witness to hope. This segment is not focused on the prayers of intercession; it is a stand-alone liturgical element. It also has a ritual form that I think adds another dimension to the support that can be offered in and through worship.

If a worshiping community is going to witness to hope for one of its members, it is necessary for her to "show" herself in some way. She needs to let the community know that something is troubling her. There is therefore a degree of risk involved. The set of rituals presented below consists of two options that involve an element that could be perceived as quite threatening, and two options in which the threat level would be viewed by most as quite low.

Rituals of Witnessing: Option 1

At an appropriate time in the service (after the sermon), the worship leader invites anyone with a personal concern to share it with the congregation. After the time of sharing, the leader acknowledges the pain of those who have spoken and lights small candles from the Christ candle to present to each person. In this way, each one is pointed toward the Light in the darkness.

You will note that the leader lights a candle for others who are suffering—near and far. This candle should be placed on the communion table after the liturgy. Thus, the candle will need to have a base, or if it doesn't, it could be placed in a small box of sand.

The liturgy is as follows:

Leader
Loving God,
we thank you that you called a covenant people
to be a light to the nations.
Through the prophets you spoke your word of hope;
a shaft of truth cutting into the darkness of injustice.
In the fullness of your grace, you sent your Son
to bring us peace, healing, and new life. Amen.

*The leader invites those who have shared to again come forward
and presents a lit candle to each one. She or he then lights a candle
and holds it. She or he says:*

This candle is for those who have held
their hurts within their hearts.
It is also for people everywhere who are suffering.

She or he then prays:

Concern and distress are casting shadows in your life.
This is a trying time for you.
God is with you, and we are with you.

Christ is our light as we walk in the shadows.
In him there is peace and hope.
Rest secure in his abundant love and grace. Amen.

*Those who have come forward are then invited to return to their seats.
The lit candle the leader is holding is placed on the communion table.*

103

Option 2

After the sharing of concerns segment, the participants are invited to join the leader at the front. Members of their families, together with the other leaders in the congregation, are invited to form a semi-circle around them. The intention is to communicate to those who have shared that they are enveloped in the love and compassion of the congregation. The leader proceeds as in Ritual 1.

Option 3

Some people will, of course, be unwilling to come out to the front and share their story of distress. They will find this simply too daunting. The means for the articulation of concern in this ritual of witnessing is less threatening. It can only be used, however, in small congregations. People are invited to name their issues while remaining in their places. For example, someone may call out, "I'd like prayer for the surgery I've got coming up." Another may say, "My concern is with a really stressful situation at work." After people have had a chance to share their concerns in this way, the leader proceeds to pray:

Loving God,
we thank you that you called a covenant people
to shine your light before the nations.
Through the prophets you spoke your word of hope;
a shaft of truth cutting into the darkness of injustice.
In the fullness of your grace, you sent your Son
to bring us peace, healing, and new life. Amen.

She or he then lights a candle from the Christ candle and says:
I light this candle on behalf of those
who have shared their concerns,
and also on behalf of those
who have held their concerns in their hearts.

She or he then prays:

Concern and distress are casting shadows in your life.
This is a trying time for you.
God is with you, and we are with you.

Christ is our light as we walk in the shadows.
In him there is peace and hope.
Rest secure in his abundant love and grace. Amen.

The leader places the lit candle on the communion table.

Option 4

This option is also less threatening than options 1 and 2. Those with personal concerns are invited to come to the front. They are not asked to tell their story; they simply stand there. It is quite possible for the community to act as a witness of hope without knowing what it is exactly that is troubling the individuals who have assembled. The members of the community know that *something* is wrong; that is enough. Once the group has assembled, the leader proceeds to pray as follows:

Loving God,
we thank you that you called a covenant people
to shine your light before the nations.
Through the prophets you spoke your word of hope;
a shaft of truth cutting into the darkness of injustice.
In the fullness of your grace, you sent your Son
to bring us peace, healing, and new life. Amen.

She or he then lights a candle from the Christ candle and says:
I light this candle on behalf of those gathered before me,
and also on behalf of others in the
congregation who are carrying a burden.

She or he then prays:

Concern and distress are casting shadows in your life.
This is a trying time for you.
God is with you, and we are with you.

Christ is our light as we walk in the shadows.
In him there is peace and hope.
Rest secure in his abundant love and grace. Amen.

The people return to their seats. The leader places the lit candle on the communion table.

6

Hope Needs an Ironic Imagination

The New Testament is replete with paradox. The Jesuit theologian, William Lynch, has established this idea as the *leitmotif* in his theological system. Required in the life of faith, according to Lynch, is an analogical imagination that allows an embrace of contraries such as faith and unfaith, acceptance and criticism, and seriousness and humor. It is argued below that finding hope in times of distress is aided by engaging the ironic imagination. As we saw in the previous chapter, psychologists define hope variously. The kind of hope that will feature here is the meaning-making variety. Those who are suffering from an affliction find it more bearable if they can make some sense out of it. A paradoxical approach is often very helpful in this regard. People suffering from a life-threatening disease, for example, report that some light broke in for them when they came to see their illness as a gift or a vocation. Or to take another case, people suffering from mental illness have given testimony to the hope and healing that is associated with seeing their illness as not only an enemy but also as a friend. These people will hasten to point out to you, of course, that they wish they didn't have this "friend." They are not being romantic in speaking in this way about their affliction. It is simply that they have found that what on one level is clearly very bad—serious illness, depression, anxiety—is on another level something that is good. Here we see the power of the ironic imagination at work in generating meaning and hope.

In this chapter, I hope to show that worship has a capacity to stimulate and form a capacity for ironic thought. The ironic imagination can be promoted through preaching, prayer, hymns, drama, symbols, and more. I have chosen to focus on the first two of these possibilities.

Faith's Ironic Imagination

Many have remarked on the fact that the gospels are filled with paradox. In the gospel vision, the humble are exalted, the poor are the blessed ones, in weakness there is strength, and, most importantly, a shameful death is declared a glorious victory. William Lynch makes the irony that is such a feature of New Testament teaching the central principle in his theological method. Lynch is particularly interested in the relationship between theology and the arts. He takes the dynamic that is central in the creative life, the power of imagination, and describes its relationship to theology. Lynch suggests that faith is a way of experiencing and imagining the world. When the faith perspective is brought to bear on the world, it recomposes it according to its vision. Ideas, practices, structures, and values that the surrounding society accepts as the norm are turned upside down when viewed through the ironic Christic imagination.

To the Infinite through the Finite

The starting point in Lynch's theological system is the conviction that the path to God is through the actuality of the human situation. Some hope to live as pure spirits and thereby escape all the messiness and pain of the human condition. But such a magical approach can only ever be wishful thinking; there are no short-cuts in the journey into the fullness of God. There is only one way to the infinite and that is by "passing through all the rigors, densities, limitations, and deci-sions of the actual."[1] Our biological form, together with the forms of personal and social existence that we construct, establishes for us the shape of our human actuality. There are certain existential, devel-opmental, familial, socio-political, and cultural issues and struggles that are simply given to us. The temptation for some is to try to find a way to hover over the top of the human experience and to meet God in the pure air. Lynch, however, rejects this super-spiritual vision; the way to the infinite is through "wallowing around in the human."[2]

Faith becomes "embodied" through this engagement with the actual.[3] Lynch observes that the way Christians individually and cor-porately live this engagement over time results in a certain sensibility. People of faith, he says, live and move in an "atmosphere and general sensibility."[4] It is not simply an ideology that they embrace, but rather an historical ethos. The body of faith is given expression in "books, actions, histories, lives, deaths, in the endless areas of a thing called an atmosphere, and above all, in the person of Christ . . ."[5] Lynch observes that this tradition has produced what he calls a "body of sensibility."[6] People of faith perceive and interpret reality, the world they inhabit, in certain characteristic ways. Think of a person with an artistic sensibility.

She views the world in a particular way. She possesses a special ability to grasp that which truly expresses the essence of a person, object, or scene and she then proceeds to give it a rich and evocative expression. Similarly, due to her participation in a great tradition of human spirituality, a Christian person engages with the world in a particular way. Her "reading" of human existence is informed by certain vitally important categories—categories such as sin and grace, law and gospel, and death and resurrection. In particular, Lynch suggests, the Christian person's reading is an ironic one.

Lynch contrasts this tradition of entering fully into human existence with the tendency in the contemporary culture to seek to bypass the finite in the quest for the infinite. "We cannot quite trust that the exploration of [life's] full, finite concreteness will really lead us anywhere." And so we exchange its "tenuous, non-cognitive, vague, suggestive power for the evoking of quick infinities in our souls."[7] Facing squarely the limits of the human condition is not attractive for us, and so we construct ourselves as pure spirits. Magic and psychologism become escape routes for those of us who do not want to deal with the actual. People daily surround themselves with potions, charms, and tricks in the hope of leaping upward into "false heavens and cheap infinities."[8] If magic does not suit, one can just as easily lose oneself in the illusory world created by Hollywood, television, and the press.[9]

This flight from reality is the absolute antithesis, Lynch contends, of the way of life that Christ embraced. He engaged in a "total and actual, positive and 'athletic' penetration of the finite."[10] Jesus was tempted in the desert to choose magic, tricks, and a leap over the human into glory and the infinite.[11] But he chose instead the human way. Christ's life exemplifies absolutely the path to the infinite through the finite. In descending into the pain, messiness, and lowliness of human existence he is greatly exalted:

> He is the Sun, but the course of this sun is through man. Above all He is a bridegroom . . . and an athlete . . . running with joy . . . through the whole length and depth of the human adventure . . . He dares more *as a way* than had ever been dared before, marching into the ultimate of the finite . . . into the underworld of man . . . Wherefore he has been exalted and every knee shall bow to him, of all the things that are in heaven or on earth or under the earth [emphasis in the original].[12]

The Analogical Imagination

Central in Lynch's theological approach is the observation that the rigor, density, and actuality of human finitude can only be captured through the analogical imagination. For Lynch, the imagination is not a single or special faculty, but rather

> all the resources of man, all his faculties, his whole history, his whole life, and his whole heritage, all brought to bear upon the concrete world inside and outside of himself, to form images of the world, and thus to find it, cope with it, shape it, even make it. The task of the imagination is to imagine the real.[13]

Imagining the real involves an appreciation for the fact that all existents have an analogical structure. It is of their essence that they contain the same and the different. That is, reality has a dipolar structure. But that does not mean that it is marked by conflict. The analogical imagination allows a person to approach the world in such a way that the two poles in any particular existent are seen as holding together in a creative tension. The analogical imagination is the "habit of perception which sees that different levels of being are also somehow one and can therefore be associated in the same image, in the same and single account of perception."[14] Those who lack the analogical perspective tend to adopt a univocal interpretation of existence—one that attempts to capture it with a unitary image. This drive to absolutize things and experiences, to only deal with the ideal, shrinks the height, depth, and breadth of human existence. "The mind and imagination is crippled by the gathering intensity of the single approach, the approach that finally reaches a pinpoint in its range of vision and flexibility."[15]

The univocal perspective is a very limited one; it fails to appreciate that the contrary dimensions in a thing, idea, or experience can be held together in a proper proportion (*ana-logon* means "according to proper proportion").[16]

Contraries such as life and death, belief and unbelief, the finite and the infinite should be imagined together. This "undissociated imagination," Lynch observes, is exemplified by John Donne in a poem set around his experience in the sick room where he may die:[17]

> I joy that in these straights I see my west;
> For though their currents yield return to none,

109

What shall my west hurt me? as west and east
In all flat maps (and I am one) are one,
So death doth touch the resurrection.

Donne is not afraid of the sting of death because he knows that his dying and his rising are one. Christ's gift to us is a sharing in the unity he established between death and the resurrection. Right at the center of Christian faith, then, we find the analogical imagination.

The Ironic Christic Imagination

Lynch develops his system by positing that the person and work of Christ embodies a particular form of the analogical imagination— namely, an ironic one. We saw above that faith finds itself through an engagement with the actuality of human existence. The religious imagination does not simply produce images of what it finds in existence, it actually makes reality.[18] It rearranges existing patterns to compose a new pattern of the way things are. This new paradigm is shaped by irony and ironic images.

The main task of irony is to keep opposites together. It is only through the appreciation of the unity of contraries that one can penetrate to the depths of human experience. On the surface, it appears that the rich and the mighty have the power. But Christians share in a sensibility, that of the Beatitudes, that sees just the opposite. Through the grace of Christ, it is the poor and the weak who are the strong ones.

Lynch points out that it is only a certain way of imagining opposites as forming a unity that is ironic. There is nothing particularly ironic, for example, about the coexistence of the one and the many.[19] This simply represents the form of existence that things actually possess. In any existent thing (except purely spiritual realities) there is both unity and multiplicity. The unity that is a table, for example, is made up of many parts. It is the one table, but it has legs, a top, sides, screws holding it together, etc. There is also nothing ironic about contradiction.[20] Good and evil are contradictory forces; they tend to cancel each other out. The ironic imagination deals not in contradictories but in contraries. In the suffering of a person, for example, there is both good and bad. It is the fact that these contraries can be imagined as coexisting in the experience of one person, and form, moreover, a unity therein, that constitutes the power of the ironic imagination:

[T]he usual quality of irony is the unexpected coexistence, to the point of identity, of certain contraries. Usually the words *contraries* and *contrariety* are employed in a metaphysical sense. The philosophical understanding is that contraries come in pairs and the pairs in each case are the two most widely separated members of the one species or class, or the two most widely separated subspecies. Thus the very hot and the very cold as the contraries within the situations referred to by the word *temperature*. The very mad and the very wise among mankind would be a pair of contraries and a contrariety that begins to be metaphysical. They are the most widely separated. But suddenly we realize, ironically, that in man, and in one and the same man, they are not widely separated [emphasis in the original].[21]

In the pre-Christian world, observes Lynch, Socrates is the outstanding exemplar of irony.[22] Even on the physical level, irony is evident. Socrates is an ugly man who expresses the most sublime and beautiful truths. There is also the fact that he makes light of the truth he tells, but yet at the same time he presents as deeply serious because he will not retract it.

Christ's irony, on the other hand, is quite different. There is no trace of mockery in his life and work. His ironies, Lynch points out, do not need parody or laughter. They operate on quite a different plane. Christ asks us to unite the majesty of his vision and promises with the ordinariness of so much of human existence.

There are the great thoughts, the great visions, the great promises, the great things that are here and are to come . . . Then there are the common human thoughts, the extremely common human feelings, the common human tasks and needs . . . There is the part that thinks divine thoughts, almost without limit; there is the other part that is weakness itself and that shall die.[23]

Christ also requires of us a willingness to unite a confident faith with a holy fear.[24] Lynch contends that faith exists in a "dynamic partnership" with fear. He draws on the thought of Luther in developing this understanding. The Reformer is careful not to split apart fear of God and trust in divine grace and loving kindness. Luther on the one hand posits faith as holding to the utter trustworthiness of the mercy of God. But faith also contains appropriate fear—one that is grounded in a deep respect for the righteousness and justice of God. The faith which is confidence is in the end stronger than the fear, but it nevertheless gives it its due.

To give one last, and most important, example of Christ's ironic vision, there is the exaltation of Christ through his embrace of the lowliness of human existence.[25] In absolute obedience the Son accepts the way of suffering and death; in total love and fidelity the Father raises the Son and establishes him in glory as Lord of all. Death and resurrection are united in Christ.[26] Christ helps us imagine a world in which the way to power is through death and weakness. In this paradigm, power is defined ironically. "Weakness becomes one of the great forms of power. Age, sickness and death lose their power over man and take on another form of power. Precisely what we are becomes the ironic mode of transcendence of what we are."[27]

Those who lack an ironic imagination want to construct Christian faith only in terms of ideals. In this vision, the pinnacle of Christian living is expressed through the absolutes of pure goodness, unswerving belief, and total seriousness. But this mocks the real existence that we all must live.

The body of sensibility that is faith that has been built up over centuries rejects the absolutizing tendency. It suggests that "we come with faith and unfaith, with a sense of reality and illusion, belief and criticism, high seriousness and mockery, to the same reality in the one and same act."[28]

Hope and Ironic Imagination

In what follows, I attempt to show that what Lynch has observed about the Christian life—namely, that irony is at the heart of it—can be applied in a particular way to the challenge of finding hope in the face of suffering. In my experience, those who find a way out of the pall of gloom that envelopes them as they struggle with adversity commonly possess the power of ironic imagination. These people come to a point of profound insight in which they view what up till now they have perceived only as an enemy as also a friend. That which they have come to hate intensely, they now also see as a gift. In order to illustrate this generation of hope through the use of paradoxical thinking, I have chosen the cases of depression and living with a life-threatening illness.

112

Depression and Ironic Cognition

Virtually everyone suffers from occasional bad moods or bouts of dysphoria, to use the technical psychological term. Typically, a person usually experiences a general sense of well-being and purpose, but she occasionally feels quite dissatisfied, irritable, and depressed. Most often, the "blue" feelings are associated with a particular frustration, setback, or disappointment.

The occasional experience of dysphoria needs to be distinguished from depression. Transient bad moods are normal reactions to the disappointments and losses that everyone experiences at one time or another. If the negative affective state persists over time, however, depression is beginning to take hold. Depression is difficult to define in an abstract way; this is why many people turn to images or metaphors in the attempt to communicate to others what it is that they are experiencing. It's like being trapped inside a black balloon; like hauling oneself through an empty desert, unable to find water; like finding oneself in an empty boat on an empty ocean.[29] For one person, the experience of observing a large vine that seemed to be smothering a grand old oak tree spoke powerfully to him of his feeling of being suffocated by depression.[30]

Depressed persons feel unhappy most of the time, but depression should not be referred exclusively to mood. Rather, it should be understood as a complex of experiences including also physical, mental, and behavioral components.[31] Affective symptoms include sadness, feeling low, empty, and irritable. However, not all people who are depressed make reference to feelings of sadness. What is most prominent—and deeply upsetting—for some, is the loss of interest or pleasure.[32] In the past, a person may have found enjoyment in activities such as sports and hobbies, social interaction, and walking on the beach or in the mountains; these were things that she really looked forward to. But now that depression has taken hold, she simply cannot find any pleasure in these activities. It's as if the color has drained out of life and everything is now in black and white.

There are also very clear cognitive symptoms associated with depression. Since the pioneering work of Aaron Beck,[33] many have come to think of the illness as a disorder of thinking as much as a disorder of mood. Depressed people typically think negatively about themselves, the world around them, and the future. When they reflect on who they are they construct personal identity in terms of incompetence, defectiveness, and inferiority. They have an inner critic that is relentless in its attacks on personal worth and capability. The way life is, the structure of the world, is also viewed in a gloomy light. It's perceived to be set up in such a way that one cannot get what one needs or deserves; it is unfair and will always defeat one's best efforts in the end. Inevitably, the future looks very bleak to the depressed person. There is nothing to look forward to; no rewards lying ahead waiting to be reaped. Depression strips a person of the hope that a situation or relationship can be changed for the better. It is simply pointless to try to change things; one is bound to fail, so why bother.

Along with its affective and cognitive dimensions, depression has a behavioral component. Depressed persons are apathetic and lack motivation. They simply lack the interest and energy required to maintain work, social, and other activities. Sometimes the depression keeps a person in bed for extended periods. When it is mild, a person may still be able to maintain her lifestyle, but it is a struggle and a grind:

> [D]ysthymia [chronic mild depression] is a mood disorder that drains your energy and dampens your mood. You can still manage to go to work and do what needs to be done, but you are run down, apathetic, negative, passive, and self-loathing. That makes it harder and harder to function well at home, school, or work . . . Going through the motions of daily living, day in and day out, life comes to feel like a chore, a struggle, a grim grind of desperation.[34]

Finally, there are physical symptoms associated with depression. Changes in appetite, sleep, and energy are frequently reported. Depressed persons often complain of very low energy levels. They feel listless, lethargic, heavy, and leaden. A change in sleep patterns is a central characteristic of the illness. It takes different forms: difficulty falling asleep, staying asleep, or sleeping too long. Appetite, lastly, is very often affected. It can either increase or decrease.

Mention was made above of dysthymia. This can be contrasted with major depression and its devastating capacity to drain the life out of, to twist and distort, to break a person down. Andrew Solomon, writing out of his own bitter experience, describes it this way:

> The first thing that goes is happiness. You cannot gain pleasure from anything . . . But soon other emotions follow happiness into oblivion: sadness as you have known it, the sadness that

seemed to have led you here; your sense of humour; your belief in and capacity for love. Your mind is leached until you seem dim-witted even to yourself. If your hair has always been thin, it seems thinner; if you have always had bad skin, it gets worse. You smell sour even to yourself. You lose the ability to trust anyone, to be touched, to grieve. Eventually, you are simply absent from yourself.[35]

The most common treatments for depression are medication, cognitive therapy, and interpersonal therapy. Cognitive therapy is reported to be as effective as anti-depressant pills.[36] Behind this form of talk therapy is the conviction that negative thinking constitutes a pre-existing vulnerability to depression. Just as some people develop bad behavioral habits, some can also develop destructive cognitive habits. When a person's mental life is shaped by defeatist, self-critical, and hopeless thoughts she is prone to depression. Such a person, as we have seen, thinks of herself as flawed, defective, and inferior. She has difficulty finding a purpose for her life, and the future presents as empty and futile. These negative thoughts are automatic, according to Beck. That is, they arise spontaneously; a person has not consciously developed them and does not intentionally invoke them in a given situation. There are also thought patterns that connect not with particular situations or experiences, but rather with one's sense of personal identity. These are beliefs that define the core of the self. Aaron Beck's daughter, Judith, captures well the distinction:

> *Core beliefs* are the most fundamental level of belief; they are global, rigid, and overgeneralized. *Automatic thoughts,* the actual words or images that go through a person's mind, are situation specific and may be considered the most superficial level of cognition.[37]

A core belief such as "I am a loser" is obviously strongly associated with depressive tendencies. It becomes the lens through which all of life's setbacks and disappointments are viewed. The blame is sheeted ruthlessly and relentlessly home to self; the undesirable outcome is seen as yet another confirmation of absolute personal inadequacy and deficiency.

Cognitive therapists work with people in challenging both their automatic thoughts and their core beliefs. Therapists have found that almost always these basic cognitive patterns go completely unrecognized and therefore unchallenged. In the most general terms, the aim of the cognitive therapist is to help the client identify her distorted thinking habits and reframe them in a constructive way.

Interpersonal therapy is founded on the observations that, first, grief and loss, forming new relationships, and maintaining old ones that are difficult produce stress, and, second, that poor social skills result in social isolation.[38] Interpersonal conflict and stress are therefore important factors in the onset of depression. The therapist directs her attention to helping the client to develop and apply interpersonal skills and problem-solving strategies to enhance the quality of relationships.

Even this overly brief discussion of the phenomenology and treatment of depression indicates some of the complexities involved. It would be naïve in the extreme to offer an ironic approach to healing the illness as some kind of break-through. It is nonetheless important to observe that a pathway of hope opens up for some when they begin to exercise the ironic imagination. What I offer here is simply one piece of the puzzle, but I believe it is an important one. There are those who have come to see that the darkness of depression can be held together with the light of a deeper, broader, and richer connection with the inner self. "I hated being depressed," writes Andrew Solomon, "but it was also in depression that I learned my own acreage, the full extent of my soul."[39] A turning point for Parker Palmer came when he was helped by his therapist to see that on one level depression is an enemy, but on another it is a friend. While he was initially resistant to the idea, it began to take hold in his imagination:

> After hours of careful listening, my therapist offered an image that helped me eventually reclaim my life. "You seem to look upon depression as the hand of an enemy trying to crush you," he said. "Do you think you could see it instead as the hand of a friend, pressing you down to ground on which it is safe to stand?"
>
> Amid the assaults I was suffering, the suggestion that depression was my friend seemed impossibly romantic, even insulting. But something in me knew that down, down to the ground, was the direction of wholeness, thus allowing that image to begin its slow work of healing in me.[40]

What the image did for Palmer is that it helped him to see that he had been living up in the heights and that his depression could serve him by pulling him back to earth. Living "at altitude" was a metaphor that pointed up for Palmer four areas of his life where he had lost his hold on solid ground. First, he had been trained as an intellectual and had drifted into the lofty places where ideas and theories live. This meant that to an extent he had lost contact with the earthy realities that are so important. Second, he was living a form of Christianity that centers on abstract notions of God rather than on experiential contact with the divine. Third, his ego had caused him to put himself up on high. Although, he remarks that his pride was actually a defense against his fear of inadequacy. Finally, Palmer indicates that a distorted ethic led him into living by images of who he ought to be rather than of who he really is. He began to see that his "friend" would help him by leading down into the reality of his true self.

> Depression was, indeed, the hand of a friend trying to press me down to ground on which it was safe to stand—the ground of my own truth, my own nature, with its complex mix of limits and gifts, liabilities and assets, darkness and light.[41]

This personal insight by Palmer affirms the indissoluble connection between the analogical imagination and personal wholeness that William Lynch so insistently argues for. If we insist on trying to live through ideals and absolutes—only giftedness, only goodness, only light—the soul will fragment. The true self is not a pure form but rather a composite entity in which there is a dynamic and creative interplay of opposites.

The pastoral psychologist, Siroj Sorajjakool, had a similar experience to that of Palmer. There is of course a negative side to depression—it's an absolutely horrible affliction—but it does have a positive aspect. This positive side is associated with its power to lead one into authenticity. Sorajjakool came to see that his feeling of emptiness was not something to be overcome but rather an invitation to return to his true self:

> When I went through depression, I remember feeling very empty. I tried to get rid of this feeling of emptiness. I did not realize that this emptiness symbolizes the fact that I journeyed away

from myself. I journeyed from myself in search for myself not realizing that in this pursuit, I slowly got rid of myself until it was empty. I did not realize that this emptiness is not something I need to or can overcome. It was, rather, a voice or an invitation for me to come back to myself, to return home.[42]

This realization that the path to healing is found not by fighting against emptiness but by embracing it points up for Sorajjakool the wisdom of the Taoist concept of *wu wei*. *Wu wei* is itself an ironic concept. It expresses the idea that sometimes the most effective action is non-action. It is effortless effort, acting spontaneously and in tune with nature.[43] While *wu wei* can certainly be translated as non-action ("*wu*" means "not" or "no", while "*wei*" means "to do" or "to act"), Eastern religions expert, Ray Billington, points out that

> [a] more accurate translation of *wu wei* would be . . . "spontane-ous action," not far removed from Zen's idea of hitting the target without taking aim. It means behaving intuitively, even uninten-tionally: expressing one's real feelings based on the real self, rather than on any kind of projected image that one may create of oneself.[44]

What Sorajjakool found through hard and painful experience is that fighting against emptiness, striving to be good and overcoming the bad, only deepens the depression. He found himself locked into a downward spiral. He tried harder and harder to overcome his inner self-hatred by being better. But he did not feel like he was making progress. The perceived failure was fuel for the inner critic, who became even more vehement in his attacks. *Wu wei* is an intuitive and spontaneous embrace of the real self. "*Wu wei* invites depressed indi-viduals to return to themselves, to stop analyzing themselves, to stop trying to fix themselves. *Wu wei* invites them to stay right where they are even in the experience of negativity."[45]

His personal experience changed the way Sorajjakool worked with people suffering from depression. One of his clients conveyed to him the fact that she was constantly disappointed with herself for being so sensitive. Sensitivity was something that she thought she had to over-come if she was to get out of her depression. In response, Sorajjakool asked his client to exercise her ironic imagination:

[I]n the spirit of *wu wei* I said to her, "It is ok to be sensitive. Depressed people are sensitive. If they are not sensitive, they are not depressed. Why don't you give yourself permission to be sensitive. Enjoy being sensitive." There was a little pause. Then I saw a smile on her face. "I feel so relieved," she uttered.[46]

Another source of significant distress for people is living with a life-threatening illness. Some who are living with dying have also found that an ironic approach to their suffering has created a pathway of hope. Looking paradoxically at their illness has helped them make some sense out of it. It is to this insight that we now turn.

Living/Dying and the Ironic Imagination

A person who is suffering from a life-threatening illness is still very much alive. The dying person, in general, wants to know that she is loved and wants to be afforded the opportunity of living life as fully as she can in the time that is left. One of the lasting contributions made by the pioneer in the field of death and dying research, Elisabeth Kübler-Ross, is her call for healthcare professionals, chaplains, social workers, and family members and friends to humanize their relationship with the dying person by offering a gift of self. In the preface of her classic book, *On Death and Dying*, she expresses this succinctly in her plea to her readers to "refocus on the patient as a human being."[47] Later, she suggests that "[a] patient who is respected and understood, who is given attention and a little time . . . will know that he is a valuable human being, cared for, allowed to function at the highest possible level as long as he can."[48]

People who are living with dying are forced to face very difficult and painful questions and challenges. These questions and challenges impact on the physical, psychological, social, and spiritual levels. Kübler-Ross famously attempted to capture the experience of the dying person in her stages model. In her empirical research she found that a person who is living with dying typically engages in the "defence mechanisms" of denial, anger, bargaining, depression, and acceptance. Kübler-Ross also discovered that "the one thing that usually persists through all these stages is hope."[49] Though she does not develop this observation in this way, it is evident that the focus of hope shifts throughout the dying process.[50] The hope that the symptoms are not related to a terminal illness is replaced by hope for a cure.

When informed by the oncologist that the condition is incurable, a person hopes for more time—time to complete "unfinished business." At the point when one's time is almost up, there is hope for a relatively comfortable, pain-free end phase in which one is enveloped in the love and kindness of those who matter most. In the most general terms, when hope for a cure is gone, the hope that meaning can be found emerges. Hope, it seems, is a particularly strong drive in the human person. Even when faced with death—or perhaps we should say especially when faced with it—the flame of hope keeps burning. It does not die out at any point; it "flickers back now and then throughout the entire sequence."[51]

Despite the warm embrace of Kübler-Ross' approach on the popular level, it has been the subject of criticism from scholars and by those who offer care to the dying.[52] It is not necessary for us to survey all aspects of the critique; it will perhaps suffice to concentrate on a major concern—namely, the problematic nature of a stages model. Robert Kastenbaum notes that the existence of the stages has never been demonstrated. "Although nearly four decades have passed," he writes, "since this model was introduced, there is no clear evidence for the establishment of stages in general, for the stages being five in number, to be those specified, or to be aligned in the sequence specified."[53] There is no doubt that dying persons do generally experience the five responses that Kübler-Ross specifies (although any given individual might not necessarily experience all of them). The problem is with the stages language. It seems better to refer to denial, anger, bargaining and so on as reactions rather than stages.[54] When one talks about stages in the dying process, it gives the impression that for a person to die appropriately she must move through each of the five in a linear fashion. Although we should note that this "modern myth of how people *ought* to cope with dying"[55] stands in contrast to what Kübler-Ross actually intended. She did not conceive of the dying process in such a neat and rigid way. The defense mechanisms, she states, "will last for different periods of time and will replace each other or exist at times side by side."[56]

If we agree to jettison the stages language and in its stead talk about reactions, we need to recognize that the five identified by Kübler-Ross do not exhaust the possibilities. Dying persons *do* experience denial; they *do* get angry and depressed; they *do* bargain with family, with caregivers, and with God; and they *do* reach a point of letting go, of ending the struggle. But they also experience shock, alienation from the body, anxiety, guilt, hope, social isolation, social connected-ness, reconciliation (with others and with God), a level of autonomy, loss of control, hope, a search for meaning, and more.

I particularly want to focus here on the spirituality of dying and, within this, on the search for meaning. It is here that the ironic imagi-nation is especially important. It is commonly recognized that the spirituality of dying can take either a secular or a religious form.[57] People who do not have a religious commitment may still value the spiritual dimension of life. In the search for meaning, in enhancing healthy relationships and in seeking to repair ones that have broken down, and in establishing a connection with the transcendent dimen-sion of life, people of a variety of religious persuasions, or none, express their spirituality in coping with dying.

The search for meaning is absolutely central. There is a strongly felt desire to experience one's life in the midst of the illness as full of worth and purpose. In the drive to wholeness and integration, dying persons ask questions such as: Why is there so much suffering? And what is this experience telling me about myself and about the nature of human existence?

When Corr refers to a connection to the transcendent dimension, he means going beyond the mundane to experience that which is of ultimate meaning and worth (although, of course, the Ultimate is often experienced in and through everyday realities). Hope is a cen-tral feature of the relationship with the transcendent. The hope for a deeper relationship with God is commonly expressed. Many people hope for something beyond the pain and imperfection of this life—the joy of eternal life with God, or the blissful state of liberated consciousness. Others simply hope for a deeper insight into, and expe-rience of, the true meaning of being human.

In their survey of personal narratives of death and dying entitled *First Person Mortal*, Lucy Bregman and Sara Thierman contrast two spiritualities of living with dying—namely, fighting the illness and the "wisdom of surrender."[58] The authors choose Max Lerner[59] as representative of the combative spirituality. "Cancer and death are enemies, but against old Max . . . they really do not have a fighting chance. Lerner exerts autonomy and self-determination on a scale worthy of a mythic hero."[60] Lerner draws his inspiration from Jacob's struggle with God: "Your name will no longer be Jacob, but Israel, because you have struggled with God and with men and have over-come" (Gen. 32.28).

Bregman and Thiermann make the point that not everyone is prepared to take on the heroic struggle described by Max Lerner. There are those who have instead embraced the "wisdom of surrender." What I find striking is that those who opt for this way have learned the power of the ironic imagination. In a number of the personal narratives studied by the authors,

> [a] turning point . . . . comes as they recognize how an alternative path opens up an even deeper kind of blessing. Not in relation to doctors and hospitals, but in relation to a universe where surrender is wiser and truer than never-ending struggle.[61]

Life-threatening illness and blessing, strangely, are imagined together. One traveler on this road expresses her experience through a paradoxical juxtaposition of cancer and adventure. Elizabeth Gee has come to see her illness as a calling to a deeper experience of her humanity:

> In an important sense cancer is a calling, a calling to adventure that if accepted culminates in the passage to a new humanity and an even greater understanding of the wonder of life. The other response, the other view of cancer or any crisis—that rejects the call, that refuses to look for meanings, other sorts of wellness and possibilities—transforms the potential adventure into a disaster, a void, a state where promise and hope are relinquished, and where the protagonist is a victim.[62]

Another person on the path of surrender is George Sheehan. That does not mean, however, that he cannot appreciate the important contribution that Max Lerner's approach makes. "[T]hose of us at or over the biblical span," he says, "or going into hand-to-hand combat with a deadly disease, can take some good advice from Lerner."[63] It's just that George tried the combative style and found that it wasn't for him. The treatment for his cancer of the prostate involves daily injections of Gn-RH designed to reduce his testosterone to an extremely low level. It is a form of chemical castration. George surrendered to what was happening to him, and in the process surprised himself with the discovery that the curse of Gn-RH brought with it an unexpected gift. "Is this new curse a blessing?" he wonders. "Is this death of desire the gift of life?"[64] He describes this gift of life as a "return to that Eden of my childhood."[65] In this lovely place, the aged share the space with children:

> It is a land where seven and seventy are kin. Where there are no concerns other than playing and learning and loving. The inhabitants of this land are in no hurry. Our days are dense with experiences. We have, as the Spanish say, more time than life . . .
>
> But I am a very wise child seeing things quite differently. The activities and interests of adults mystify me. They appear senseless. It is like watching the TV with the sound off—and suddenly realizing how ridiculous people actually are.
>
> I expect adults will in turn regard me as ridiculous. Actions people might accept in a child may not seem appropriate to a grandfather. I won't be distressed. I am looking forward to new heroes and new adventures. And if you ask me where I've been I'll say "out"; and if you ask me what I've been doing I'll say "nothing."[66]

If there is one thing that is clear about the experience of suffering it is that the way people cope with it is a very individual matter. People find hope in their pain and distress in all kinds of different ways. It has not been any part of my argument to suggest that the exercise of ironic imagination will help everyone. Rather, I have simply been attempting to highlight through the use of the case studies of depression and living with dying the fact that for some a paradoxical way of approaching their suffering has resulted in meaning-making and a breakthrough to hope. This approach accords well with the New Testament. As Lynch and many others have observed, this paradoxical imagination is a prominent feature in Jesus' message. The central themes of hope that he proclaimed have an ironic form: New life through death, blessed are the poor, the last shall be first, and boasting in suffering.

Worship and the Ironic Imagination

With these observations in mind, I want now to show how the resources of worship and liturgy can be used to stimulate the ironic imagination.

I am not attempting to be comprehensive here. There are a number of candidates for the task of demonstrating an approach to forming the ironic imagination—sermons, prayers, symbols, drama, songs, and more. For the purposes of illustration, it will perhaps be sufficient to focus on the first two options.

In the sermon below, I begin by discussing the logic in Jesus' association in the Sermon on the Mount of happiness with poverty and mourning. I then make the transition to the way in which people today use a paradoxical imagination to cope with pain and distress.

Sermon on Hope and the Ironic Imagination

"Isn't it Ironic? Suffering Folk are the Happy Ones" (Mt. 5.3–12)

"Happy are the poor in spirit . . . Happy are those who mourn." We've heard these words a thousand times. We tend to take them for granted. But I want you to have another think about what Jesus is saying. Doesn't it strike you as strangely ironic? Jesus is asking us to imagine the terms "happy" or "fortunate" as fitting together with poverty and mourning. This is a pretty tough mental exercise. We'd probably find it easier if he said, "Happy are the affluent, the powerful, the people in good health." But according to Jesus' teaching it's the poor and the mourners who are fortunate. How can he say that? A person who didn't know Jesus might think that he's guilty of mocking the suffering of the poor?[67] Obviously it's not Jesus' style to poke fun at the disadvantaged; he's deadly serious. But what does he mean by his affirmation that the poor in spirit are fortunate?

If we have a think about some of the key terms in Jesus' sermon—terms like "poor in spirit," "meekness," and "mourning"—things will become a little bit clearer. We're looking at Matthew's Beatitudes, but Luke also has a set. For Luke it's simply "happy are the poor." Matthew adds "in spirit." Luke's straight-forward poor stresses the humiliation of poverty. In referring to the "poor in spirit," Matthew's tells us that we should have an attitude of relying on God within the spirit.[68] His addition points to an attitude of relying on God within the spirit as opposed to depending on concrete possibilities for support such as wealth or favors from the powerful.[69] The situation at the time was that the Jewish people were under the oppression of the Roman Imperial system. Some would naturally look to violent revolution as a means of ousting the oppressors. The poor in spirit reject this way. They don't want to try to force God's hand; they will wait faithfully and patiently for God to act.

We also need to think a bit about that term, "meekness." Meekness is not a word that we hear much today. And when we do, it doesn't have great connotations. We think of a meek person as being timid, a bit of a pushover. But Jesus didn't mean it in this sense. Humility and meekness are closely related. Actually the word "kindness" can also be used for meekness. The meek are those whose humility is expressed through kindness.[70] They seek to live in love toward all people, even their enemies. A disciple who values meekness is not a doormat, but she seeks to resolve conflicts as lovingly and humbly as possible.

Thinking about this quality of meekness takes me back to an experience I had in one of my parishes. It relates to my involvement in two particular committees. On each of these committees there were individuals—"Jack" and "Tom"—whom I regularly had a difference of opinion with. Both had quite strong views and strong personalities to match. But I related to them very differently. I was thinking about this one day and I thought, "I have these clashes with both Jack and Tom. Why is it that Jack upsets me so, puts my stomach in knots, whereas I really like Tom?" The answer that I came up with is that Jack construes everything in terms of winning and losing. I'm his opponent—his enemy really—and he has to beat me at all costs. Tom, on the other hand, is a person who sees his service on the committee as his contribution to advancing the Realm of God. His puts his views firmly but graciously. If others come up with something better, he'll struggle for a while but in the end he'll be happy to hear it. His love for God and for people comes across even when he's in the middle of a hot debate. Tom is a good example of meekness.

The last term that we need to reflect on to get ourselves inside Jesus' teaching in the Beatitudes is "mourning." In referring to those who mourn Jesus isn't just talking about a deep sadness over the oppression, injustice, and deprivation that are the unhappy lot of Palestine. He is thinking more broadly. This is a generalized reference to the experience of all those who are broken, who suffer grief and oppression, and who respond humbly and faithfully.[71]

"Happy are the poor in spirit." These are people who are materially and socially deprived. Their extreme deprivation works as a striking symbol of their absolute need of divine grace.[72] In this sense they are no different to the rich and powerful—everyone is ultimately totally dependent on God and God's gracious love. It's just that the affluent tend to find it more difficult to grasp hold of this truth. The poor in spirit are fortunate because they are truly humble and meek. They look only to God's grace. They are not building their hope on the shaky foundation of material assets or the favors of the powerful. Their hope is in the coming reign of God that is already powerfully manifesting in

the ministry of Jesus. "Happy are the poor in spirit, for theirs is the kingdom of heaven."

God's grace and love are breaking into this world of pain, injustice, and suffering. The broken are being made whole; the oppressed are being blessed. Though the humble poor must wait for the final reversal of all that is evil and unjust, even now things are being turned around. The disciples can be glad **now** *because Jesus' ministry of healing and reconciliation is the guarantee of a glorious future under God. Jesus' promises are absolutely trustworthy. But the poor are already getting a taste of what God has in store for them. Some of the boundless joy of the future is spilling over into the present.*[73]

There is this wonderful promise of grace in the Beatitudes. But it fits hand in hand with a call to right action. Jesus expresses a very clear expectation that those who share in the promises of the Realm of God will live faithful to its ethical demands. Having received God's gift, the heart needs to be changed. The blessed hunger and thirst for righteousness. They conform themselves to Christ and his teaching. The blessed are merciful, says Jesus. In Matthew's gospel we find a number of examples of an ethic of mercy being demonstrated.[74] *Joseph shows mercy to Mary by not subjecting her to public shame. A husband is to show mercy to his wife by not divorcing her. And lastly, the parable of the debtors teaches us that forgiveness is an act of mercy.*

The blessed are the peacemakers, says Jesus. Those who are committed to God's way, co-operate with God in the divine project of bringing all things into a just relation with each other.

The blessed are pure in heart, says Jesus. The heart in Jewish thinking is the center of human desire, thinking, feeling, and deciding.[75] *The heart that is pure expresses itself through mercy, justice, and peacemaking.*

All of these righteous attitudes—and more—are the fitting response to an experience of the beauty of God's grace. God's grace is something that people can really put their trust in. In God's gracious action in Christ there is hope. Indeed, that Jesus is even now bringing in the Reign of God is cause for celebration. Those who have known only oppression and the poverty and humiliation that go with it can actually be happy. The poor in spirit can celebrate because they know in whom to trust. It's not in the powerful who might be able to do them some favors. They look only to God and to what God is doing in and through Jesus.

Now it begins to make some sense. The logic behind Jesus' ironic association of happiness on the one hand with poverty and mourning on the other becomes clear. God's grace is so powerful, Jesus' promises so absolutely trustworthy, that the celebrations can begin now. The future joy of the coming Realm of God is spilling over into the present.

That was then. We have heard the story of the poor in spirit. But what about us and our contemporary situation? Where is our suffering? Fortunately, we don't suffer from oppression and domination in _____. The abject poverty that was such a feature of life in Palestine in Jesus' day is quite far from our experience. Indeed, most of us are reasonably well off. And here, of course, is a spiritual danger. We are tempted to build our world around the material things in our lives. We can too easily find ourselves trusting in our skills, in our material resources, in the economic policies and processes of the day—in anything except divine grace.

But let me get back to the original question: Where is our suffering? We may not be oppressed by grinding poverty, but we do suffer. We mourn; we know what it is to be broken-hearted. Life is not always a bed of roses for us. We have experienced the reversals of fortune that are so painful and disorienting. Grief, serious illness, emotional suffering, job losses, and more, have touched many of our lives.

The striking thing for me is that the way in which some people—the hopeful ones—deal with their pain and misfortune is a lot like the poor in spirit. The context is very different, but there is the same paradoxical imagination. These suffering folk find that the opposites of blessedness and misfortune fit together for them. "Jane" was dying of cancer. In one of our conversations she really surprised me, and reminded me of something that is incredibly important at the same time.

"You know," she said, "I've come to see my cancer as a gift. It's a gift I didn't want, of course. I'd be very happy to have it taken away from me!

"I don't quite get what you mean. How can cancer be a gift?"

"Well, I used to feel confident because I was so in control of my life. I had a successful business, I worked hard and I thought I knew exactly where I was going in life. Then the cancer struck. I used to get to church when I could. I used to give God as much of my time as I had available. I probably half convinced myself that I trusted in him. But now I know that I was largely kidding myself. Now I know what it is to place myself completely in God's hands. I used to rush around doing everything I needed to do to take care of business. And it all seemed so important. And I think I really enjoyed it. But now the best part of my day is just sitting on the beach each morning and being with God. I wouldn't trade this new relationship I've got with him for anything."

Happy are those who know whom to trust. Happy are those who are so confident in God's grace that they gladly place their futures in God's hands. The rich, the powerful, those in blooming good health usually find it harder to surrender to grace. Perhaps it doesn't seem so ironic, then, that Jesus can utter the words "happy" and "poor" and "mourning" all in the same breath. Amen.

The Ironic Imagination in Prayer

The first example of a prayer adopting a paradoxical approach to hope comes from a collection of responsive prayers called *Be Our Freedom Lord* and is entitled, "Waiting in Darkness".[76] The author of the prayer takes the metaphor of darkness, something that usually has a negative connotation in the Christian tradition, and associates it with positive experiences in the spiritual life. It is not necessary to reproduce the whole prayer; an extract serves the purpose of illustration.

For the darkness of waiting,
Of not knowing what is to come,
Of staying ready and quiet and attentive,
We praise you, O God.

For the darkness and the light
are both alike to you.

For the darkness of loving
in which it is safe to surrender,
to let go of our self-protection,
and to stop holding back our desire,
we praise you, O God.

For the darkness and the light
are both alike to you.

For the darkness of hoping
In a world which longs for you,
For the wrestling and the laboring
Of all creation,
For the wholeness and justice
and freedom,
we praise you, O God.

For the darkness and the light
are both alike to you.

While joining in the Eucharistic worship of the Mustard Bush community in Brisbane, Australia, I was struck by the following section in the prayer known as the Song of Ascents (it leads into confession).

128

It reminds the worshiper that human existence is lived in the tension of opposites:

> We come defeated, we come dancing,
> We come traumatized, we come trusting,
> We come aggrieved, we come adoring.

The next prayer is my own; it is inspired by an essay by Daniel Louw on hope and imagination in practical theology.[77] Louw shows how Christ's passion reconciles beauty and ugliness. The prayer could be used as a collect during the season of Lent.

> Almighty God,
> in his suffering on the Cross,
> your dear son Jesus brought together
> the beautiful and the ugly.
> In him, death and new life are one;
> the beauty of his disfigurement is our hope.
> We give thanks that through
> dying with him we have been raised to new life.
> Amen.

The final prayer that is offered as illustrative of an approach to stimulating the ironic imagination is a modification of an intercessory prayer from the Church of Scotland's *Common Order*.[78] The part in italics has been added by me.

> Remember, O Lord,
> those who are sick,
> those who suffer pain or
> loneliness or grief,
> those who draw near to death,
> and those who we name in our hearts before you . . .
> Comfort them with your presence,
> sustain them by your promises,
> grant them your peace.
> *Help them to find fullness in their emptiness,*
> *light in their darkness,*
> *meaning in the absurdity of suffering.*
> In Jesus' name we pray. Amen.

I am not intending to give the impression by including these examples that simply by preaching on hope and paradox and by using certain prayers it is guaranteed that worshipers will instinctively employ an ironic imagination when adversity strikes. Rather, I suggest that it is important for pastors to regularly highlight through their liturgies the ironic nature of hope that is such a feature of the gospels. Through regular exposure to sermons, prayers, and other liturgical elements that proclaim the paradoxical nature of Christian hope, worshipers will be formed in an attitude that will sustain them in the midst of the hardships and distresses of life. As indicated above, a central task in witnessing to hope is helping others to make meaning in their distress. The gospel message of new life through death and blessing in poverty establishes a powerful perspective for dealing with adversity. In and through worship that highlights the paradoxical nature of all human experience and of God's saving action in the world, seeds of hope are planted. What the individual members of the worshiping community do with these seeds is, of course, up to them and God.

PART 4

COMMUNION: LIFE TOGETHER
IN CHRIST

An important aspect of pastoral ministry is working with others to develop strong bonds of *koinonia*. A commitment to building community was something that the writers of the New Testament highlighted often. In Acts 2.42, Luke describes the life of togetherness made possible in and through the Spirit: "they devoted themselves to . . . fellowship"; and in Acts 4.32ff he paints an idyllic picture of communal life in which people reacted freely and generously to ensure that no one was in need. When Paul refers to the *koinonia*, he has in mind much more, of course, than simply a group of people united by a common interest. For him, the dynamic power driving the communion of the faithful comes from the grace of Christ and the power of the Spirit. In corporate worship, it is our privilege to be the beneficiaries of these wondrous divine gifts.

We have learnt a great deal about skills for interpersonal relations from psychology. Many pastors have used such knowledge profitably in facilitating a healthier congregational life. However, building up the life of the Christian community is not only a matter of attending to patterns of communication and developing good conflict resolution skills. The Holy Spirit is already at work in moving the community to actualize its true identity as the Body of Christ.

In Chapter 7, the way in which the Holy Spirit works in and through Baptism and the Eucharist to form the Christian is discussed. The process of individualization has resulted in a widespread tendency for individuals to pay excessive attention to their own personal needs and goals. What has been lost to a significant degree is a commitment to building community and promoting the common good. Christians are obviously not immune to this disease. It is argued that Baptism and the Eucharist have the power to 're-Christianize' us when we begin to lose our way.

While self-giving in community is a core Christian value, it is possible to go too far in this direction. The issue that is discussed in the final chapter is what the psychologists call unmitigated communion. There are some people—and this appears to be especially the case with women—who invest themselves so completely in relationships with others that they lose themselves in the process. Loss of self through unmitigated self-giving may not be nearly as common a problem as its opposite—paying too much attention to self—but it nevertheless requires our serious attention. There are two major thrusts in this chapter. First, there is an attempt to identify an adequate love ethic in which mutuality is established as a desideratum. Second, the issue of how this ethic can be integrated into worship is addressed.

It will be obvious from what has been said above that ethics plays a major role in these final two chapters. Throughout most of its history, pastoral care has had two major concerns. First, pastors have traditionally offered comfort and support to those who are experiencing the harsh side of life. And second, they have attempted to form their parishioners in the normative vision of life promoted by the Gospel. It is this second pastoral task that in recent times many have lost sight of. In introducing this ethical element into my work, I align myself with those who have argued strongly for a renewed commitment to this aspect of pastoral care. There is a "moral context"[1] to the pastoral ministry.

7

Individualization, Christianization, and the Sacraments

Many have commented that Western societies have for some time now been subject to a process of individualization or institutionalized individualism. Certain social institutions—namely the labor market, the education and welfare systems—have developed in such a way that those of us who participate in them are virtually forced to adopt an individualistic stance. Individualism is a complex phenomenon and it is understood in a variety of ways. A common interpretation is that it is "the habit of being independent and self-reliant; behavior that can lead to self-centered feeling or conduct."[1] Straight away it is clear that there is a clash between this lifestyle and the Christian one. A certain level of independence and self-reliance, to be sure, is a good thing. However, the fact that Christians are incorporated into the Body of Christ through Baptism, and are called to live out their Baptism through service of others , means that the fullest expression of the life of faith involves giving and receiving in community. It is the failure in self-giving and the lack of concern for the common good that is associated with the individualistic perspective that creates the most distance from the gospel.

The cultural air is thick with the spirit of individualism. It is difficult for Christians to avoid sucking some of it in. They can easily lose sight of their calling in Christ to co-operate in God's project of love, justice, and reconciliation in the world. Their lifestyle begins to look more like that of the carefree tourist than that of the dedicated pilgrim. This reality points to the need for an on-going process of "Christianization."[2] The sacraments play a crucial role in this renewal process. Sacramental worship proclaims the central values of belonging to God and to others (saving covenant) and service to the world (mission), on the one hand, and upholds a view of selfhood as person-in-community, on the other.

133

If the sacraments really do militate against the corrupting effects of individualization, it must be the case that those who participate in them in an active and open manner are formed in Christian character. Some have argued that sacramental worship only rarely penetrates this deeply.[3] I hope to show that this is an overly pessimistic assessment. Evidence from empirical psychological research on individualism and interdependence will be presented that provides a strong indication that sacramental words and actions are efficacious in inculcating central Christian values. It is recognized, though, that we are dealing here with just one aspect of the process; there is much more involved in formation through worship than a cognitive appropriation of central Christian ideas and values. Moreover, it needs to be acknowledged that the triune God is the primary agent of Christianization. Thus, I will also show that through a whole-of-person (body, mind, and spirit) performance of the sacramental actions, worshipers open themselves to the God of grace who is forming them in their identity in Christ.

Some may wonder if the pastoral approach that I am proposing should really be thought of as pastoral care. Pastoral care, after all, is most commonly viewed as the act of supporting and guiding persons faced with existential, developmental, or interpersonal crises. However, the ministry of care, as Don Browning and others have been arguing so insistently and so rightly for at least thirty years, is also concerned with shaping values and maintaining a structure of meaning.[4]

Pastoral care, then, can be construed, in part, as involving the utilization of the resources of the Christian tradition in forming people in core moral values advocated in the Scriptures. Those who engage in this pastoral activity must deal with the fact that for some time now the grasp of the tradition has been growing weak. It is not just a case of the Christian heritage waning in influence. Other religious and social institutions have suffered a similar fate. What we have been witnessing is a process of "detraditionalization." It is this process that has contributed so significantly to the growth of individualism.

Individualization and Detraditionalization

The German sociologists, Ulrich Beck and Elisabeth Beck-Gernsheim, are surely right when they comment that "[t]here is hardly a desire more widespread in the West today than to lead 'a life of your own'."[5] The desire for personal fulfillment and the drive to achieve are powerful forces in the postmodern society. People today in the West very commonly see themselves as autonomous, free agents endowed with the right to construct the trajectories of their lives. I am the author of my life; I am the creator of my own individual identity. This is the view of self-in-the-world that is ubiquitous today.

A significant factor in the emergence of the culture of individualism is the high level of differentiation in contemporary society.[6] The social domain today is broken down into separate functional spheres. When we engage with others in the everyday world we do so through a variety of roles and personal representations. In these engagements, we function not simply as John Smith or Mary Jones—namely as a single or unified identity—but rather as a taxpayer, a voter, a parent, someone's partner, a consumer, and much more. The postmodern self is a "pastiche personality" (K. Gergen). She is "a social chameleon, constantly borrowing bits and pieces desirable in a given situation."[7] Because we are forced to constantly switch between various roles and sub-selves—all expressing their own style and governed by their own logic and social rules—there is the feeling that our sense of self is slipping through our fingers. We therefore feel the need to take control of our own lives.

Taking control of our own lives does not mean, though, that the social space is totally open. That is simply not our experience; indeed, we know that quite the opposite is true. We may live a life of our own, but at the same time we are also almost completely dependent on institutions.[8] Our lives are tightly regulated by governmental and private sector guidelines, rules, and regulations. However, many of these regulations and protocols—in the educational system, in the labor market, and in the welfare system—push strongly in the direction of personal decision. The guidelines and rules set the parameters for legitimate or acceptable action, but the individual is given the responsibility of shaping her own life within those parameters. The way that the society has organized itself in recent decades has shoved us all in the direction of individualism. This way of life is not so much the result of individuals making a free choice about how they want to express themselves in their day to day living, but more the consequence of a particular approach to social organization and order.

Seen in this way . . . individualization is a compulsion, albeit a paradoxical one, to create, to stage manage, not only one's own biography but the bonds and networks surrounding it . . . while

135

constantly adapting to the conditions of the labor market, the educational system, and the welfare state.[9]

It was once the case that a biography was decided to a large extent by forms, structures, and values established by the timeless orders of tradition. A person was born into a particular class and into a particular religion, and consequently shaped her life around the rules, mores, expectations, and responsibilities associated with her lot. That is, one's way of life had already largely been decided by others—by the guardians of the tradition. With the wane of the influence of tradition, however, the locus of authority has shifted from without to within.[10] Many consider this to be a very positive shift. Detraditionalization has resulted in an increased level of liberty and autonomy for the individual, supporters point out. The push behind the Reformation, the Enlightenment, the Romantic movement, the liberal ethic, and democracy—the very significant differences in the various assumptions, values, and motivation notwithstanding—was to free people from unthinking and forced submission to external authorities. These developments have weakened the grasp of tradition by cultivating the authority of the individual.

Freedom of choice is considered by a vast number of people to be one of the major gains associated with detraditionalization. Set free from the hold of an external locus of authority, we have become autonomous agents who decide the shape of our own lives. We are not bound any longer by the assumptions and values of the guardians of tradition. The decisions we make are based on our personal preferences and on an autonomous exercise of reason.

Most people today simply take the view that we have been liberated from the shackles of tradition; this is the age of personal autonomy. It may be fairly asked, however, whether we are as free as we like to think we are. The depth psychologists, for a start, point to the fact that choices are often steered, or even blocked altogether, by unconscious drives and conflicts.[11]

It is also true that a hefty chunk of our lives is governed by routine and habit. Both our private and our working lives are largely conducted according to set patterns involving little or no self-reflexivity. Often we do not think about what we are doing; we simply operate through force of habit. "To focus on biographically significant life choices is to forget that they are few and far between, whilst everyday life is made up of myriad minor decisions which rapidly crystallize into routine."[12]

Personal autonomy is rightly considered to be an important societal value (although it should not be adopted as an absolute value). However, the degree of our freedom to choose is often overrated. We are free, but we are also constrained by certain psychological and social forces and necessities.

There is a positive side to detraditionalization, but it also has its drawbacks. The negative side of the ledger is actually quite extensive. Consumerism and economic rationalism have moved in and rudely pushed many of our finer traditional meanings to one side. The *raison d'être* of the marketing professionals is to package everything in terms of a commodity to be bought and sold. Cultural activities and social events are drained of their integrity and meaning in a frenetic drive to generate a profit for this or that organization. Armed conflicts are "sold" as media spectacles. Leaders in the tertiary education sphere too often and too readily compromise their commitment to the humanization of the society in the push to spin out marketable programs. Even religion is not immune to these pressures. There are plenty of churches and synagogues who are happy to construct their programs around what "the consumer" wants.

In this environment in which high culture is weakened and trivialized, there is less for people to believe in, and little to arrest the free fall into egoism and narcissism. Everywhere in the West, vast numbers of people are preoccupied with style and appearance.[13] There is a massive and growing market for cosmetics, fashion, diet and health products, home furnishings and interior design, and luxury cars and accessories. In one sense, this preoccupation with personal titillation is not new. If we look back to the salons of France in the eighteenth century and to the courts and palaces of Europe before the time of the new regime, and even further back in history than this, we find the same trivial pursuits. In those days, however, fussing over one's appearance was a privilege largely reserved for the idle rich. Now it is preoccupation that a majority can afford.

Nothing is certain in the world of style and fashion. No one is sure in which direction it will head next. Everyone is open and everything is possible. Style takes us into the epicenter of the postmodern phenomenon—namely contingency.

> Postmodernity is the condition of *contingency* which has come to be known as beyond repair. Nothing seems impossible, let alone unimaginable. Everything that "is," is until further notice.

Nothing that has been binds the present, while the present has but a feeble hold on the future.[14]

This environment of continual movement in philosophies, spiritualities, and fashions has produced a new form of selfhood—namely, what Robert Jay Lifton calls the "protean self."[15] With this term, Lifton attempts to capture the propensity for both mutation and pluralism in selfhood that is associated with life in the contemporary social milieu. Not only does the self change its form over time, but the way it expresses itself in a single day may change a number of times. Due to the effects of rapid historical change, the mass media revolution, and the threat of human extinction, the self is becoming fluid and multi-dimensional.

In this environment in which little seems dependable or enduring, the moral life is under threat. The building of character is a life-long project; it demands a certain level of stability on the one hand and long-term vision on the other. In a time when social life is driven largely by contingency, these building blocks are in short supply. With this in mind, the sociologist Zygmunt Bauman suggests that the moral capacity of many people today has fallen so low that they can only be thought of as "tourists."[16] Tourists are characterized by a focus on pleasure and amusement on the one hand, and the possession of almost total freedom to structure their daily activity on the other. The tourist lives his or her short-term existence as "independence, as the right to be free, to be free to choose; as a licence to re-structure the world to fit his [or her] wishes and to quit the world that refuses to fit."[17] There are many today living a kind of permanent holiday-maker existence. Moral responsibility is jettisoned in the interests of securing a pleasant, unencumbered, light and breezy existence. Here we find ourselves confronted by the dark side of the freedom and autonomy won by detraditionalization. Every person living with the privilege of personal liberty carries a burden of responsibility. She can either choose to make her contribution to the common good, or to opt out and live a comfortable and self-absorbed existence.

Tourists, Pilgrims, and Christianization

Tourists travel light; they do not carry with them any kind of moral vision. A big part of the pleasure of going on vacation is the temporary release from commitments and responsibilities. One can simply please oneself. Tourists do not want to be tied down. They have no interest in lugging the load of concern for others.

A holiday is set within a short timeframe. Therefore the tourist operates with a short-term vision; anything sitting on the far horizon simply does not exist for her. She has no interest in making a sacrifice now for the sake of a future good.

Detraditionalization spawns a tourist morality. Despite the fact that Christians are part of a traditioning community—one that sponsors faith and service—we are not immune to this disease. We can so easily lose sight of our calling to contribute vigorously and courageously to Christ's mission to the world. If we are to live faithful to our vocation, we need to be continually engaging in a process of Christianization.

I find it helpful to think of this process of Christianization as one of conversion from a tourist to a pilgrim morality. Here it is instructive to reflect on how the two travelers differ from each other. I should say at the outset that when I use the term "pilgrim," I am referring primarily to the experience of Israel and of the Church as these communities journey under God toward their destiny. When we compare tourists with the pilgrim People of God, there are (at least) four sets of polarities that distinguish the two. They are as follows: (i) Contract vs. covenant, (ii) rights vs. responsibilities, (iii) self vs. community, and (iv) short-term vs. long-term vision.

The tourist contracts—either in a written or (most often) in an unwritten form—for the various services that she needs to enjoy her holiday. For her part, she pays the fee that is required and she agrees to adhere to the conditions that are attached to provision of the service. The contract between the tourist and the service provider allows for a time-limited exchange between two parties who have little or no prior relationship through which they are able to conduct their business smoothly, efficiently, and pleasantly. It is very appropriate for the short-term relationships that characterize the holiday-maker milieu.

Pilgrims, on the other hand, need something more expansive and weighty to sustain them on their journey than a commercial contract. Along the way that God is showing them, they encounter all manner of challenging and trying situations. There are times when their emotional, physical, and spiritual strength is all but gone. The shadows seem to be closing in on them and they feel as if the darkness will soon swallow them. They are on the verge of giving up when they hear the voice of hope: "Fear not, for I am with you." The "fear not" is at the center of God's loving commitment in the covenantal relationship with God's people. The pilgrim is invited to trust deeply in the loving kindness and providence of God.

For their part, the pilgrims are called to commit themselves to certain responsibilities. Tourists, to be sure, are not completely free of responsibilities. There are both "good" and "bad" tourists. Good tourists pay their bills, respect the local culture, ensure that their air travel is carbon neutral, wait patiently in line, and are courteous and respectful when in public places. Given that these responsibilities amount to little more than observing the rules of decent behavior—something that is largely second nature for most people—tourists are usually more focused on their rights. They have paid good money for services and they have a strong expectation that those services will meet their standards. If what is offered falls short, tourists are usually quick to express their displeasure and to seek rectification and/or compensation. Their primary concern is with having a relaxing and enjoyable holiday. Tourists both expect and demand that those who contract to facilitate leisure and enjoyment will fulfill their obligations.

The experience of pilgrims, in contrast, revolves more around joy than pleasure. Living in covenant with God is a very demanding enterprise; it's not exactly a barrel of laughs. There are many occasions when pilgrims fail to fulfill their covenantal responsibilities. But when they do manage to live faithful to the command to love God and neighbor, there is a deep experience of joy. Paul Hanson has clearly shown in his comprehensive study of community in the Bible that life for the people of God is structured around a pattern of divine initiative and human response.[18] God acts graciously on behalf of the people to secure their freedom and well-being, and they respond in love and fidelity. The shape of their response can be described quite precisely. It has three fundamental elements—namely, worship, righteousness, and compassion.

Worship, justice, and compassion are the fundamental acts and virtues required to sustain and enrich the life of a pilgrim people. These are alien terms for tourists. They are focused largely on themselves and on their enjoyment of their brief respite from the rigors, routines, and demands of everyday life. In a very loose sense, it can be said that tourists form a community. Lazing on the beach, or hiking in the mountains, one looks around and feels a sense of joy in observing the fun that one's fellow tourists are having. At that moment, one has a sense of sharing in the communion of holiday-makers. But it is a very weak sense of communion that is felt. One feels virtually no sense of responsibility for the happiness and well-being of the others in the "playground."

Richard Niebuhr once observed that a "deep characteristic of human nature" is "the desire to travel, to be in motion."[19] Tourists travel to a location; pilgrims journey toward a *telos*. The latter meaning is of course what Niebuhr primarily had in mind. What is significant about human existence is not so much the desire for physical motion, but the need for mental, emotional, and spiritual movement. We are questing beings. There is an inner drive impelling us toward a destination and a destiny. In theological terms, our destiny is to share in the unsurpassed joy of full communion with God and others. In the Bible, this experience of total communion is set within an eschatological framework. What the faithful ones have now is only a sampling of the wonderful experience that awaits them in the glorious future God has prepared for them. Pilgrims are required to think long-term. Indeed, they are asked to project right to the end of time. At the end of all things, all God's people will sit down at table and share in a sumptuous meal of love and goodness. Along this line, Isaiah speaks of the future feast in which death is abolished and all rejoice in the blessings of God's saving grace:

> On this mountain the Lord of hosts will make for all peoples a feast of rich food, a feast of well-aged wines, of rich food filled with marrow, of well-aged wines strained clear.
>
> And he will destroy on this mountain the shroud that is cast over all peoples, the sheet that is spread over all nations; he will swallow up death forever. Then the Lord God will wipe away the tears from all faces, and the disgrace of his people he will take away from all the earth, for the Lord has spoken. It will be said on that day, Lo, this is our God; we have waited for him, so that he might save us.
>
> This is the Lord for whom we have waited; let us be glad and rejoice in his salvation. For the hand of the Lord will rest on this mountain (Isa. 25. 6–9).

This final banquet is marked by freedom from the power of death and sharing in everlasting joy. God's love and mercy know no bounds. The riches of the feast are not just for the chosen few but for all people.

Christianization through Baptism and the Eucharist

In the inter-testamental period, this messianic banquet imagery became associated with the Passover.[20] Given the Passover setting for the Last Supper, it seems very likely that this association was carried over to the Eucharist that Jesus instituted. As we celebrate the Lord's Supper, we sample a little of the great heavenly feast that awaits us all.

> In the earthly liturgy, by way of foretaste, we share in the heavenly liturgy which is celebrated in the holy city of Jerusalem, the goal toward which we journey as pilgrims, where Christ is sitting at the right hand of God as the minister of the sanctuary and of the true tabernacle.[21]

Our pilgrimage begins at Baptism and ends in the heavenly banquet that marks the end of all things and the start of an endless celebration of full communion with God. Through the sacraments we have a foretaste of the wondrous experience that awaits us. In our earthly liturgies we share in a partial experience of the perfect communion that lies in the future. As the Holy Spirit draws us into relationship with the triune God, we are Christianized. Ellen Charry captures this particularly well:

> The Holy Spirit is the specific agent of Christianization in the sacraments, binding Christians into the trinitarian life in Baptism, and feeding them on the dramatic reenactment of redemption played out through the death and resurrection of Christ in the Eucharist.[22]

In the act of Baptism, union with God in Christ is a central dynamic. In his letter to the church at Rome, Paul ties our union with Christ to our dying and rising with him:

> Do you not know that all of us who have been baptized into Christ were baptized into his death? . . . For if we have been united with him in a death like his, we will certainly be united with him in a resurrection like his (Rom. 6.3,5).

Our union with Christ is both the source of our joy and freedom and the call to share in Christ's mission.[23] In Christ there is freedom, and in Christ there is responsibility. Indeed, to be fully free is to respond fully to the call to mission. The responsibilities associated with the grace of Baptism are recognized through the "Commitment to Mission" that is included in the liturgy for "A Congregational Reaffirmation of Baptism" in *Uniting in Worship 2*, the worship book of the Uniting Church in Australia:

> I ask you now to pledge yourselves
> to Christ's ministry in the world.
>
> Will you continue in the community of faith,
> the apostles' teaching,
> the breaking of bread and the prayers?
> **With God's help, we will.**
>
> Will you proclaim by word and example
> the good news of God in Christ?
> **With God's help, we will.**
>
> Will you seek Christ in all people,
> and love your neighbor as yourself?
> **We God's help, we will.**
>
> Will you strive for justice and peace,
> and respect the dignity of every human being?
> **With God's help, we will.**
>
> May almighty God,
> who has given us new birth by water and the Holy Spirit,
> keep us steadfast in the faith,
> and bring us to eternal life;
> through Jesus Christ our Lord.
> **Amen.**[24]

The other central aspect of our union with Christ that is germane to the individualization issue is that this union constitutes us as members of the family of God. To share life with Christ is to have a share in the communion of his Body. In his earthly ministry, Jesus gathered around himself a new family. He declared that his disciples are members of his household. When his mother and his brothers (and sisters) came looking for him, he said, "Who are my mother and my brothers?" And looking at those who sat around him, he said, "Here are my mother and my brothers! Whoever does the will of God is my brother and sister and mother" (Mk 3.31–35).

Great demands were made of the disciples called into the new family established by Jesus. They were to leave behind brothers and sisters, fathers and mothers, children and fields. Jesus called them to a costly act of substitution, namely, the old life and all that it meant for a new life under the coming Reign of God.[25] However, in leaving behind everything they had, everything that was precious to them, they received back a hundredfold (Mk 10.29–30). Every time that we share in the celebration of the sacrament of Baptism, or participate in a service of reaffirmation, we are reminded that we have been grafted into this family of faith.

As this community gathers around the table of the Lord, it receives the food and drink it needs to sustain it on its journey. In this pilgrimage into a deeper communion with God, it will inevitably lose its way from time to time. The history of the People of God as narrated in the Bible provides abundant evidence of this. The waywardness and rebellion of Israel indicates a failure to internalize the *Torah*. It is this failure which prompts God to inaugurate a new covenant. The prophet Jeremiah announces this new move of God with these words: "I will put my law within them, and I will write it on their hearts; and I will be their God, and they shall be my people" (Jer. 31.33).

The renewal of the covenant announced by Jeremiah has been definitively fulfilled through Christ's self-offering. As the writer of the Letter to the Hebrews puts it:

> Now even the first covenant had regulations for worship and an earthly sanctuary ...
>
> But when Christ came as a high priest of the good things that have come ... he entered once for all into the Holy Place, not with the blood of goats and calves, but with his own blood, thus obtaining eternal redemption ... For this reason he is the mediator of a new covenant, so that those who are called may receive the promised inheritance.(Heb. 9.1, 11–12, 15)

Our word "Eucharist" comes from the Greek term *eucharistia*, meaning thanksgiving. The fullest expression of thanksgiving is found in the one who offers her- or himself for others. The writer to the Hebrews reminds us that the new covenant is established through the self-gift of Christ. The Son of God is therefore "the highest Eucharist" and "the most expressive form known to [us] of God's communion of love."[26]

As we participate in the Eucharist, we are formed in the ethos of self-giving. We are reminded that to share in the life of Christ is to share in his mission of healing, reconciliation, and liberation.

Participation in the Sacraments: Formation or Simply Exposure?

The assumption that I have been working with in the discussion above on Christianization through the sacraments is that active participation in the celebration of Baptism and the Eucharist is a genuinely formative experience. Byron Anderson captures my thinking well when he declares that "even as we 'perform' liturgy, liturgy is also 'performing' us. It is inscribing a form of the Christian faith in body, bone, and marrow as well as in mind and spirit."[27] With this thought in mind, I have suggested that faithful involvement in the sacramental life of the Church serves to inculcate the central values of belonging to God and others (saving covenant) and service to the world (mission), on the one hand, and a view of selfhood as person-in-community, on the other. In this way, protection is offered against the corrupting effects associated with the individualization process. The question that must be faced, though, is this: How effective is participation in the sacraments in creating a communitarian and missional vision? In his essay on worship and the problem of individualism, Robert Hovda contends that Christianization through the sacraments is a rare experience:

> Sometimes we speak of ourselves, euphemistically, as "formed" by our biblical/liturgical sources in saving, ritual actions of reading and singing and praying. It would be more truthful to say we are in liturgy "exposed" to those saving sources, perhaps even desiring formation, but all the while enclosed in a cultural shell so thick and so resistant that only in relatively rare instances are we able to either really *go to* these sources, or really respond.[28]

It is my contention that we are entitled to feel quite a bit more optimistic about the formative power of worship and the sacraments than Hovda allows. It is true, of course, that some people sit in the pews Sunday after Sunday and despite a constant exposure to the powerful story of Israel and Jesus nothing much seems to be happening in terms of response to the call of God. It is very possible to resist the formative force of the liturgy. But when people come with a genuine openness to the grace of God, the worship experience is transformative. In Baptism and the Eucharist we are constantly exposed to the meta-narrative of salvation in Christ. The ritualized telling of the meta-narrative draws the worshiper into a particular identity and into a particular way of seeing the world. Inhabiting the master story in this way shapes the way she thinks, feels, and acts. It is much like the experience that an actor has in rehearsing her role.[29] In talking like her character, in embodying her mannerisms and gestures, in thinking her thoughts, the actor becomes the character for a time. The phrase "for a time" indicates where the metaphor breaks down. Actors take time off from their craft. When they are away from the set or the stage, they slip quickly out of the role and become themselves again. Christians seek to inhabit the identity of a son or daughter of God on a full-time rather than a part-time basis.

An important part of playing a role well is to practice the gestures of one's character. As an actor assumes the posture and mannerisms of her character her sense of herself is changed and she is "in the role." Gestures are also at the center of the moral life. "Nothing in life is more important than gestures, as gestures embody as well as sustain the valuable and the significant. Through gestures we create and form our worlds."[30] Stanley Hauerwas suggests that we should think of the sacraments as gestures.[31] Baptism and the Eucharist, he avers, initiate us into God's life by drawing us into Jesus' life, death, and resurrection. Without these sacramental gestures, "we are constantly tempted to turn God into an ideology to supply our wants and needs rather than have our needs and wants transformed by God's capturing of our attention through the mundane life of Jesus of Nazareth."[32]

There is empirical research in psychology that offers support to this view that the way we think, the way we understand ourselves, is shaped by the words, gestures, and ideas that constitute the liturgy. Research on the relationship between individualism and interdependence demonstrates the impact on cognition of exposure to particular prompts or "primes." The activity, for example, of circling the pronouns "we" and "us" while reading a story shifts an individual's focus from private to collective self-cognitions. Marilynn Brewer and Wendi

Gardner set out to test the hypothesis that "the concept 'we' primes social representations of the self that are more inclusive than that of the personal self-concept."[33] The third experiment that they conducted is of most interest to us. In this experiment, participants read a descriptive paragraph (a story about a trip to the city) and were instructed to circle all pronouns that appeared in the text. The text was varied so that the same materials were presented to subjects with almost all of the pronouns referring either to *we* or *us*, or to *they* or *them*, or to *it*. After completing this task, the participants were asked to complete a Twenty Statement Test (TST) as a means of producing spontaneous self-descriptions. Brewer and Gardner report that in keeping with the individualistic orientation in the American society, another piece of research utilizing the TST found that 58% of responses generated by White college students were personal traits and attributes, and less than 10% referred to social relations or affiliations. After applying the TST, the researchers found, by way of a contrast, that "the overall production of social self-descriptions was greatly enhanced by the *we* prime, compared to the baseline proportions found in the *they* and *it* conditions."[34]

The same effect as the *we* pronoun circling exercise was achieved through getting subjects to read a story about a warrior that highlighted family loyalty and prestige.[35] The story begins thus:

> Sostoras, a warrior in ancient Sumer, was largely responsible for the success of Sargon I in conquering all of Mesopotamia. As a result he was rewarded with a small kingdom of his own to rule.
>
> About 10 years later, Sargon I was conscripting warriors for a new war. Sostoras was obligated to send a detachment of soldiers to aid Sargon I. He had to decide who to put in command of the detachment. After thinking about it for a long time, Sostoras eventually decided on Tilgath who was a . . .

At this point, subjects received one of two primes. In the *private self* prime, the story continues in this way:

> . . . talented general. This appointment had several advantages. Sostoras was able to make an excellent general indebted to him. This would solidify Sostoras's hold on his own dominion. In addition, the very fact of having a general such as Tilgath as his personal representative would greatly increase Sostora's prestige.

Finally, sending his best general would be likely to make Sargon I grateful. Consequently, there was the possibility of getting rewarded by Sargon I.

In the *collective self* prime, the story continues thus:

member of his family. This appointment had several advantages. Sostoras was able to show loyalty to his family. He was also able to cement their loyalty to him. In addition, having Tilgath as the commander increased the power and prestige of the family. Finally, if Tilgath performed well, Sargon I would be indebted to the family.

After reading the story, subjects completed a self-attitudes test that required completion of 20 sentences that begin with "I am." The researchers differentiate between *idiocentric responses* that "refer to personal qualities, attitudes, beliefs, or behaviors that do not relate to others", on the one hand, and *group responses* that "refer to demographic categories or groups with which the subject is likely to be experiencing 'common fate',", on the other.[36] They found that exposure to the *collective self* prime "stimulated the retrieval of . . . group cognitions."[37]

Given these research findings, it follows that we should expect that constant exposure in sacramental worship to prayers, songs, and narratives that highlight the value of community, covenant, self-giving, and justice will form the worshiper in both a communal and a missional orientation. The simple fact that these words are used so often primes these orientations. There is also the fact that worshipers are repeatedly exposed to the message that these values reflect God's will and purpose and should therefore be central in their lives. The activities of circling "we" pronouns and reading a story with a family focus present as not especially powerful instruments for forming collectivist self-cognitions. It is perhaps surprising that they have the effect that they do. The language and the symbolism of the sacraments are much richer and much more evocative than that of these research instruments. Moreover, Baptism and the Eucharist are multi-layered ritual acts that impact on selfhood and identity at a number of levels.

It is important to note that the sacraments are transformative on a level much deeper than that of cognition. The act of being formed in the Christian ethos is a profound and multi-faceted process; it involves much more than mental appropriation of certain fundamental Christian values. At its core, to worship is to perform one's identity in Christ.[38] It is in engaging in all of the various acts that constitute the sacramental liturgies that one is formed and transformed. Doing and knowing are indissolubly linked in living the Christian story; the Christian self is formed through ritual performance.

Baptism and the Eucharist can be construed on one level as rich systems of symbols. It is imperative to recognize, though, that it is not simply the act of engaging mentally with the various symbols that is transformative. It is not that the bread, wine, water, and oil *mean* something that is the crucial fact; rather, it is that the performance of the ritual signs and gestures *constitutes a people* shaped by these meaning structures. The ritual action "creates an alternative ontology, a counter-community, a different polis, another way of being."[39]

If we take this perspective, Baptism should not be viewed primarily as a signifying ritual act—one that symbolizes the new birth in Christ. It is fundamentally a sacred action that inducts persons into a new people. "To be immersed and to rise from the waters of the *mikvah* may be said to symbolize death and resurrection, but really it makes you a member of the historical community of the new age."[40] The members of this alternative community identify with Christ and his egalitarianism and total commitment to service.

Similarly, the deepest meaning of breaking bread and sharing wine is not found in the fact that these acts symbolize unity in the community of Christ and thus a form of social life that transcends individualism. Eating bread and drinking wine together *is* community, *is* the transcendence of individualism.[41] In faithfully participating in the Eucharistic words and gestures, an alternative community of love and service is constituted.

To give another example, sharing the peace of Christ in the Eucharist should not be construed first and foremost as a symbol of non-violence and solidarity with the poor. To share the peace, as Debra Dean Murphy points out, is to make a powerful political statement:

> In sharing the peace, we extend our bodies toward one another, gesturing our willingness to risk living in peace with one another; we are not simply offering a pious morning greeting, but are in fact making a radical political claim—materially, bodily—about the nature of Christian community and eucharistic fellowship.[42]

It is in the doing of this liturgical gesture that Christian identity is formed.

The act of singing in community, to give one last example, draws isolated individuals out of themselves into a relationship with others. To sing well with others is to be attentive to them. If I go off into my own world and simply sing as I want to, I have subverted the process of congregational praise. As David Ford puts it, "singing together embodies joint responsibility in which each singer waits on the others, is attentive with the intention of serving the common harmony."[43] The simple invitation to sing in worship is actually a call to the individual to be transformed by a community of voices responding thankfully and joyously to the presence and blessing of the triune God.

What all this points to is that the Holy Spirit is the agent of formation. The deepest meaning of formation is found not in performing certain sacred words and actions, but in the spiritual power that these words and actions mediate—namely, the love and grace of the triune God. "The life of the eucharist is the life of God Himself . . . It is the life of communion with God, such as exists within the Trinity and is actualized within the members of the Eucharistic community. Knowledge and communion are identical."[44]

8

Maintaining Self in Communion

In the last chapter, the individualistic orientation of the tourist was contrasted with the communitarian commitment of the pilgrim. Whereas tourists tend to be focused on the self and its needs and desires, pilgrims commit themselves to self-giving and service of others. The argument was that communion needs to be promoted to counteract the corrosive effects of the culture of individualism. Here attention is given to developing an understanding of the true nature of communion with others. While a loving concern for the well-being of others expressed in acts of care and service lies at the heart of the Christian ethic, it is possible to go too far in this direction. Some psychologists have identified an unhealthy modality that they call "unmitigated communion."[1] They use the term "communion" to indicate a balanced approach to care in relationships. On the one hand, it involves thinking of the needs of others and making oneself available to help and support them. On the other hand, it entails being ready to ask for help and to graciously receive it when it is needed. In a word, communion involves both giving and receiving. Unmitigated communion indicates an unbalanced approach to relationships. It involves a tendency to define oneself almost exclusively through care and concern for others and to thereby lose one's self. That is, it is too much concern for others and too little concern for oneself.

In the terms of theological ethics, unmitigated communion is the result of constructing one's Christian identity around self-sacrifice. A pure, sacrificial love—one in which a person pays no heed to self—is taken to be the ideal for the Christian. A number of moral theologians have argued that this is unhealthy and that, moreover, it is not actually mandated by the Scriptures.[2] Their reading of the Bible and of the theological tradition indicates to them that mutuality in loving relations is a more adequate ideal than self-sacrifice. They are joined in this by feminist theologians and philosophers who have observed that the self-sacrifice ethic feeds into the cultural construction of the exemplary woman as the one who is prepared to sacrifice significant personal desires and ambitions in order to support the personal and professional goals of the members of her family.[3]

Unmitigated communion has been associated with a range of psychological and physical health problems. Communion, on the other hand, is typically unrelated to such problems, and some research even indicates a small positive association with good mental health.[4] With this in mind, it is argued in what follows that worship leaders have a pastoral responsibility to promote mutuality in giving as the Christian ideal for love. In the prayers and songs we use and in the sermons we preach, communion needs to be held up as normative in the Christian life.

Communion and the Covenant Service

I want to begin our reflections by briefly analyzing the Covenant Service that is part of the liturgical tradition of, among others, the Congregational, Methodist, and Presbyterian Churches. This service highlights a central theme of the last chapter—namely, the intimate relationship that exists between covenant and communion. It is not primarily with individuals but rather with a community that God makes a covenant. The liturgy centers on the covenant with Israel founded on fidelity to God's law and on the new covenant established in and through the death and resurrection of Christ. In the Church of Scotland service, the minister says: "In the strength of the covenant/ which he has made with his people/let us bind ourselves anew to God/who has so graciously bound himself to us."[5] The communion that is established through the covenant began at Baptism and is strengthened every time the Eucharist is celebrated. In the liturgy of the Covenant Service, worshipers are reminded that they were initiated into the new covenant by baptism through dying and rising with Christ. They are also asked to recall that every time the Lord's Supper is celebrated, the covenant is renewed.

In renewing their commitment to the covenant, worshipers are reminded that a life of faithful and obedient living is often challenging. There are times when much is asked of the disciple of Christ. The minister says:

Christ has many services to be done:
some are easy, some are difficult;

some are suited to our natural inclinations
and material interests,
others are contrary to both.
In some we please Christ and please ourselves,
in others we cannot please Christ
except by denying ourselves.[6]

The minister continues by inviting the worshipers to take upon themselves "the yoke of glad obedience":

We are no longer our own, but yours.
Put us with what you will,
rank us with whom you will;
put us to doing, put us to suffering;
let us be employed for you
or laid aside for you,
exalted for you or brought low for you;
let us be full, let us be empty;
let us have all things, let us have nothing;
we freely and wholeheartedly
yield all things
to your pleasure and disposal.[7]

There is the recognition here that self-sacrifice is a part of faithful Christian service. The liturgy indicates that it is simply not possible to loyally serve Christ if we insist on always pleasing ourselves. The demands of love are such that sometimes our needs and desires must be set aside in order to provide the help or care that others need from us. It is important for us to acknowledge the role of self-denial in Christian service. What will be argued below, though, is that *while it has an important place in a love ethic, it is not the ideal.* The ideal is mutuality in giving. We both serve our neighbors and allow them to serve us. There is no implied criticism of the Covenant Service here. It is quite right to declare that Christian service will not always be comfortable for us. There is indeed an important place for self-denial in faithful discipleship. What I aim to do in what follows is to mount an argument that in the totality of our worship life a balanced approach to the requirements of love is essential if we are to avoid encouraging the unhealthy tendency of some—and this seems to be especially true of women—to pour all of themselves into the care and self-development of others. It is appropriate to concentrate in a Covenant Service on our commitment to costly discipleship. In other services we need to promote the ideal of mutuality in loving relations. We need to monitor the overall pattern of our worship life lest through its prayers, songs, and messages we unwittingly exacerbate the problem of unmitigated communion.

Unmitigated Communion

Psychologists researching unmitigated communion have taken their lead from David Bakan's work on two fundamental modalities for human existence—namely, agency and communion.[8] Agency refers to the existence of a person as an individual, and communion denotes her participation in social life. Agency manifests itself in "self-protection, self-assertion, and self-expansion."[9] Communion expresses itself in the desire for, and the experience of, union and unity with others. Isolation and aloneness are features of agency. Contact, openness, and union are expressions of the life of communion. Bakan's thesis is that psychological, spiritual, and social wholeness requires a balance of agency and communion. Here he is inspired by Rabbi Hillel: "If I am not for myself, who will be for me? But if I am only for myself, what am I?"[10] His observation is—and as we saw in the last chapter, virtually all social commentators agree with him on this—that agency is dominating the landscape of modern Western societies.[11] If we are to build a society that embodies the good, then agency needs to be mitigated by communion.

Bakan is well aware, then, of the dangers of unmitigated agency. But at no point in his book does he discuss the problem of unmitigated communion. A number of empirical psychologists have noted this oversight and have set about the challenge of researching this phenomenon. Unmitigated communion is focusing on others to the exclusion of the self. To be more specific, "it involves placing others' needs before one's own, worrying excessively about others' problems, and helping others to one's own detriment."[12] In ethical discourse, it is referred to as a self-sacrificial approach to interpersonal life. Self-sacrifice is a gendered concept. By that I do not mean that women are necessarily more self-sacrificial than men, or vice versa. What I intend to indicate through this phrase is that men and women express self-sacrifice differently.[13] Some men are prepared, for example, to work two or more jobs in order to provide a decent standard of living for their family. Associated with this commitment is the sacrifice of time that could be spent building relationships and simply having fun with their partner and their children. Many middle-aged men look back with profound regret on an overly busy life in which there was too little time spent with the family.

Alongside the traditional male role of provider is that of protector. Here too we find a commitment to self-sacrifice. Large numbers of men are prepared to risk injury or worse in defending their loved ones against aggressors. A preparedness to risk one's life in armed conflict is another expression of this commitment to protect others.

What men have most often not been prepared to sacrifice are opportunities for self-development and self-actualization through their careers. The role of the man has been constructed around autonomy, independence, and competitiveness in the workplace. Men are expected to energetically and vigorously pursue advancement in their careers. The sacrifice that is asked of them is the minimization of their opportunities for leisure and pleasure in order to devote themselves to success in their chosen vocation. The role of the woman in modern Western societies, on the other hand, has been constructed in terms of nurture and care. The women's movement has of course strongly challenged this view, but it is still commonly considered that in order to fulfill her role a woman should put the personal development goals of the other members of the family ahead of her own. The result is that men tend to be focused on agency, and women on communion. Men generally root their sense of self in their achievements and self-development; women tend to find their identity in building strong relationships through nurture and care. Though men are not immune to unmitigated communion, it is more often a problem for women. A woman is much more likely than a man to lose her personal center in caring for others. Brita Gill-Austern clearly illustrates this strong tendency in women through the following clinical vignette. Ann is asked to introduce herself to the group with the invitation from the counselor: "Tell us about yourself."

Ann:	"I take care of people. I'm a nurse. I'm a mother. I take care of my daughter; I am a daughter. I take care of my mother, who has Alzheimers. She lives with us."
Counselor:	"Tell us about yourself."
Ann:	"I can't, I don't know who I am."[14]

155

Gill-Austern goes on to make the very apt comment that "[w]hereas men have been encouraged to bolster the 'I' at the expense of responsible connectedness to others, women have learned to sacrifice the 'I' for 'we.'"[15]

Psychological research has indicated that associated with a tendency to lose oneself in caring for others are some unhealthy psychological dynamics. A series of studies by Vicki Hegelson and Heidi Fritz on unmitigated communion (UC) have yielded the following data.[16] Individuals with a tendency to UC lack a healthy sense of self. Closely related to this is a strong susceptibility to depression. UC is associated with low self-esteem, looking to others to boost one's sense of worth, and a neglect of self in interpersonal engagements. In order to boost self-esteem, persons characterized by UC involve themselves in an excessive way in the lives of others.

Unmitigated communion is supported by a particular theological and ethical orientation—namely, one that holds up self-sacrifice as the ultimate expression of love. Christian persons who construct their identity and sense of worth almost exclusively around caring for and serving others feel encouraged in this unhealthy pattern by the theology of self-sacrificial love. A more adequate love ethic, however, is one in which mutuality in giving is established as the ideal. We should aim to give ourselves in love to others without losing ourselves in the process. The goal is to hold agency and communion in creative tension. Mutuality in loving relations is expressed most fully—perfectly in fact—in the life of the triune God.

The Trinity and Communion

Unmitigated communion can be clearly distinguished from communion.[17] Communion is a positive modality and involves an appropriate level of care and concern for others. Brita Gill-Austern suggests that looking to the doctrine of the Trinity can help us to develop a healthy approach to expressing love in relationships.[18] She notes that in the life of the Trinity there is total self-giving that is (i) mutual, (ii) respectful of difference and individuality, and (iii) completely without domination or subordination. These are very helpful observations; it is worth taking some space here to develop them.

The point that Bakan makes is that both agency and communion are required in a healthy, balanced approach to life. In making a connection with the doctrine of the Trinity, it is not legitimate to draw a direct parallel here. It is clearly inappropriate to refer to agency within the triune God. There is no push for self-assertion or self-expansion from the divine persons. However, though the Three indwell each other in perfect communion, it is also true that they maintain their distinctiveness. In the act of drawing near to each other in love, they also give each other space to be. There is particularity in the Godhead as well as absolute unity. The divine persons do not have to give up their distinctiveness and identity in order to live in perfect harmony. Whenever we talk about particularity in the Trinity, however, it is very difficult to avoid the notion that the persons represent three individual centers of consciousness. The way to overcome this is to see the Trinity as an event of relationality. Father, Son, and Holy Spirit indicate a particular set of relations.

Relationality is the central focus in Catherine Mowry LaCugna's Trinitarian theology.[19] LaCugna builds her relational theology of God around the notion of persons in communion. She then uses the life of the Godhead to shed light on the true nature of human existence. Persons, she notes first, are not isolated, self-contained entities. To be a person is to be in relationship. Here LaCugna picks up on an idea that was first developed by dialogical philosophers such as Buber, Rosenzweig, and Macmurray. They asserted that prior to the ego and subjectivity is the I–Thou relation. Following a similar line, Ted Peters observes that attending to the Trinity points up the folly of unmitigated agency: "Our identity grows continually through interaction with other individuals . . . Gone is the image of the self-defined and autonomous individual, the island of personhood standing over against society."[20]

Through her Trinitarian theology, LaCugna makes the point that human life expresses its true nature and meaning when persons come together in a fellowship of love. The essential meaning of the Trinity for LaCugna is that God reaches out to the world in Christ and through the power and presence of the Spirit calling all creatures into a loving communion of human and divine persons.

> [T]he perfection of God is the perfection of love, of communion, of personhood. Divine perfection is the antithesis of self-sufficiency, rather it is the absolute capacity to be who and what one is by being for and from another. The living God is the God who is alive in relationship, alive in communion with the creature, alive with desire for union with every creature.[21]

God reaches out in love to the world through Christ and the Spirit and invites us to share in the communion of God's love. David Cunningham captures this notion of an interlocking connection between the inner life of God and God for us through the metaphor of "producing."[22] He observes that the divine "production" encompasses both "God producing God" and "God producing the world." The idea of the production of the world points not only to the act of creation, but also to the missions of the Word and the Spirit. "God producing God" is Cunningham's way of referring to Aquinas' understanding of the processions and relations within God. In Aquinas' scheme, God produces God through the processions of "begetting" (the Word) and "breathing forth" (the Spirit).[23] These processions imply, in turn, four kinds of "real relation," namely begetting, being begotten, breathing out, and being breathed. There are, however, only three unique relations because the actions through which the Word and the Spirit are produced (begetting and breathing out are of the same general type). Thus the three unique relations are begetting (which includes breathing out), being begotten, and being breathed forth. What Aquinas is describing here, then, is the network of relations that is the Trinity. The term he uses to describe these unique relations is "subsistent." What he means by this is that their ground of existence is in themselves. There are no persons at each end of a relation; Father, Son, and Holy Spirit are simply the relations.

Now Aquinas goes on to say that the subsistence of these relations can be explained by the fact that they are identical with the one divine substance, which itself is the ground of its own existence. The three relations subsist because they are the same as the one divine substance which itself is self-grounded. Despite the very important contribution that Aquinas makes through his demonstration that the Trinity does not consist of three "somethings" who subsequently enter into relationships, but is purely and simply a network of subsistent relations, his work suffers from its tie with the metaphysics of substance. What is required is a more dynamic understanding of the triune God.

Paul Fiddes takes up this challenge by introducing the idea of God as "an event of relationships."[24] He suggests that we refer to "movements of relationship" or to "three movements of relationship subsisting in one event."[25] There is, of course, no way to imagine or visualize three interweaving relationships. When we think of relations we naturally picture two subjects who share in communion. The fact that we cannot picture the inner life of God is no bad thing, however. God is not simply one more being alongside all others. It is not even accurate to depict God as the Supreme Being. All such attempts to capture God's reality ultimately represent a failure to recognize that there is an infinite qualitative distinction between time and eternity (Kierkegaard). God's exists in a manner that is absolutely other, and as such God is beyond objectification.

Cunningham uses the term *participation* to describe this "event of relationships." In using this descriptor, he indicates that the divine life is first and foremost an event of mutual indwelling. It was this way of thinking about the Trinity that the early Greek theologians sought to capture with the term, *perichoresis*. It means "being-in-one-another, permeation without confusion. No person exists by him/herself or is referred to him/herself . . ."[26] Other terms that describe this notion of being-in-one-another are interpenetration and "mutual reciprocal participation."[27] The divine persons participate together in the intimacy of love and self-giving.

The metaphor of dancing is commonly used to express the meaning of *perichoresis*. The Three flow together in a continuous movement of love. "In this love the Father and the Son are intertwined like dancers moving to the music of the Spirit."[28] There is eternal order and symmetry in this dance, but at the same time there is diversity.

The connotation of dynamism that is associated with the dance metaphor is picked up in the first of two Latin words used to translate *perichoresis*, namely *circumincessio*.[29] It refers to a continual movement of the persons into the life of the others. The other Latin word that is used is *circuminsessio*. It also indicates mutual indwelling, but it conveys the sense of indwelling as a completed act. In and through the act of co-inherence, there is complete satiation of the need for love; the divine persons rest in each other.

Participation is both a divine and a human virtue. If the doctrine of the Trinity has anything to teach us about the nature of our human existence it is that *koinonia* is at the center of authentic living. There is a place for autonomy and personal freedom, but these values should not be allowed to take over. Agency needs to be mitigated by communion. Cunningham puts it this way:

[T]he focus on *participation* suggests that human beings are called to understand themselves, not as "individuals" who may (or may not) choose to enter into relationships, but rather as mutually indwelling and indwelt, and to such a degree that—echoing the mutual indwelling of the Three—all pretensions to wholly independent existence are abolished.[30]

Participation is another way of talking about what Bakan and the psychologists that are inspired by him refer to as communion. It is a human modality in which connection to others and giving and receiving love are assigned a high priority. The doctrine of the Trinity can help us further in identifying a healthy approach to interpersonal life. In the life of the triune God, there is mutual indwelling but there is also space to be. Father, Son, and Holy Spirit maintain their individuality and distinctiveness as they participate in each other in loving intimacy. There is no question of the persons "losing themselves" through their intense and deeply intimate relational engagement. There is also no hint of control or domination. Jürgen Moltmann observes that the Three draw close to each other in the intimacy of perfect love, but at the same time provide each other with an open space. In this space, the divine persons are free to give fully and free to be themselves. "[T]he divine persons," he says, "are 'habitable' for one another, giving one another open life-space for their mutual indwelling. Each person is indwelling and room-giving at the same time."[31]

Communion and the Love Ethic

In looking to the doctrine of the Trinity as a model, we have established that genuine love involves giving in a spirit of mutuality. There is both giving and receiving. Each person gives fully while maintaining her personal center. A commitment to love and care for others should not involve losing ourselves in the process. If we are to hold onto the "I" while giving to the "We," it is necessary to balance regard for others with regard for self. If I love others less than I love myself, I am in the grip of egoism. If I love others more than myself, I am afflicted by low self-esteem. What is required for a positive love ethic is equal regard.

Equal Regard

A compelling theological rationale for the principle of equal regard is supplied by Gene Outka.[32] We should love ourselves, he suggests, for the same reason that we should love others. The notion that every other person is to be loved simply because he or she is a child of God has an application to my relationship with myself. Others are neither more nor less deserving of my love than I am. I should regard others and myself equally.

Outka develops his argument in this way. Christians are called to love others. We are called to love not only those who are likable, or who have done something good for us, but *all* people. Loving only our "favorites" is not an option. We must love each and every person God puts in our path. The theological rationale is based around our status as children of God. Each and every person is created in the image of God. He or she is someone Christ died for. It follows that each and every person possesses an inherent dignity and worth. Just as God recognizes that value through the gift of divine love, so it is to be with us. God does not have favorites, and neither should we. This leads Outka to refer to the principle of impartiality. It is clear that we are to love others simply because of their status in God's eyes: a person created out of love and offered the loving gift of Christ on the cross. We need to apply, Outka suggests, the same theological rationale to ourselves. We are to love self for the same reason that we love others. There is, therefore a principle of "equal regard." We should love self neither more nor less than we love others.

Don Browning has taken up Outka's suggestion and developed it in a number of contexts.[33] He helpfully points out that the principle of equal regard constitutes a middle way between the extremes of independence, on the one hand, and self-sacrifice, on the other. In the independence or self-actualization model of love, it is assumed that self-love comes first, and that love of neighbor will follow automatically. That is, the focus is largely on self-fulfillment and the extent to which a particular act or relationship is likely to contribute to it. At the other end of the scale is an understanding of love that requires sacrificing the self for others. The equal regard approach, Browning suggests, picks up values from the other two models, but it manages to avoid their excesses. A person living according to the principle of equal regard will take the needs and claims of the other as seriously as her own. The needs of others are seen to be very important, but so are one's own. Love for others and self-love are assigned an equal weighting.

Reciprocal Giving as the Ideal

The principle of equal regard is closely associated with an ethic of reciprocal giving in relationships. If I have a healthy love of self, when it comes to my relationships I will expect that the other will give to me, just as I give to her. Stephen Post builds a strong argument in support of his view that mutual love is the only appropriate basic norm for interpersonal relations.[34] He refers to this reciprocal love as "communion." He argues that there is a true self-love that is expressed through a desire for a triadic fellowship involving God, self, and other(s).[35] One pursues one's own needs and aspirations, but only in the context of a loving commitment to the needs and aspirations of those with whom one shares life. Such a reciprocal love, argues Post, is not inferior to selfless love, as many believe:

> The moral excellence of communion (giving and receiving love) is too often lost sight of . . . Frequently selfless love . . . is thought to be ethically superior to communion and alone worthy of the designation "Christian." The equilibrium of communion that allows each participant to find fulfillment through the process of mutuality is set aside to make room for the rare genius of selflessness. However, in our view, a "true" or proper self-love defined as the pursuit of one's own good within the context of triadic communion can be distinguished from both selfishness (the pursuit of one's own separate interests) and self-infatuation.[36]

Post argues, then, that it is legitimate to pursue one's own good within the context of a triadic fellowship. Such self-love must be distinguished from both selfishness and self-infatuation. Selfishness means pursuing one's own interests without due regard for the interests of others. But when one is committed to a life of communion, one pays due attention to the needs and desires of others. A person who is self-infatuated, on the other hand, simply cannot manage fellowship with others. She is so attracted to self that she finds no interest in getting to know others in any depth. The good of personal fulfillment, by contrast, is pursued through a relationship of reciprocity. One desires fulfillment for oneself, but one is equally concerned with helping others find it.

Post makes the point that the ideal of a love stripped of all self-concern is grounded in a mistaken conceptualization of divine love. Self-concern, it is important to recognize, is very different from selfishness. There are legitimate concerns that the self has and these need to be taken care of. God's relationship with us is not marked by disinterest. God has as a central concern the mutual good of communion with human persons. In the Bible we read often of the grief that God feels when God's offer of communion is rejected. This makes no sense if God's love is disinterested. Human love, like divine love, appropriately entails a level of self-concern.

Universal Love

Equal regard and communion are important elements in an adequate love ethic. Outka rightly points out that it is also important to acknowledge the place of what he calls "universal love."[37] Though it is closely associated with impartiality, it also moves beyond it to incorporate the Christian commitment to being for the other. That is to say, he is acknowledging the importance of cross-bearing. Let me point out that though he does not use the term "universal love," Browning is clearly aware of the importance of the principle. "Self-sacrifice and the demands of the cross," he writes, "are still required in this love ethic. Sometimes we must love even when circumstances do not permit us to be loved fully in return."[38]

Outka lists four challenges to the principle of impartiality.[39] It is the first two that are particularly relevant to our discussion. They are these. First, impartiality cannot find a place for the radically other-regarding elements in *agape*. Secondly, it does not take seriously the fact that we are more likely to be tempted by selfishness than by altruism. Outka is prepared to align himself with impartiality to the extent that altruism is not given endorsement if it is of the radical kind that is dismissive of self-love. However, in taking these two objections seriously, he suggests that it is necessary to go beyond impartiality and incorporate "a practical swerve" away from self and toward the other.[40] Given the fact that we tend to have great difficulty in being even-handed when it comes to balancing our own needs against those of the other, we need to build in a bias toward her well-being.

In sum, the Christian ideal for communion is reciprocal giving. What we should aim for in relationships is both giving and receiving love. To be sure, there will be times when we are asked to forget about ourselves and our needs in order to provide the love and care that another person needs. Self-sacrifice has an important role to play in communion. Further, though it is legitimate to give attention to our own interests as we engage in relationships with others, we need to be mindful that there is a sinful tendency in all of us to give a little more attention to those interests than is justified. We therefore need to build in a "practical swerve" toward the other.

Worship and Maintaining Self in Communion

It is these theological principles and values that need to be inculcated through worship. What has been offered will hopefully provide a useful guide for choosing songs and for preparing sermons when the theme of love and self-giving presents itself. It is not necessary for me to pursue this line any further. The individual reader will decide how he or she wants to apply the principles that have been developed. However, I would like to make one final contribution, and that is through offering the litany below. It is not possible, of course, to capture the nuances of a complex theological discussion in a prayer. What I have aimed to do with my "litany of love" is simply to encapsulate the major emphases in the love ethic that has been developed.

Litany of Love

Leader:
Love is our gift.
Christ calls us to give it generously.
Are you willing?

People:
By the grace of God, we are.

Leader:
Love seeks out the needs of others.
The Spirit who leads us is waiting.
Will you respond?

People:
By the grace of God, we will?

Leader:
Love is costly.
Christ calls us to deny ourselves and to take up our cross.
Are you ready?

People:
By the grace of God, we are.

Leader:
Love is not just for others.
God's intention is that we also love ourselves.
Are you able?

People:
By the grace of God, we are.

Leader:
Love regards self and others equally.
God wants us to care for ourselves as we love and serve others.
Will you follow him?

People:
By the grace of God, we will.

Leader:
Regard for others and regard for self should be held in balance.
Christ warns us against selfishness.
Will you hear him?

People:
By the grace of God, we will.

Leader:
Great and Blessed God,
Father, Son, and Holy Spirit,
we renew today our commitment to loving service.
Forgive our failures in love for others.
Infuse us with your grace that we may more fully give of
    ourselves.
As we give generously in caring for others,
remind us also to care for ourselves.
Help us to hold love for others in balance with love for
    ourselves.

All: Amen.

Notes

Introduction

1 There are a variety of approaches that writers have taken to according a more central role to the faith community in providing pastoral care. For representative approaches focusing on worship and liturgy, see W.H. Willimon, *Worship as Pastoral Care* (Nashville: Abingdon Press, 1979), and idem, *Pastor: The Theology and Practice of Ordained Ministry* (Nashville: Abingdon Press, 2002), chp. 4; D. Capps, *Life Cycle Theory and Pastoral Care* (Minneapolis: Fortress Press, 1983), chp. 3; E. Ramshaw, *Ritual and Pastoral Care* (Philadelphia: Fortress Press, 1987), and idem, "Ritual and Pastoral Care: The Vital Connection," in E. Berstein (ed.) *Disciples at the Crossroads* (Collegeville: Liturgical Press, 1993), pp. 92–105; R. Kinast, *Sacramental Pastoral Care* (New York: Pueblo, 1988); R.L. Underwood, *Pastoral Care and the Means of Grace* (Minneapolis: Fortress Press, 1993); G.L. Ramsey, *Care-full Preaching: From Sermon to Caring Community* (St. Louis: Chalice Press, 2000); R.J. Allen, *Preaching and Practical Ministry* (St. Louis: Chalice Press, 2001), chp. 3; D. Lyall, "The Bible, Worship, and Pastoral Care," in P. Ballard and S.R. Holmes (eds) *The Bible in Pastoral Practice* (Grand Rapids: Eerdmans, 2005), pp. 225–240.

2 This is how Marva Dawn describes it. See her *Reaching Out without Dumbing Down* (Grand Rapids: Eerdmans, 1995), pp. 75–82. The same idea is presented in J.D. Witvliet, "The Opening of Worship: Trinity," in L. van Dyk (ed.) *A More Profound Alleluia* (Grand Rapids: Eerdmans, 2005), pp. 1–5.

3 J.D. Crichton uses the divine initiative–human response theme to structure his very helpful essay, "A Theology of Worship," in C. Jones, G. Wainwright, and E. Yarnold (eds) *The Study of Liturgy* (London: SPCK, 1985), pp. 1–29.

4 R. Byars, *The Future of Protestant Worship* (Louisville: Westminster John Knox Press, 2002), p. 29.

5 W.H. Willimon, *Worship as Pastoral Care*, p. 48.

6 See, for example, ibid., pp. 100–165; P.P.J. Sheppy, *Death Liturgy and Ritual: A Pastoral and Liturgical Theology* (Aldershot: Ashgate, 2003); and G. Fowler, *Caring through the Funeral* (St. Louis: Chalice Press, 2004). For a briefer

but nonetheless helpful treatment, see D. Lyall, "The Bible, Worship, and Pastoral Care."

7 See, for example, E.P. Wimberly, *Moving from Shame to Self-worth: Preaching and Pastoral Care* (Nashville: Abingdon Press, 1999); G.L. Ramsey, *Care-full Preaching*; R.J. Allen, *Preaching and Practical Ministry*, chp. 3; and L.H. Aden and R.G. Hughes, *Preaching God's Compassion* (Minneapolis: Fortress Press, 2002).

Introduction to Part 1

1 See E. Thurneysen, *A Theology of Pastoral Care* (Richmond: John Knox Press, 1962), p. 154.

2 Ibid., p. 154.

3 See A. Purves, *Reconstructing Pastoral Theology: A Christological Foundation* (Louisville: Westminster John Knox Press, 2004), p. 176.

4 S. Pattison, *A Critique of Pastoral Care* (London: SCM Press, 1993), p. 13.

5 D. van Deusen Hunsinger, *Pray without Ceasing: Revitalizing Pastoral Care* (Grand Rapids: Eerdmans, 2006), p. 156.

6 See W.A. Clebsch and C.R. Jaekle, *Pastoral Care in Historical Perspective* (Englewoods Cliffs: Prentice-Hall, 1964).

7 See H. Clinebell, *Basic Types of Pastoral Care and Counseling*, rev. edn (Nashville: Abingdon Press, 1984), p. 43. For a comprehensive treatment of the pastoral function of nurturing, see N. Pembroke, *The Art of Listening: Dialogue, Shame, and Pastoral Care* (Edinburgh: T&T Clark & Grand Rapids: Eerdmans, 2002).

Chapter 1

1 C. Plantinga and S.A. Rozeboom, *Discerning the Spirits: A Guide to Thinking About Christian Worship Today* (Grand Rapids: Eerdmans, 2003), p. 160.

2 See, for example, Augustine, *City of God* (London: Dent, 1945), Bk. XIV, chp. 13, and idem, "The Punishment and Forgiveness of Sins and the Baptism of Little Ones," in *Answer to the Pelagians* I, in J. Rotelle (ed.) *The Works of St. Augustine*, Part I, vol. 23 (New York: New City Press, 1990), chp. 17, para. 27.

3 See R. Niebuhr, *The Nature and Destiny of Man*, vol. 1 (London: Nisbet & Co., 1941), chp. VII.

4 See P. Tillich *Systematic Theology*, vol. 2 (London; Nisbet & Co., 1957), chp. XIV.

5 See K. Barth, *Church Dogmatics* IV.1 (Edinburgh: T&T Clark, 1951), pp. 413–478.

6 Ibid., p. 421.

7 K. Barth, *Church Dogmatics* IV.2 (Edinburgh: T&T Clark, 1958), p. 404.

8 See M. Biddle, *Missing the Mark: Sin and Its Consequences in Biblical Theology* (Nashville: Abingdon, 2005), pp. 54–57.

9 Ibid., p. 57.

10 See ibid., pp. 63–66.

11 See K. Barth, *CD* IV.2, pp. 403–483.

12 Ibid., p. 405.

13 Ibid., p. 406.

14 Ibid., p. 415.

15 See ibid., p. 416.

16 Ibid., p. 419.

17 Ibid., p. 437.

18 See ibid., p. 438.

19 See ibid., p. 452–467.

20 Ibid., p. 454.

21 Ibid., p. 455.

22 Ibid., p. 460.

23 See C. Daniel Batson et al, "In a Very Different Voice: Unmasking Moral Hypocrisy," *Journal of Personality and Social Psychology* 72, no. 6 (1997), pp. 1335–1343; C. Daniel Batson et al, "Moral Hypocrisy: Appearing to be Moral to Oneself Without Being So," *Journal of Personality and Social Psychology* 77, no. 3 (1999), pp. 525–537; C. Daniel Batson et al, "Moral Hypocrisy: Addressing Some Alternatives," *Journal of Personality and Social Psychology* 83, no. 2 (2002), pp. 330–339.

24 C. Daniel Batson et al, "In a Very Different Voice," p. 1336.

25 See ibid., p. 1337.

26 Ibid., p. 1342.

27 See C. Daniel Batson et al, "Moral Hypocrisy: Appearing to be Moral," pp. 527–529.

28 See ibid., pp. 529–532.

29 See Barth, *CD* IV.1, pp. 358–413.

30 Barth, ibid., p. 390.

31 On Zwingli's pattern of confession after the sermon, see H.V. Taylor, "The General Confession of Sin," *Reformed Liturgy and Music* 26 (1992), pp. 179–183, p. 182; and J. Paarlberg, "Genuine Sorrow ... Wholehearted Joy: The Why, When, and How of Confession," *Reformed Worship* 34 (1994), pp. 4–8, p. 5.

32 See Paul Scott Wilson, *The Four Pages of the Sermon* (Nashville: Abingdon Press, 1999).

Chapter 2

1 Cf. R. Karen, "Shame," *The Atlantic Monthly* (Feb. 1992), pp. 40–70, p. 40.

2 S. Tomkins, "Shame," in D. Nathanson (ed.) *The Many Faces of Shame* (New York: Guilford Press, 1987), pp. 133–161, p.155.

3 S. Pattison, *Shame: Theory, Therapy, Theology* (Cambridge University Press, 2000), p. 39.

4 Two leading shame researchers who have developed typologies are Robert Karen and James Fowler. The former suggests four categories, namely *existential shame* (the individual suddenly becomes aware of his failings), *class shame* (related to my category of *inherited identity shame*), *narcissistic shame* (one's personal identity is shame-based), and *situational shame* (a category I also use). See R. Karen, "Shame," pp. 40–70, p. 58. Moving from "normal" shame to increasingly pathological variations, James Fowler describes five types and degrees. These are: *healthy shame, perfectionist shame, shame due to enforced minority* (cf. my *inherited identity shame*), *toxic shame* (cf. Karen's *narcissistic shame*), and *shamelessness*. See J. Fowler, *Faithful Change: The Personal and Public Challenges of Post-modern Life* (Nashville: Abingdon Press, 1996), chp. 7.

5 See R. Karen, "Shame," p. 58.

6 Ibid., p. 58.

7 See M. Babcock and J. Sabini, "On Differentiating Embarrassment from Shame," *European Journal of Social Psychology* 20 (1990), pp. 151–169, p. 153.

8 Ibid., p. 154.

9 See J. Fowler, *Faithful Change*, p. 119.

10 See G. Thrane, "Shame," *Journal for the Theory of Social Behavior* 92 (1979), pp. 139–166, p. 144.

11 See D. Nathanson, *Shame and Pride: Affect, Sex, and the Birth of the Self* (New York: W.W. Norton & Co., 1992).

12 See A. Heller, *The Power of Shame: A Rational Perspective* (London: Routledge & Kegan Paul, 1985), p. 17.

13 See ibid., p. 19.

14 See ibid., p. 20.

15 See G. Thrane, "Shame," pp. 139–166, esp. pp. 139, 152–154, 157–158.

16 Ibid., p. 152.

17 Ibid., p. 154.

18 See C. Schneider, *Shame, Exposure, and Privacy* (New York: W.W. Norton, 1992), pp. 18–20.

19 Ibid., p. 20.

20 Exposure is an important theme in studies by Helen Merrell Lynd and Carl Schneider. See H.M. Lynd, *On Shame and the Search for Identity* (New York: Harcourt, Brace & World, Inc., 1958) and C. Schneider, *Shame, Exposure and Privacy*.

21 Cf. P. Gilbert, "What is Shame? Some Core Issues and Controversies," in P. Gilbert and B. Andrews (eds) *Shame: Interpersonal Behavior, Psychopathology, and Culture* (Oxford University Press, 1998), pp. 3–38, p. 23.

22 See D. Ausubel, "Relationships between Shame and Guilt in the Socializing Process," *Psychological Review* 62, no.15 (1955), pp. 379–390, p. 382.

23 H.M. Lynd, *On Shame*, p. 32.

24 See L. Wurmser, "Shame: The Veiled Companion of Narcissism," in D. Nathanson (ed.) *The Many Faces of Shame* (New York: Guilford Press, 1987) pp. 64–92, p. 82.

25 Ibid., p. 83.

26 W.H. Auden, *The New Yorker*, (Dec. 18, 1954), pp. 142–143. Cited in H.M. Lynd, *On Shame*, p. 32.

27 See H.B. Lewis, *Shame and Guilt in Neurosis* (New York: International Universities Press, 1971), p. 38.

28 See ibid., p. 53.

29 This discussion of the link between shame and incongruence is informed by H.M. Lynd, *On Shame*, pp. 34–42.

30 See ibid., p. 43.

31 Ibid., p. 46.

32 L. Wurmser, *The Mask of Shame* (Baltimore: The John Hopkins University Press, 1981), p. 93.

33 S. Pattison, *Shame*, p. 90.

34 L. Wurmser, *The Mask*, pp. 96–97.

35 See L. Wurmser, "Shame: The Veiled Companion," p. 86.

36 See D. Capps, *The Depleted Self: Sin in a Narcissistic Age* (Minneapolis: Fotress Press, 1993).

37 See ibid., pp. 3, 71.

38 I began the process in my first book. See N. Pembroke, *The Art of Listening: Dialogue, Shame, and Pastoral Care* (Edinburgh: T&T Clark and Grand Rapids: Eerdmans, 2002), chp. 9.

39 C. Plantinga, "Not the Way It's S'pposed to Be: A Breviary of Sin," *Theology Today* 50, no. 2 (1993), pp. 179–192, p. 184.

40 V. Saiving Goldstein, "The Human Situation: A Feminine View," *Journal of Religion* 40 (1960): pp. 100–112, p. 108. The author later decided to go under the name Valerie Saiving.

41 See J. Plaskow, *Sex, Sin, and Grace: Women's Experience and the Theologies of Reinhold Niebuhr and Paul Tillich* (Lanham: University Press of America, 1980).

42 Ibid., p. 65.

43 Cf. M. Biddle, *Missing the Mark: Sin and Its Consequences in Biblical Theology* (Nashville: Abingdon Press, 2005), p. 66. Biddle puts it this way: "Human beings can and should grow into full personhood . . . The process is, unfortunately, rife with opportunities to be stunted by perversion and suppression: sin."

44 N.H. Gregersen, "Guilt, Shame, and Rehabilitation: The Pedagogy of Divine Judgment," *Dialog: A Journal of Theology* 39, no. 2 (Sum. 2000), pp. 105–118, p. 111.

45 P. Kettunen, "The Function of Confession: A Study Based on Experiences," *Pastoral Psychology* 51, no. 1 (Sep. 2002), pp. 13–25, p. 21.

46 J. Harold Ellens, "Sin or Sickness: The Problem of Human Dysfunction," in *Seeking Understanding: The Strob Lectures, 1986–1998* (Grand Rapids: Eerdmans, 2001), pp. 439–489, p. 454.

47 See E. Moltmann-Wendel, *A Land Flowing with Milk and Honey: Perspectives on Feminist Theology* (New York: Crossroad, 1986), p. 151.

48 E. Moltmann-Wendel, "Self-love and Self-acceptance," *Pacifica* 5 (Oct. 1992), pp. 288–301, p. 292.

49 N.H. Gregersen, "Guilt, Shame, and Rehabilitation," p. 111.

50 See P. Goodliff, *With Unveiled Face: A Pastoral and Theological Exploration of Shame* (London: Darton, Longman & Todd, 2005), pp. 96–99.

51 J-L Marion, *God without Being* (University of Chicago Press, 1991), p. 12.

52 Cf. M. Quenot, *The Icon: Window on the Kingdom* (Crestwood: St.Vladimir's Seminary Press, 1991), p. 93.

53 R. Williams, *The Dwelling of the Light: Praying with Icons of Christ* (Norwich: Canterbury Press, 2003), xix.

54 Note that I have not used the words "right" and "good" from Moltmann-Wendel's formula here. The reason for this is that it may be confusing to some worshipers. They may wrongly think that the worship leader wants to affirm them as morally good. The intention, rather, is to declare that God sees us as beautiful and full of quality despite our human frailty.

Introduction to Part 2

1 W. Brueggemann, "The Friday Voice of Faith," *Calvin Theological Journal* 36, no. 1 (2001), pp. 12–21, p. 16.

2 Virtually all worship books largely, or even completely, ignore the lament. On this see, K.D. Billman and D.L. Migliore, *Rachel's Cry: Prayer of Lament and Rebirth of Hope* (Cleveland: United Church Press, 1999), p. 13; and N. Duff, "Recovering Lamentation as a Practice of the Church," in S.A. Brown and P.D. Miller (eds) *Lament: Reclaiming Practices in Pulpit, Pew, and Public Square* (Louiseville: Westminster John Knox Press, 2005), pp. 3–14, p. 4. I am pleased to report, though, that a notable exception is the worship resource of my own denomination, the Uniting Church in Australia. See *Uniting in Worship 2* (Sydney: Uniting Church Press, 2005).

3 Cf. W. Brueggemann, "The Friday Voice of Faith," p. 14; M. Boulton, "Forsaking God: A Theological Argument for Christian Lamentation," *Scottish Journal of Theology* 55, no. 1 (2002), pp. 58–78, p. 59.

Chapter 3

1 On the relationship between the sovereignty and providence of God on the one hand, and lament on the other, see E.T. Charry, "May We Trust God and (Still) Lament? Can We Lament and (Still) Trust God?" in S.A. Brown and P.D. Miller (eds) *Lament: Reclaiming Practices in Pulpit, Pew, and Public Square* (Louisville: Westminster John Knox Press, 2005), pp. 95–108; and N. Wolterstorff, "If God is Good and Sovereign, Why Lament?" *Calvin Theological Journal* 36 (2001), pp. 42–52.

2 Augustine, *Confessions*, trans. Henry Chadwick (Oxford: Oxford University Press, 1991), IV.iv.9.

3 Ibid.

4 Ibid., IV.vi.11.

5 Cf. N. Wolterstorff, "If God is Good," p. 46.

6 Augustine, *Confessions*, IV.vi.11.

7 Ibid., IV.x.15.

8 Ibid.

9 Ibid., IX.xii.29.

10 Ibid., IV.xii.33.

11 Cf. N. Wolterstorff, "Suffering Love," in T.V. Morris (ed.) *Philosophy and the Christian Faith* (Notre Dame: University of Notre Dame Press, 1988), pp. 196–237, p. 197.

12 Ibid., IV.xii.30.

13 Ibid., IV.xi.16.

14 See J. Calvin, *Institutes of the Christian Religion*, trans. Henry Beveridge (Grand Rapids: Eerdmans, 1989), III.viii.2.

15 Ibid., III.viii.5.

16 N. Wolterstorff, "If God is Good," p. 49.

17 Calvin, *Institutes*, III.viii.11.

18 Ibid., III.viii.10.

19 Ibid.

20 Ibid., III.viii.1.

21 See K. Barth, *Church Dogmatics* III.4 (Edinburgh: T & T Clark, 1961), p. 378.

22 See K. Barth, *CD* III.3 (Edinburgh: T & T Clark, 1960), p. 293.

23 Barth, *CD* III.4, p. 383.

24 Ibid.

25 Ibid.

26 Ibid.

27 Barth, *CD* III.3, p. 3.

28 See ibid., p. 28. For more on the "fatherly lordship" of God, see ibid., p. 142.

29 See ibid., p. 155.

30 See ibid., p. 91.

31 Ibid., p. 132.

32 E.T. Charry, "May We Trust God," p. 96.

33 C. Westermann, "The Complaint against God," in T. Linafelt and T.K. Beal (eds) *God in the Fray* (Minneapolis: Fortress Press, 1998), pp. 233–241, p. 239.

34 W. Brueggemann, "A Shape for Old Testament Theology I: Structure Legitimation," *Catholic Biblical Quarterly* 47 (1985), pp. 28–46, p. 42.

35 C. Westermann, "The Complaint," p. 238.

36 On this, see R.E. Clements, *Jeremiah* (Atlanta: John Knox Press, 1988), pp. 121–122.

37 See A. Laytner, *Arguing with God: A Jewish Tradition* (Northvale: Jason Aronson, 1990), p. 20; and W. Brueggemann, "A Shape for Old Testament Theology, II: Embrace of Pain," *Catholic Biblical Quarterly* 47 (1985), pp. 395–415, p. 405.

38 On this, see N. Whybray, *Job* (Sheffield: Sheffield Academic Press, 1998), p. 18.

39 W. Brueggemann, "The Friday Voice of Faith," *Calvin Theological Journal* 36, no. 1 (2001), pp. 12–21, p. 21.

40 W. Brueggemann, "The Shape II," p. 400.

41 Ibid., p. 400.

42 D.R. Ames and F.J. Flynn, "What Breaks a Leader: The Curvilinear Relation between Assertiveness and Leadership," *Journal of Personality and Social Psychology* 92, no. 2 (2007), pp. 307–324, p. 307.

43 See, for example, D.R. Ames and F.J. Flynn, "What Breaks a Leader"; A.H. Gervasio, "Assertiveness Techniques as Speech Acts," *Clinical Psychology Review* 7 (1987), pp. 105–119; R.J. Delamater and J.R. McNamara, "Perceptions of Assertiveness by Women Involved in a Conflict Situation," *Behavior Modification* 15, no. 2 (1991), pp. 173–193; and K. Wilson and C. Gallois, *Assertion and Its Social Context* (Oxford: Pergamon Press, 1993), p. 2.

44 See K. Wilson and C. Gallois, *Assertion*, p. 28.

45 See C. Westermann, *Praise and Lament in the Psalms* (Atlanta: John Knox Press, 1981), pp. 181, 185.

46 Cf. ibid., p. 184.

47 See N.J. Duff, "Recovering Lamentation as a Practice of the Church?" in S.A. Brown and P.D. Miller (eds) *Lament: Reclaiming Practices in Pulpit, Pew, and Public Square* (Louisville: Westminster John Knox Press, 2005) pp. 3–14, pp. 8–9.

48 See, for example, *Uniting in Worship 2* (Sydney: Uniting Church Press, 2005); T.C. Falla, *Be Our Freedom Lord*, 2nd edn (Adelaide: OpenBook Publishers, 1994).

49 See A. Laytner, *Arguing with God*, chp. 7.

50 This is David Blumenthal's term. See his "Liturgies of Anger," *CrossCurrents* 52, no. 2 (2002), pp. 178–199.

Chapter 4

1 See W. Brueggemann, "Prerequisites for Genuine Obedience: Theses and Conclusions," *Calvin Theological Journal* 36 (2001), pp. 34–41, pp. 34–35.

2 Ibid., p. 34.

3 N. Wolterstorff, "If God is Good and Sovereign, Why Lament?" *Calvin Theological Journal* 36 (2001), pp. 42–52, p. 44.

4 Cf. Brueggemann, "Prerequisites," p. 36.

5 Ibid., p. 36.

6 Cf. D. Blumenthal, *Facing the Abusing God: A Theology of Protest* (Louiseville: Westminster/John Knox Press, 1993), p. 40.

7 D. Blumenthal, "Liturgies of Anger," *CrossCurrents* 52, no. 2 (2002), pp. 178–199, p. 195.

8 W. Brueggemann, "The Friday Voice of Faith," *Calvin Theological Journal* 36, no. 1 (2001), pp. 12–21, p. 15.

9 See W. Brueggemann, "A Shape for Old Testament Theology, II: Embrace of Pain," *Catholic Biblical Quarterly* 47 (1985), pp. 395–415, p. 400.

10 D. Blumenthal, *Facing the Abusing God*, p. 102.

11 Cf. A.E. Roffman, "Is Anger a Thing-to-be-Managed?" *Psychotherapy: Theory, Research, Practice, Training* 41, no. 2 (2004), pp. 161–171, p. 161.

12 Cf. J.P. Tangney et al, "Assessing Individual Differences in Constructive Versus Destructive Responses to Anger Across the Lifespan," *Journal of Personality and Social Psychology* 70, no. 4 (1996), pp. 780–796, p. 780.

13 See A. Roffman, "Is Anger a Thing-to-be-Managed?" p. 165.

14 See ibid., p. 168.

15 J.R. Averill, *Anger and Emotion: An Essay on Emotion* (New York: Springer-Verlag, 1982, p. 195).

16 See R.R. Holt, "On the Interpersonal and Intrapersonal Consequences of Expressing or Not Expressing Anger," *Journal of Consulting and Clinical Psychology* 35, no. 1 (1970), pp. 8–12.

17 Holt, ibid., p. 9.

18 C. Christ, "Expressing Anger at God," *Anima* 5 (1978), pp. 3–10, p. 7.

19 Cf. S. Carney, "God Damn God: A Reflection on Expressing Anger in Prayer," *Biblical Theology Bulletin* 13 (1983), pp. 116–120, p. 118.

20 D. Blumenthal, "Liturgies," p. 198.

21 S. Carney, "God Damn God," p. 119.

22 See J. Littrell, "Is the Reexperience of Painful Emotion Therapeutic?" *Clinical Psychology Review* 18, no. 1 (1998), pp. 71–102; and E. Kennedy-More and J.C. Watson, "How and When Does Emotional Expression Help?" *Review of General Psychology* 5, no. 3 (2001), pp. 187–212.

23 E. Kennedy-More and J.C. Watson, "How and When," p. 196.

24 R.A. Green and E.J. Murray, "Expression of Feelings and Cognitive Reinterpretation in the Reduction of Hostile Aggression," *Journal of Consulting and Clinical Psychology* 43, no. 3 (1975), pp. 375–383. Both these research projects are also discussed by E. Kennedy-More and J.C. Watson, in "How and When."

25 Ibid., p. 381.

26 See A. Bohart, "Role Playing and Interpersonal-Conflict Reduction," *Journal of Counseling Psychology* 24, no. 1 (1977), pp. 15–24.

27 Ibid., p. 22.

28 M.A. Lieberman, I.D. Yalom, and M.B. Miles, *Encounter Groups: First Facts* (New York: Basic Books, 1973).

29 See W. Brueggemann, *The Message of the Psalms* (Minneapolis: Augsburg, 1984), p. 57.

30 Ibid., p. 57.

31 See W. Brueggemann, *The Message*, p. 57; and H.G.M. Williamson, "Reading the Lament Psalms Backwards," in B.A. Strawn and N.R. Bowen (eds) *A God So Near* (Winona Lake: Eisenbrauns, 2003), pp. 3–15, p. 5.

32 M.M. Adams, *Wrestling for Blessing* (London: Darton, Longman & Todd, 2005).

33 Ibid., pp. 51–53.

Introduction to Part 3

1 On hope in pastoral care, see A. Lester, *Hope in Pastoral Care and Counseling* (Louisville: Westminster John Knox, 1995); D. Capps, *Agents of Hope: A Pastoral Psychology* (Minneapolis: Fortress Press, 1995); D. Lyall, *Integrity of Pastoral Care* (London: SPCK, 2001, pp. 104–107, 158–159, and idem, "The Bible, Worship, and Pastoral Care," in P. Ballard and S.R. Holmes (eds) *The Bible in Pastoral Practice* (Grand Rapids: Eerdmans, 2005), pp. 225–240, esp. pp. 238–240.

2 D. Lyall, "The Bible, Worship, and Pastoral Care," p. 240.

3 See D. Capps, *Agents of Hope.*

Chapter 5

1 On hope and temporality, see A, Lester, *Hope in Pastoral Care and Counseling* (Louiseville: Westminster John Knox Press, 1995), pp. 13–24.

2 See K. Weingarten, "Witnessing, Wonder, and Hope," *Family Process* 39, no. 4 (2000), pp. 389–402; idem, "Cancer, Meaning Making, and Hope: The Treatment Dedication Project," *Families, Systems, and Health* 23, no. 2 (2005), pp. 155–160; and idem, "Hope in a Time of Global Despair."

Unpublished paper delivered at the International Family Therapy Association Conference, Reykjavick, Iceland, October 4–7, 2006.

3 Cf. K. Herth, "Fostering Hope in Terminally ill People," *Journal of Advanced Nursing* 15 (1990), pp. 1250–1259, p. 1250.

4 Cf. S.R. Staats and M.A. Stassen, "Hope: An Affective Cognition," *Social Indicators Research* 17 (1985), pp. 235–242, p. 235.

5 Cf. W.F. Lynch, *Images of Hope: Imagination as Healer of the Hopeless* (Notre Dame: University of Notre Dame Press, 1974), p. 32.

6 D. Capps, *Agents of Hope: A Pastoral Psychology* (Minneapolis: Fortress Press, 1995), p. 53.

7 R.S. Lazarus, "Hope: An Emotion and a Vital Coping Resource against Despair," *Social Research* 66, no. 2 (Sum. 1999), pp. 653–678, p. 653.

8 S.R. Staats and M.A. Stassen, "Hope," p. 235.

9 See G. Marcel, *Homo Viator: Introduction to a Metaphysic of Hope* (London: Victor Gollancz Ltd., 1951), p. 30.

10 Ibid., p. 31.

11 W.F. Lynch, *Images*, p. 25.

12 Cf. I.N. Korner, "Hope as a Method of Coping," *Journal of Consulting and Clinical Psychology* 34, no. 2 (1970), pp. 134–139, p. 135; and D. Capps, *Agents*, p. 59.

13 W.F. Lynch, *Images*, p. 135.

14 Ibid., p. 141.

15 See S.R. Staats and M.A. Stassen, "Hope," p. 235; and R.S. Lazarus, "Hope," p. 663.

16 See R.S. Lazarus, "Hope," p. 663.

17 See I.N. Korner, "Hope as a Method," p. 136.

18 See D. Capps, *Agents*, pp. 53–54.

19 See S.R. Staats and M.A. Stassen, "Hope," p. 235.

20 I.N. Korner, "Hope as a Method," p. 137.

21 On the centrality of the goal aspect in the psychological literature on hope, see S.E. Hobfoll, M. Briggs-Phillips, and L.R. Stines, "Fact or Artifact: The Relationship of Hope to a Caravan of Resources," in R. Jacoby and G. Keinan (eds) *Between Stress and Hope: From a Disease-centered to a Health-centered Perspective* (New York: Greenwood, 2005), pp. 81–104, p. 94; and J.F. Miller and M.J. Powers, "Development of an Instrument to Measure Hope," *Nursing Research* 37, no. 1 (1988), pp. 6–10, p. 7.

22 See C.R. Snyder et al, "The Will and the Ways: Development and Validation of an Individual Differences Measure of Hope," *Journal of Personality and Social Psychology* 60 (1991), pp. 570–585; C.R. Snyder, J. Cheavans, and S.C. Sympson, "Hope: An Individual Motive for Social Commerce," *Dynamics: Theory, Research, and Practice* 1, no. 2 (1997), pp. 107–118; C.R. Snyder, "Hypothesis: There is Hope," in C.R. Snyder (ed.) *Handbook of Hope: Theory, Measures, and Applications* (New York: Academic

Press, 2000), pp. 3–21; and C.R. Snyder, J. Cheavans and S.T. Michael, "Hope Theory: History and Elaborated Model," in J.A. Eliott (ed.) *Interdisciplinary Perspectives on Hope* (New York: Nova Science Publishers, 2005), pp. 101–118.

23 C.R. Snyder et al, "The Will and the Ways," p. 571.

24 C.R. Snyder, "Hypothesis," p. 9.

25 See C.R. Snyder et al, "Hope Theory," pp. 105–106.

26 C.R. Snyder, "Hypothesis," p. 9.

27 C.R. Snyder et al, "Hope: An Individual Motive," p. 108.

28 Cf. S.E. Hobfoll et al, "Fact or Artifact," p. 85.

29 C. Pearson, "The Future of Optimism," *American Psychologist* 55, no. 1 (Jan. 2000), pp. 44–55, p. 47.

30 G. Marcel, *Homo Viator*, p. 34.

31 Ibid., p. 60.

32 Ibid., p. 58.

33 G. Marcel, "Desire and Hope," in N. Lawrence and D. O'Connor (eds) *Readings in Existential Phenomenology* (Englewood Cliffs: Prentice-Hall, 1967), pp. 277–285, p. 285.

34 See K. Weingarten, "Witnessing, Wonder, and Hope."

35 See K. Weingarten, "Hope in a Time of Global Despair," pp. 2–3.

36 Ibid., p. 3.

37 See ibid., p. 5.

38 See K. Weingarten, "Witnessing, Wonder, and Hope" p. 399–401.

39 Ibid., p. 400.

40 G. Marcel, *Homo Viator*, p. 60.

41 Cf. W. Brueggemann, *Hope within History* (Atlanta: John Knox Press, 1987), p. 73.

42 Cf. ibid., pp. 16, 20.

Chapter 6

1 William Lynch, "Theology and the Imagination II: The Evocative," *Thought* 29 (1954), pp. 529–554, p. 545.

2 Lynch, "Theology and the Imagination," *Thought* 29 (1954), pp. 61–86, p. 68.

3 See Lynch, *Images of Faith: An Exploration of the Ironic Imagination* (Notre Dame: University of Notre Dame Press, 1973), pp. 12–13.

4 Lynch, *Images of Faith*, p. 64.

5 Ibid., p. 64.

6 Lynch, "Images of Faith II: The Task of Irony," *Continuum* 7 (1969), 478–492, p. 478.

7 Lynch, "Theology and the Imagination II," p. 538.

8 Ibid., p. 541.

9 See Lynch, "Theology and the Imagination," p. 69.

10 Ibid., p. 61.

11 See ibid., p. 72.

12 Ibid., p. 73.

13 Lynch, *Christ and Prometheus: A New Image of the Secular* (Notre Dame: University of Notre Dame Press, 1970), p. 23.

14 Lynch, "Theology and the Imagination," p. 66.

15 Lynch, *Images of Faith*, p. 78.

16 Cf. Gerald J. Bednar, *Faith as Imagination: The Contribution of William F. Lynch* (Kansas City: Sheed & Ward, 1996), p. 54.

17 Donne's poem is discussed in Lynch's "Theology and the Imagination," p. 74.

18 See Lynch, "Images of Faith II," pp. 187–194; 190; *Christ and Prometheus*, p. 23.

19 See Lynch, *Images of Faith*, p. 84.

20 See ibid., p. 84.

21 Ibid., p. 85.

22 See Lynch, "Images of Faith II," p. 489.

23 Lynch, *Images of Faith*, p. 88.

24 See ibid., pp. 90–92.

25 See Lynch, "Images of Faith II," p. 491.

26 Others have noted the relationship between Christian paradox and our imaginative capacity. See, for example, D. Louw, "Creative Hope and Imagination in Practical Theology," *Religion and Theology/Religie and Teologie* 8, nos. 3–4 (2001), pp. 327–344. He suggests that it is the aesthetic imagination that allows us to hold together the contraries of ugliness and beauty in the suffering of God:

> While theoretical reason involves the values of true and false, and practical reason involves good and evil or the right and wrong, aesthetic reason seeks to portray the beautiful and the ugly, the sublime and lowly, or the deep and the superficial. To perform this act, an aesthetic reason needs imagination and creativity (p. 334).

27 Lynch, "Images of Faith II," p. 492.

28 Lynch, *Images of Faith*, p. 93.

29 These images come from Dorothy Rowe. See her *Breaking the Bonds: Understanding Depression, Finding Freedom* (London: Fontana, 1991), pp. 9–10.

30 See Andrew Solomon, *The Noonday Demon: An Anatomy of Depression* (London: Vintage, 2002), p. 18.

31 See Constance Hammen, *Depression* (Hove, East Sussex: Psychological Press, 1998), pp. 4–7.

32 See ibid., p. 4; and Michael E. Thase and Susan S. Lang, *Beating the Blues: New Approaches to Overcoming Dysthymia and Chronic Mild Depression* (New York: Oxford University Press, 2004), p. 27.

33 See Aaron T. Beck, *Depression: Clinical, Experimental, and Theoretical Aspects* (New York: Harper & Row, 1967).

34 Thase and Lang, *Beating the Blues*, p. 18.

35 Solomon, *Noonday Demon*, p. 19.

36 See Thase and Lang, *Beating the Blues*, p. 89.

37 J. Beck, *Cognitive Therapy: Basics and Beyond* (New York: The Guilford Press, 1995), p. 16.

38 See Thase and Lang, *Beating the Blues*, p. 12.

39 Solomon, *Noonday Demon*, p. 24.

40 Parker J. Palmer, *Let Your Life Speak: Listening for the Voice of Vocation* (San Francisco: Jossey-Bass, 2000), p. 66.

41 Palmer, ibid., p. 67.

42 Siroj Sorajjakool, "*Wu Wei* (Non-doing) and the Negativity of Depression," *Journal of Religion and Health* 39, no. 2 (Sum. 2000), pp. 159–166, p. 165.

43 See ibid., p. 160.

44 Ray Billington, *Understanding Eastern Philosophy* (London: Routledge, 1997), 92.

45 Sorajjakool, "*Wu Wei*," pp. 165–166.

46 Ibid., p. 166.

47 Elisabeth Kübler-Ross, *On Death and Dying* (London: Tavistock Publications, 1970), xi.

48 Ibid., p. 46.

49 Ibid., p. 122.

50 Cf. Lynne A. De Spelder and Albert L. Strickland, *The Last Dance: Encountering Death and Dying*, 6th edn (Boston: McGraw Hill, 2002), p. 158.

51 Robert J. Kastenbaum, *Death, Society, and Human Experience*, 9th edn (Boston: Pearson, Allyn & Bacon, 2007), p. 134.

52 See ibid., pp. 134–136, and Charles A. Corr, Clyde M. Nabe, and Donna M. Corr, *Death and Dying, Life and Living*, 5th edn (Belmont.: Thomson Wadsworth, 2006), pp. 134–137, for critiques of the Kübler-Ross model.

53 Kastenbaum, *Death*, p. 134.

54 Cf. Robert Buckman, *I Don't Know What to Say* (Melbourne.: Sun, 1990), p. 39.

55 De Spelder et al, *Last Dance*, p. 156.

56 Kübler-Ross, *On Death*, p. 122.

57 On this, see C.A. Corr, "A Task-Based Approach to Coping with Dying," *Omega: Journal of Death and Dying* 24, no. 2 (1991–1992), pp. 81–94.

58 See L. Bregman and S. Thiermann, *First Person Mortal: Personal Narratives of Dying, Death, and Grief* (New York: Paragon House, 1995), pp. 171–173.

59 They refer to Max Lerner's personal account of his fight against two cancers and a heart attack set out in his book *Wrestling with the Angel* (New York: W.W. Norton, 1990).

60 Bregman and Thiermann, *First Person*, p. 172.

61 Ibid., p. 173.

62 E. Gee, *The Light Around the Dark* (New York: National League for Nursing Press, 1992), 71; cited in Bregman and Thiermann, *First Person*, p. 171.

63 G. Sheehan, *Going the Distance: One Man's Journey to the End of His Life* (New York: Villard, 1996), p. 86.

64 Ibid., p. 87.

65 Ibid., p. 87.

66 Ibid., pp. 88, 90.

67 Cf. Donald Senior, *Invitation to Matthew* (New York: Image Books, 1977), p. 60.

68 See Ulrich Luz, *Matthew 1–7: A Continental Commentary*, trans. W.C. Linss (Minneapolis: Fortress Press, 1992), 237. Luz points out that "poor in spirit" refers not to a circumstance but to an attitude. It means "lowly in spirit", humble.

69 See Robert H. Gundry, *Matthew: A Commentary on His Handbook for a Mixed Church Under Persecution*, 2nd edn (Grand Rapids: Eerdmans, 1994), p. 67; Craig S. Keener, *A Commentary on the Gospel of Matthew* (Grand Rapids: Eerdmans, 1999), pp. 168–169.

70 See Luz, *Matthew 1–7*, p. 236.

71 See Keener, *A Commentary*, 170; Donald Senior, *Matthew* (Nashville: Abingdon, 1998), p. 71.

72 Cf. Senior, *Invitation*, p. 61.

73 See Senior, *Invitation*:

> [T]he "poor in spirit," the "gentle," or meek, the "mournful," those who hunger and thirst for what is right … are promised happiness or blessing *now* in view of a *future* reward. The disciples of Jesus can begin to be happy now, because their future is so assured that its promise gladness spills over into the present. (p. 60)

74 See Gundry, *Matthew*, p. 71.

75 See Luz, *Matthew 1–7*, p. 237; Warren Carter, *Matthew and the Margins* (Sheffield: Sheffield Academic Press, 2000), p. 135.

76 See T.C. Falla, *Be Our Freedom Lord*, 2nd edn (Adelaide: OpenBook Publishers, 1994), pp. 99–100.

77 See D. Louw, "Creative Hope and Imagination."

78 Panel of Worship of the Church of Scotland, *Common Order* (Edinburgh: Saint Andrew Press, 1994), p. 163.

Introduction to Part 4

1 The term comes from Don Browning. See his *The Moral Context of Pastoral Care* (Philadelphia: Westminster Press, 1976). See also, J. Poling,

"Ethical Reflection and Pastoral Care: Part 1," *Pastoral Psychology* 32, no. 2 (Win. 1983), pp. 106–114, and idem, "Ethical Reflection and Pastoral Care: Part 2," *Pastoral Psychology* 32, no. 2 (Spr. 1984), pp. 160–170; G. Noyce, *The Minister as Moral Counselor* (Nashville: Abingdon Press, 1989); R. Miles, *The Pastor as Moral Guide* (Minneapolis: Fortress Press, 1998); and N. Pembroke, *The Art of Listening: Dialogue, Shame, and Pastoral Care* (Grand Rapids: Eerdmans, 2002), chp. 5.

Chapter 7

1 P. Hopper, *Rebuilding Communities in an Age of Individualism* (Aldershot: Ashgate, 2003), p. 3.

2 On renewal in faith through the sacraments, see E.T. Charry, "Sacraments for the Christian Life," *The Christian Century* (Nov. 15, 1995), pp. 1076–1079, p. 1076.

3 See, for example, R. Hovda, "Individualists are Incapable of Worship," *Worship* 65, no. 1 (1991), pp. 69–74, p. 72.

4 D. Browning, *The Moral Context of Pastoral Care* (Philadelphia: The Westminster Press, 1976), p. 12.

5 U. Beck and E. Beck-Gernsheim, *Individualization* (Thousand Oaks: SAGE Publications, 2002), p. 22.

6 See ibid., p. 23.

7 K.J. Gergen, *The Saturated Self* (New York: Basic Books, 2000), p. 150.

8 Cf. U. Beck and E. Beck-Gernsheim, *Individualization*, p. 23.

9 Ibid., p. 4.

10 Cf. P. Heelas, "Introduction: Detraditionalization and Its Rituals," in P. Heelas, S. Lash, and P. Morris (eds) *Detraditionalization* (Oxford: Blackwell Publishers, 1996), pp. 1–20, p. 2.

11 Cf. A. Giddens, "Living in a Post-Traditional Society," in U. Beck, A. Giddens, and S. Lash, *Reflexive Modernization* (Cambridge: Polity Press, 1994), pp. 56–109, p. 75.

12 C. Campbell, "Detraditionalization, Character, and the Limits of Agency," in P. Heelas et al (eds), *Detraditionalization* (Oxford: Blackwell Publishers, 1996), pp. 149–169, p. 163.

13 On this trend, see P. Hopper, *Rebuilding Communities*, p. 41.

14 Z. Bauman, "Morality in the Age of Contingency," in P. Heelas et al (eds) *Detraditionalization* (Oxford: Blackwell Publishers, 1996), pp. 49–58, p. 51.

15 See R.J. Lifton, *The Protean Self* (New York: Basic Books, 1993).

16 See Z. Bauman, "Morality in the Age of Contingency," pp. 52–58.

17 Ibid., p. 53.

18 See P. Hanson, *The People Called: The Growth of Community in the Bible* (San Francisco: Harper & Row, 1986), p. 3.

19 Niebuhr made this statement in the course entitled "Pilgrimages" at the Harvard Divinity School in 1982. It is cited in C.F. Senn, "Journeying as Religious Education: The Shaman, the Hero, the Pilgrim, and the Labyrinth Walker," *Religious Education* 97, no. 2 (Spr. 2002), pp. 124–140, p. 124.

20 Cf. R. Kuiken, "Hopeful Feasting; Eucharist and Eschatology," in W.H. Lazareth (ed.) *Hope for Your Future: Theological Voices from the Pastorate* (Grand Rapids: Eerdmans, 2002), pp. 192–198, p. 194.

21 *Sacrosanctum Concilium* 8, the documents of the Second Vatican Council; cited in A. Dulles, "The Eucharist and the Mystery of the Trinity," in R.A. Kereszty (ed.) *Rediscovering the Eucharist: Ecumenical Conversations* (Mahwah: Paulist Press, 2003), pp. 226–239, p. 232.

22 E. Charry, "Sacraments," p. 1076.

23 Cf. P. Atkins, *Memory and Liturgy* (Aldershot: Ashgate, 2004), p. 43.

24 *Uniting in Worship 2* (Sydney: Uniting Church Press, 2005), p. 93.

25 Cf. G. Lohfink, *Jesus and Community* (London: SPCK, 1985), p. 41.

26 P. Casarella, "Eucharist: Presence of a Gift," in R.A. Kereszty (ed.) *Rediscovering the Eucharist: Ecumenical Conversations* (Mahwah: Paulist Press, 2003), pp. 199–225, p. 201.

27 E. Byron Anderson, *Worship and Christian Identity: Practicing Ourselves* (Collegeville: Pueblo Books, 2003), p. 58. Ron Byars makes a similar point when he says, "Worship not only expresses a faith already present, but it forms and nurtures it ... We grow into the faith represented in our worship" [*The Future of Protestant Worship* (Louiseville: Westminster John Knox Press, 2002), p. 26].

28 R. Hovda, "Individualists are Incapable of Worship," pp. 69–74, p. 72.

29 Cf. J. Fodor, "Reading the Scriptures: Rehearsing Identity, Practicing Character," in S. Hauerwas and S. Wells (eds) *The Blackwell Companion to Christian Ethics* (Oxford: Blackwell, 2004), pp. 141–155, p. 150.

30 S. Hauerwas, *Christian Existence Today* (Durham: The Labyrinth Press, 1988), p. 106.

31 See ibid., p. 107.

32 Ibid., p. 107.

33 M.B. Brewer and W. Gardner, "Who is this 'We'? Levels of Collective Identity and Self Representations," *Journal of Personality and Social Psychology* 71, no. 1 (1996), pp. 83–93, p. 87.

34 Ibid., p. 90.

35 See D. Trafimow, H.C. Triandis, and S.G. Goto, "Some Tests of the Distinction Between the Private Self and the Collective Self," *Journal of Personality and Social Psychology* 60, no. 5 (1991), pp. 649–655.

36 Ibid., p. 650.

37 Ibid., p. 653.

38 This point is made by a number of theologians. See, for example, E. Byron Anderson, *Worship and Christian Identity*; D. Ford, *Self and Salvation: Being*

Transformed (Cambridge: Cambridge University Press, 1999); C. Pickstock, *After Writing: On the Liturgical Consummation of Philosophy* (Oxford: Blackwell, 1998); and D.D. Murphy, "Worship as Catechesis: Knowledge, Desire, and Christian Formation," *Theology Today* 58, no. 3 (Oct. 2001), pp. 321–332.

39 Murphy, "Worship," pp. 326–327.

40 J.H. Yoder, "Sacrament as Social Process: Christ the Transformer of Culture," *Theology Today* 48, no. 1 (Apr. 1991), pp. 33–44, p. 38.

41 Cf. Yoder, ibid.

42 Murphy, "Worship," p. 326.

43 Ford, *Self*, p. 122.

44 J. Zizioulas, *Being as Communion: Studies in Personhood and the Church* (London: Darton, Longman & Todd, 1985), p. 81.

Chapter 8

1 See D.M. Buss, "Unmitigated Agency and Unmitigated Communion: An Analysis of the Negative Components of Masculinity and Femininity," *Sex Roles* 22, nos 9/10 (1990), pp. 555–568; V.S. Hegelson, "Relation of Agency and Communion to Well-being: Evidence and Potential Explanations," *Psychological Bulletin* 116, no. 3 (1994), pp. 412–428; H.L. Fritz and V.S. Hegelson, "Distinctions of Unmitigated Communion from Communion: Self-Neglect and Overinvolvement with Others," *Journal of Personality & Social Psychology* 74, no. 1 (1998), pp. 121–140; and V.S. Hegelson and H.L. Fritz, "Unmitigated Agency and Unmitigated Communion: Distinctions from Agency and Communion," *Journal of Research and Personality* 33 (1999), pp. 131–158.

2 See, for example, D. Browning, *Religious Thought and the Modern Psychologies* (Philadelphia: Fortress Press, 1987), pp. 150–156; S. Pope, "Expressive Individualism and True Self-Love: A Thomistic Perspective," *The Journal of Religion* 71, no. 3 (Jul. 1991), pp. 384–399; S. Post, "Communion and True Self-Love," *The Journal of Religious Ethics* 16 (Fall 1988), pp. 345–362, and idem, "The Inadequacy of Selflessness," *Journal of the American Academy of Religion* 56, no. 2 (1989), pp. 213–228; G. Outka, "Universal Love and Impartiality," in E. Santuri and W. Werpehowski (eds) *The Love Commandments: Essays in Christian Ethics and Moral Philosophy* (Washington: Georgetown University Press, 1992), pp. 1–103.

3 See, for example, B. Gill-Austern, "Love Understood as Self-Sacrifice: What Does It Do to Women?" in J.S. Moessner (ed.) *Through the Eyes of Women: Insights for Pastoral Care* (Minneapolis: Fortress Press, 1996), pp. 304–321; K. Ramsay, "Losing One's Life for Others: Self-Sacrifice Revisited," in S.F. Parsons (ed.) *Challenging Women's Orthodoxies in the Context of Faith* (Aldershot: Ashgate, 2000), pp. 121–133; R.E. Groenhout,

"I Can't Say No: Self-Sacrifice and an Ethics of Care," in R.E. Groenhout and M. Bower (eds) *Philosophy, Feminism, and Faith* (Bloomington: Indiana University Press, 2003), pp. 152–174.

4 See H.L. Fritz and V.S. Hegelson, "Distinctions of Unmitigated Communion from Communion," p. 121.

5 *Book of Common Order of the Church of Scotland* (Edinburgh: Saint Andrew Press, 1996), p. 346.

6 Ibid., p. 346.

7 Ibid., p. 347.

8 See D. Bakan, *The Duality of Human Existence: Isolation and Communion in Western Man* (Boston: Beacon Press, 1966).

9 Ibid., p. 15.

10 Ibid., p. 14.

11 See ibid., p. 14.

12 V.S. Hegelson and H.L. Fritz, "Unmitigated Agency and Unmitigated Communion," p. 132.

13 Cf. R.E. Groenhout, "I Can't Say No," pp. 157–158.

14 M. Glaz and J. Stevenson Moessner, *Women in Travail and Transition* (Minneapolis: Fortress Press, 1991), p. 198. Cited in B. Gill-Austern, "Love Understood as Self-Sacrifice," p. 305.

15 B. Gill-Austern, "Love Understood as Self-Sacrifice," p. 306.

16 See H.L. Fritz and V.S. Hegelson, "Distinctions of Unmitigated Communion from Communion," and V.S. Hegelson and H.L. Fritz, "Unmitigated Agency and Unmitigated Communion."

17 See ibid.

18 See B. Gill-Austern, "Love Understood as Self-Sacrifice," p. 319.

19 See C.M. LaCugna, *God For Us: The Trinity and Christian Life* (San Francisco: HarperSanFrancisco, 1992).

20 T. Peters, *God as Trinity* (Louiseville: Westminster/John Knox Press, 1993), p. 15.

21 C.M. LaCugna, *God For Us,* p. 304.

22 See D. Cunningham, These Three are One: The Practice of Trinitarian Theology (Oxford: Blackwell, 1998), chp. 2.

23 See Aquinas, *Summa Theologiae*, Ia.2,1–5. I have used the edition trans. by T. Gilby (London: Eyre & Spottiswoode, 1964, 1965).

24 See P. Fiddes, *Participating in God: A Pastoral Doctrine of the Trinity* (London: Darton, Longman, and Todd, 2000), p. 36ff.

25 Ibid., p. 36.

26 C.M. LaCugna, *God For Us,* p. 271.

27 D. Cunningham, "Participation as a Trinitarian Virtue," *Toronto Journal of Theology* 14, no. 1 (1998), pp. 7–25, p. 19.

28 T.J. Scirghi, "The Trinity: A Model for Belonging in Contemporary Society," *The Ecumenical Review* 54, no. 3 (2002), pp. 333–342, p. 334.

29 For descriptions of *circumincessio* and *circumsessio*, see R. Leupp, *Knowing the Name of God: A Trinitarian Tapestry of Grace, Faith and Community* (Downer's Grove: InterVarsity Press, 1995), pp. 161–162; and J. Moltmann, "Perichoresis: An Old Magic Word for a New Trinitarian Theology," in M.D. Meeks (ed.) *Trinity, Power and Community* (Nashville: Kingswood Books, 2000), p. 114.

30 D. Cunningham, "Participation," p. 10.

31 J. Moltmann, "Perichoresis," p. 114.

32 See G. Outka, *Agape: An Ethical Analysis* (New Haven: Yale University Press, 1972), esp. pp. 9–16 and 290–291, and idem, "Universal Love and Impartiality."

33 See D. Browning, *Religious Thought and the Modern Psychologies*, pp. 150–156; and D. Browning and C. Browning, "The Church and the Family Crisis: A New Love Ethic," *The Christian Century* 108, no. 23 (Aug. 7, 1991), pp. 746–749.

34 S. Post, "The Inadequacy of Selflessness," p. 213.

35 See S. Post, "Communion and True Self-Love," p. 345.

36 S. Post, ibid., p. 345.

37 See G. Outka, "Universal Love and Impartiality."

38 See D. and C. Browning, "The Church and the Family Crisis,", p. 749.

39 See G. Outka, "Universal Love and Impartiality," p. 4ff.

40 See ibid., p. 80ff.

Bibliography

Adams, M.M., *Wrestling for Blessing* (London: Darton, Longman & Todd, 2005).

Aden, L.H. and Hughes, R.G., *Preaching God's Compassion* (Minneapolis: Fortress Press, 2002).

Allen, R.J., *Preaching and Practical Ministry* (St. Louis: Chalice Press, 2001).

Ames, D.R. and Flynn, F.J., "What Breaks a Leader: The Curvilinear Relation Between Assertiveness and Leadership," *Journal of Personality and Social Psychology* 92, no. 2 (2007), pp. 307–324.

Anderson, E.B., *Worship and Christian Identity: Practicing Ourselves* (Collegeville: Pueblo Books, 2003).

Aquinas, T., *Summa Theologiae: Vol. 2.*, trans. T. Gilby et al. (London: Eyre & Spottiswoode, 1964, 1965).

Assembly of the Uniting Church in Australia, *Uniting in Worship 2* (Sydney: Uniting Church Press, 2005).

Atkins, P., *Memory and Liturgy* (Aldershot: Ashgate, 2004).

Augustine, *City of God* (London: Dent, 1945).

—, "The Punishment and Forgiveness of Sins and the Baptism of Little Ones," in *Answer to the Pelagians* I, in J. Rotelle (ed.) *The Works of St. Augustine*, Part I, vol. 23 (New York: New City Press, 1990).

—, *Confessions*, trans. Henry Chadwick (Oxford: Oxford University Press, 1991).

Ausubel, D., "Relationships between Shame and Guilt in the Socializing Process," *Psychological Review* 62, no.15 (1955), pp. 379–390.

Averill, J.R., *Anger and Emotion: An Essay on Emotion* (New York: Springer-Verlag, 1982).

Babcock, M. and Sabini, J., "On Differentiating Embarrassment from Shame," *European Journal of Social Psychology* 20 (1990), pp. 151–169.

Bakan, D., *The Duality of Human Existence: Isolation and Communion in Western Man* (Boston: Beacon Press, 1966).

Barth, K., *Church Dogmatics* IV.1 (Edinburgh: T&T Clark, 1951).

—, *Church Dogmatics* IV.2 (Edinburgh: T&T Clark, 1958).

—, *Church Dogmatics* III.3 (Edinburgh: T & T Clark, 1960).

—, *Church Dogmatics* III.4 (Edinburgh: T & T Clark, 1961).

Batson, C.D., Kobrynowicz, D., Dinnerstein, J.L., Kampf, H.C., and Wilson, A.D., "In a Very Different Voice: Unmasking Moral Hypocrisy," *Journal of Personality and Social Psychology* 72, no. 6 (1997), pp. 1335–1343.

Batson, C.D., Thompson, E.R., Seuferling, G., Whitney, H., and Strongman, J.A., "Moral Hypocrisy: Appearing to be Moral to Oneself without Being so," *Journal of Personality and Social Psychology* 77, no. 3 (1999), pp. 525–537.

Batson, C.D., Thompson, E.R., and Chen, H., "Moral Hypocrisy: Addressing Some Alternatives," *Journal of Personality and Social Psychology* 83, no. 2 (2002), pp. 330–339.

Bauman, Z., "Morality in the Age of Contingency," in P. Heelas, S. Lash and P. Morris . (eds) *Detraditionalization* (Oxford: Blackwell Publishers, 1996), pp. 49–58.

Beck, A.T., *Depression: Clinical, Experimental, and Theoretical Aspects* (New York: Harper & Row, 1967).

Beck, J., *Cognitive Therapy: Basics and Beyond* (New York: The Guilford Press, 1995).

Beck, U. and Beck-Gernsheim, E., *Individualization* (Thousand Oakes: SAGE Publications, 2002).

Bednar, G.J., *Faith as Imagination: The Contribution of William F. Lynch* (Kansas City: Sheed & Ward, 1996).

Biddle, M., *Missing the Mark: Sin and Its Consequences in Biblical Theology* (Nashville: Abingdon, 2005).

Billington, R., *Understanding Eastern Philosophy* (London: Routledge, 1997).

Billman, K.D. and Migliore, D.L., *Rachel's Cry: Prayer of Lament and Rebirth of Hope* (Cleveland: United Church Press, 1999).

Blumenthal, D., *Facing the Abusing God: A Theology of Protest* (Louiseville: Westminster John Knox Press, 1993).

—, "Liturgies of Anger," *CrossCurrents* 52, no. 2 (2002), pp. 178–199.

Bohart, A., "Role Playing and Interpersonal-Conflict Reduction," *Journal of Counseling Psychology* 24, no. 1 (1977), pp. 15–24.

Boulton, M., "Forsaking God: A Theological Argument for Christian Lamentation," *Scottish Journal of Theology* 55, no. 1 (2002), pp. 58–78.

Bregman, L. and Thiermann, S., *First Person Mortal: Personal Narratives of Dying, Death, and Grief* (New York: Paragon House, 1995).

Brewer, M.B. and Gardner, W., "Who is this 'We'? Levels of Collective Identity and Self Representations," *Journal of Personality and Social Psychology* 71, no. 1 (1996), pp. 83–93.

Browning, D., *The Moral Context of Pastoral Care* (Philadelphia: The Westminster Press, 1976).

—, *Religious Thought and the Modern Psychologies* (Philadelphia: Fortress Press, 1987).

Browning, D. and Browning, C., "The Church and the Family Crisis: A New Love Ethic," *The Christian Century* 108, no. 23 (Aug 7, 1991), pp. 746–749.

Brueggemann, W., *The Message of the Psalms* (Minneapolis: Augsburg, 1984).

—, "A Shape for Old Testament Theology I: Structure Legitimation," *Catholic Biblical Quarterly* 47 (1985), pp. 28–46.

—, "A Shape for Old Testament Theology, II: Embrace of Pain," *Catholic Biblical Quarterly* 47 (1985), pp. 395–415.

—, *Hope within History* (Atlanta: John Knox Press, 1987).

—, "Prerequisites for Genuine Obedience: Theses and Conclusions," *Calvin Theological Journal* 36 (2001), pp. 34–41.

—, "The Friday Voice of Faith," *Calvin Theological Journal* 36, no. 1 (2001), pp. 12–21.

Buckman, R., *I Don't Know What to Say* (Melbourne: Sun, 1990).

Buss, D.M., "Unmitigated Agency and Unmitigated Communion: An Analysis of the Negative Components of Masculinity and Femininity," *Sex Roles* 22, nos 9/10 (1990), pp. 555–568.

Byars, R., *The Future of Protestant Worship* (Louisville: Westminster John Knox Press, 2002).

Calvin, J., *Institutes of the Christian Religion*, trans. Henry Beveridge (Grand Rapids: Eerdmans, 1989).

Campbell, C., "Detraditionalization, Character, and the Limits of Agency," in P. Heelas, S. Lash, and P. Morris (eds), *Detraditionalization* (Oxford: Blackwell Publishers, 1996), pp. 149–169.

Capps, D., *Life Cycle Theory and Pastoral Care* (Minneapolis: Fortress Press, 1983).

—, *The Depleted Self: Sin in a Narcissistic Age* (Minneapolis: Fortress Press, 1993).

—, *Agents of Hope: A Pastoral Psychology* (Minneapolis: Fortress Press, 1995).

Carney, S., "God Damn God: A Reflection on Expressing Anger in Prayer," *Biblical Theology Bulletin* 13 (1983), pp. 116–120.

Carter, W., *Matthew and the Margins* (Sheffield: Sheffield Academic Press, 2000).

Casarella, P., "Eucharist: Presence of a Gift," in R.A. Kereszty (ed.) *Rediscovering the Eucharist* (Mahwah: Paulist Press, 2003), pp. 199–225.

Charry, E.T., "Sacraments for the Christian Life," *The Christian Century* (Nov 15, 1995), pp. 1076–1079.

—, "May We Trust God and (Still) Lament? Can We Lament and (Still) Trust God?" in S.A. Brown and P.D. Miller (eds) *Lament: Reclaiming Practices in Pulpit, Pew, and Public Square* (Louisville: Westminster John Knox Press, 2005), pp. 95–108.

Christ, C., "Expressing Anger at God," *Anima* 5 (1978), pp. 3–10.

Clebsch, W.A., and Jaekle, C.R., *Pastoral Care in Historical Perspective* (Englewoods Cliffs: Prentice-Hall, 1964).

Clements, R.E., *Jeremiah* (Atlanta: John Knox Press, 1988).

Clinebell, H., *Basic Types of Pastoral Care and Counseling*, rev. edn (Nashville: Abingdon Press, 1984).

Corr, C.A., "A Task-Based Approach to Coping with Dying," *Omega: Journal of Death and Dying* 24, no. 2 (1991–1992), pp. 81–94.

Corr, C.A., Nabe, C.M., and Corr, D.M., *Death and Dying, Life and Living*, 5th edn (Belmont: Thomson Wadsworth, 2006).

Crichton, J.D. , "A Theology of Worship," in C. Jones, G. Wainwright, and E. Yarnold (eds) *The Study of Liturgy* (London: SPCK, 1985), pp. 1–29.

Cunningham, D., "Participation as a Trinitarian Virtue," *Toronto Journal of Theology* 14, no. 1 (1998), pp. 7–25.

—, *These Three are One: The Practice of Trinitarian Theology* (Oxford: Blackwell, 1998).

Dawn, M., *Reaching Out without Dumbing Down* (Grand Rapids: Eerdmans, 1995).

Delamater, R.J., and McNamara, J.R., "Perceptions of Assertiveness by Women Involved in a Conflict Situation," *Behavior Modification* 15, no. 2 (1991), pp. 173–193.

De Spelder, L.A., and Strickland, A.L., *The Last Dance: Encountering Death and Dying*, 6th edn (Boston: McGraw Hill, 2002).

Duff, N.J., "Recovering Lamentation as a Practice of the Church?" in S.A. Brown and P.D. Miller (eds) *Lament: Reclaiming Practices in Pulpit, Pew, and Public Square* (Louisville: Westminster John Knox Press, 2005), pp. 3–14.

Dulles, A., "The Eucharist and the Mystery of the Trinity," in R.A. Kereszty (ed.) *Rediscovering the Eucharist: Ecumenical Conversations* (Mahwah: Paulist Press, 2003), pp. 226–239.

Ellens, J.H., "Sin or Sickness: The Problem of Human Dysfunction," in *Seeking Understanding: The Strob Lectures, 1986–1998* (Grand Rapids: Eerdmans, 2001), pp. 439–489. Falla, T.C., *Be Our Freedom Lord*, 2nd edn (Adelaide: OpenBook Publishers, 1994).

Fiddes, P., *Participating in God: A Pastoral Doctrine of the Trinity* (London: Darton, Longman, and Todd, 2000).

Fodor, J., "Reading the Scriptures: Rehearsing Identity, Practicing Character," in S. Hauerwas and S. Wells (eds) *The Blackwell Companion to Christian Ethics* (Oxford: Blackwell, 2004), pp. 141–155.

Ford, D., *Self and Salvation: Being Transformed* (Cambridge: Cambridge University Press, 1999).

Fowler, G., *Caring Through the Funeral* (St. Louis: Chalice Press, 2004).

Fowler, J., *Faithful Change: The Personal and Public Challenges of Post-modern Life* (Nashville: Abingdon Press, 1996).

Fritz, H.L., and Hegelson, V.S., "Distinctions of Unmitigated Communion from Communion: Self-Neglect and Overinvolvement with Others," *Journal of Personality & Social Psychology* 74, no. 1 (1998), pp. 121–140.

Gee, E., *The Light Around the Dark* (New York: National League for Nursing Press, 1992).

Gergen, K.J., *The Saturated Self* (New York: Basic Books, 2000).

Gervasio, A.H., "Assertiveness Techniques as Speech Acts," *Clinical Psychology Review* 7 (1987), pp. 105–119.

Giddens, A., "Living in a Post-Traditional Society," in U. Beck, A. Giddens, and S. Lash (eds) *Reflexive Modernization* (Cambridge: Polity Press, 1994), pp. 56–109.

Gilbert, P., "What is Shame? Some Core Issues and Controversies," in P. Gilbert and B. Andrews (eds) *Shame: Interpersonal Behavior, Psychopathology, and Culture* (Oxford: Oxford University Press, 1998), pp. 3–38.

Gill-Austern, B., "Love Understood as Self-Sacrifice: What Does It Do to Women?" in J.S. Moessner (ed.) *Through the Eyes of Women: Insights for Pastoral Care* (Minneapolis: Fortress Press, 1996), pp. 304–321.

Glaz, M. and Stevenson Moessner, J., *Women in Travail and Transition* (Minneapolis: Fortress Press, 1991).

Goldstein, V.S., "The Human Situation: A Feminine View," *Journal of Religion* 40 (1960), pp. 100–112.

Goodliff, P., *With Unveiled Face: A Pastoral and Theological Exploration of Shame* (London: Darton, Longman & Todd, 2005).

Green, R.A. and Murray, E.J., "Expression of Feelings and Cognitive Reinterpretation in the Reduction of Hostile Aggression," *Journal of Consulting and Clinical Psychology* 43, no. 3 (1975), pp. 375–383.

Gregersen, N.H., "Guilt, Shame, and Rehabilitation: The Pedagogy of Divine Judgment," *Dialog: A Journal of Theology* 39, no. 2 (Sum. 2000), pp. 105–118.

Groenhout, R.E., "I Can't Say No: Self-Sacrifice and an Ethics of Care," in R.E. Groenhout and M. Bower (eds) *Philosophy, Feminism, and Faith* (Bloomington: Indiana University Press, 2003), pp. 152–174.

Gundry, R.H., *Matthew: A Commentary on His Handbook for a Mixed Church Under Persecution*, 2nd edn (Grand Rapids: Eerdmans, 1994).

Hammen, C., *Depression* (Hove, East Sussex: Psychological Press, 1998).

Hanson, P., *The People Called: The Growth of Community in the Bible* (San Francisco: Harper & Row, 1986).

Hauerwas, S., *Christian Existence Today* (Durham: The Labyrinth Press, 1988).

Heelas, P., "Introduction: Detraditionalization and Its Rituals," in P. Heelas, S. Lash, and P. Morris (eds) *Detraditionalization* (Oxford: Blackwell Publishers, 1996), pp. 1–20.

Hegelson, V.S., "Relation of Agency and Communion to Well-being: Evidence and Potential Explanations," *Psychological Bulletin* 116, no. 3 (1994), pp. 412–428.

Hegelson, V.S., and Fritz, H.L., "Unmitigated Agency and Unmitigated Communion: Distinctions from Agency and Communion," *Journal of Research and Personality* 33 (1999), pp. 131–158.

Heller, A., *The Power of Shame: A Rational Perspective* (London: Routledge & Kegan Paul, 1985).

Herth, K., "Fostering Hope in Terminally ill People," *Journal of Advanced Nursing* 15 (1990), pp. 1250–1259.

Hobfoll, S.E., Briggs-Phillips, M., and Stines, L.R., "Fact or Artifact: The Relationship of Hope to a Caravan of Resources," in R. Jacoby and G. Keinan (eds) *Between Stress and Hope: From a Disease-centered to a Health-centered Perspective* (New York: Greenwood, 2005), pp. 81–104.

Holt, R.R., "On the Interpersonal and Intrapersonal Consequences of Expressing or Not Expressing Anger," *Journal of Consulting and Clinical Psychology* 35, no. 1 (1970), pp. 8–12.

Hopper, P., *Rebuilding Communities in an Age of Individualism* (Aldershot: Ashgate, 2003).

Hovda, R., "Individualists are Incapable of Worship," *Worship* 65, no. 1 (1991), pp. 69–74.

Karen, R., "Shame," *The Atlantic Monthly* (February 1992), pp. 40–70.

Kastenbaum, R.J., *Death, Society, and Human Experience*, 9th edn (Boston: Pearson, Allyn & Bacon, 2007).

Keener, C.S., *A Commentary on the Gospel of Matthew* (Grand Rapids: Eerdmans, 1999).

Kennedy-More, E. and Watson, J.C., "How and When Does Emotional Expression Help?" *Review of General Psychology* 5, no. 3 (2001), pp. 187–212.

Kettunen, P., "The Function of Confession: A Study Based on Experiences," *Pastoral Psychology* 51, no. 1 (Sept. 2002), pp. 13–25.

Kinast, R., *Sacramental Pastoral Care* (New York: Pueblo, 1988).

Korner, I.N., "Hope as a Method of Coping," *Journal of Consulting and Clinical Psychology* 34, no. 2 (1970).

Kübler-Ross, E., *On Death and Dying* (London: Tavistock Publications, 1970).

Kuiken, R., "Hopeful Feasting: Eucharist and Eschatology," in W.H. Lazareth (ed.) *Hope for Your Future: Theological Voices from the Pastorate* (Grand Rapids: Eerdmans, 2002), pp. 192–198.

LaCugna, C.M., *God For Us: The Trinity and Christian Life* (San Francisco: HarperSanFrancisco, 1992.

Laytner, A., *Arguing with God: A Jewish Tradition* (Northvale: Jason Aronson, 1990).

Lazarus, R.S., "Hope: An Emotion and a Vital Coping Resource against Despair," *Social Research* 66, no. 2 (Sum. 1999), pp. 653–678.

Lerner, M., *Wrestling with the Angel* (New York: W.W. Norton, 1990).

Lester, A., *Hope in Pastoral Care and Counseling* (Louiseville: Westminster John Knox Press, 1995).

Leupp, R., *Knowing the Name of God: A Trinitarian Tapestry of Grace, Faith and Community* (Downers Grove: InterVarsity Press, 1995).

Lewis, H.B., *Shame and Guilt in Neurosis* (New York: International Universities Press, 1971).

Lieberman, M.A., Yalom, I.D., and Miles, M.B., *Encounter Groups: First Facts* (New York: Basic Books, 1973).

Lifton, R.J., *The Protean Self* (New York: Basic Books, 1993).

Littrell, J., "Is the Reexperience of Painful Emotion Therapeutic?" *Clinical Psychology Review* 18, no. 1 (1998), pp. 71–102.

Lohfink, G., *Jesus and Community* (London: SPCK, 1985).

Louw, D., "Creative Hope and Imagination in Practical Theology," *Religion and Theology/Religie and Teologie* 8, nos. 3–4 (2001), pp. 327–344.

Luz, U., *Matthew 1–7: A Continental Commentary*, trans. W.C. Linss (Minneapolis: Fortress Press, 1992).

Lyall, D., *Integrity of Pastoral Care* (London: SPCK, 2001).

—, "The Bible, Worship, and Pastoral Care," in P. Ballard and S.R. Holmes (eds) *The Bible in Pastoral Practice* (Grand Rapids: Eerdmans, 2005), pp. 225–240.

Lynch, W.F., "Theology and the Imagination," *Thought* 29 (1954), pp. 61–86.

—, "Theology and the Imagination II: The Evocative," *Thought* 29 (1954), pp. 529–554.

—, "Images of Faith II: The Task of Irony," *Continuum* 7 (1969), 478–492.

—, *Christ and Prometheus: A New Image of the Secular* (Notre Dame: University of Notre Dame Press, 1970).

—, *Images of Faith: An Exploration of the Ironic Imagination* (Notre Dame: University of Notre Dame Press, 1973).

—, *Images of Hope: Imagination as Healer of the Hopeless* (Notre Dame: University of Notre Dame Press, 1974).

Lynd, H.M., *On Shame and the Search for Identity* (New York: Harcourt, Brace & World, Inc., 1958).

Marcel, G., *Homo Viator: Introduction to a Metaphysic of Hope* (London: Victor Gollancz Ltd., 1951).

—, "Desire and Hope," in N. Lawrence and D. O'Connor (eds) *Readings in Existential Phenomenology* (Englewood Cliffs: Prentice-Hall, 1967), pp. 277–285.

Marion, J-L., *God without Being* (Chicago: University of Chicago Press, 1991).

Miles, R., *The Pastor as Moral Guide* (Minneapolis: Fortress Press, 1998).

Miller, J.F., and Powers, M.J., "Development of an Instrument to Measure Hope," *Nursing Research* 37, no. 1 (1988), pp. 6–10.

Moltmann, J., "Perichoresis: An Old Magic Word for a New Trinitarian Theology," in M.D. Meeks (ed.) *Trinity, Power and Community* (Nashville: Kingswood Books, 2000).

Moltmann-Wendel, E., *A Land Flowing with Milk and Honey: Perspectives on Feminist Theology* (New York: Crossroad, 1986).

—, "Self-love and Self-acceptance," *Pacifica* 5 (Oct. 1992), pp. 288–301.

Murphy, D.D., "Worship as Catechesis: Knowledge, Desire, and Christian Formation," *Theology Today* 58, no. 3 (Oct. 2001), pp. 321–332.

Nathanson, D., *Shame and Pride: Affect, Sex, and the Birth of the Self* (New York: W.W. Norton & Co., 1992).

Niebuhr, R., *The Nature and Destiny of Man*, vol. 1 (London: Nisbet & Co., 1941).

Noyce, G., *The Minister as Moral Counselor* (Nashville: Abingdon Press, 1989).

Outka, G., *Agape: An Ethical Analysis* (New Haven: Yale University Press, 1972).

—, "Universal Love and Impartiality," in E. Santuri and W. Werpehowski (eds) *The Love Commandments: Essays in Christian Ethics and Moral Philosophy* (Washington: Georgetown University Press, 1992), pp. 1–103.

Paarlberg, J., "Genuine Sorrow . . . Wholehearted Joy: The Why, When, and How of Confession," *Reformed Worship* 34 (1994), pp. 4–8.

Palmer, P.J., *Let Your Life Speak: Listening for the Voice of Vocation* (San Francisco: Jossey-Bass, 2000).

Panel of Worship of the Church of Scotland, *Common Order* (Edinburgh: Saint Andrew Press, 1994.

Pattison, S., *A Critique of Pastoral Care* (London: SCM Press, 1993).

—, *Shame: Theory, Therapy, Theology* (Cambridge: Cambridge University Press, 2000).

Pearson, C., "The Future of Optimism," *American Psychologist* 55, no. 1 (Jan. 2000), pp. 44–55.

Pembroke, N., *The Art of Listening: Dialogue, Shame, and Pastoral Care* (Edinburgh: T&T Clark & Grand Rapids: Eerdmans, 2002).

Peters, T., *God as Trinity* (Louiseville: Westminster John Knox Press, 1993).

Pickstock, C., *After Writing: On the Liturgical Consummation of Philosophy* (Oxford: Blackwell, 1998).

Plantinga, C., "Not the Way It's S'pposed to Be: A Breviary of Sin," *Theology Today* 50, no. 2 (1993), pp. 179–192.

Plantinga, C. and Rozeboom, S.A., *Discerning the Spirits: A Guide to Thinking About Christian Worship Today* (Grand Rapids: Eerdmans, 2003).

Plaskow, J., *Sex, Sin, and Grace: Women's Experience and the Theologies of Reinhold Niebuhr and Paul Tillich* (Lanham: University Press of America, 1980).

Poling, J., "Ethical Reflection and Pastoral Care: Part 1," *Pastoral Psychology* 32, no. 2 (Win. 1983), pp. 106–114.

—, "Ethical Reflection and Pastoral Care: Part 2," *Pastoral Psychology* 32, no. 2 (Spr. 1984), pp. 160–170.

Pope, S., "Expressive Individualism and True Self-Love: A Thomistic Perspective," *The Journal of Religion* 71, no. 3 (Jul. 1991), pp. 384–399.

Post, S., "Communion and True Self-Love," *The Journal of Religious Ethics* 16 (Fall 1988), pp. 345–362.

—, "The Inadequacy of Selflessness," *Journal of the American Academy of Religion* 56, no. 2 (1989), pp. 213–228.

Purves, A., *Reconstructing Pastoral Theology: A Christological Foundation* (Louisville: Westminster John Knox Press, 2004).

Quenot, M., *The Icon: Window on the Kingdom* (Crestwood: St. Vladimir's Seminary Press, 1991).

Ramsay, K., "Losing One's Life for Others: Self-Sacrifice Revisited," in S.F. Parsons (ed.) *Challenging Women's Orthodoxies in the Context of Faith* (Aldershot: Ashgate, 2000), pp. 121–133.

Ramsey, G.L., *Care-full Preaching: From Sermon to Caring Community* (St. Louis: Chalice Press, 2000).

Ramshaw, E., *Ritual and Pastoral Care* (Philadelphia: Fortress Press, 1987).

—, "Ritual and Pastoral Care: The Vital Connection," in E. Berstein (ed.) *Disciples at the Crossroads* (Collegeville: Liturgical Press, 1993).

Roffman, A.E., "Is Anger a Thing-to-be-Managed?" *Psychotherapy: Theory, Research, Practice, Training* 41, no. 2 (2004), pp. 161–171.

Rowe, D., *Breaking the Bonds: Understanding Depression, Finding Freedom* (London: Fontana, 1991).

Schneider, C., *Shame, Exposure, and Privacy* (New York: W.W. Norton, 1992).

Scirghi, T.J., "The Trinity: A Model for Belonging in Contemporary Society," *The Ecumenical Review* 54, no. 3 (2002), pp. 333–342.

Senior, D., *Invitation to Matthew* (New York: Image Books, 1977).

—, *Matthew* (Nashville: Abingdon, 1998).

Senn, C.F., "Journeying as Religious Education: The Shaman, the Hero, the Pilgrim, and the Labyrinth Walker," *Religious Education* 97, no. 2 (Spr. 2002), pp. 124–140.

Sheehan, S., *Going the Distance: One Man's Journey to the End of His Life* (New York: Villard, 1996).

Sheppy, P.P.J., *Death Liturgy and Ritual: A Pastoral and Liturgical Theology* (Aldershot: Ashgate, 2003).

Snyder, C.R., "Hypothesis: There is Hope," in C.R. Snyder (ed.) *Handbook of Hope: Theory, Measures, and Applications* (New York: Academic Press, 2000), pp. 3–21.

Snyder, C.R., Harris, C., Anderson, J.R., Holleran, S.A., Irving, L.M., Sigmon, S.T., Yoshinobu, L., Gibb, J., Langelle, C., and Harney, R., "The Will and the Ways: Development and Validation of an Individual Differences Measure of Hope," *Journal of Personality and Social Psychology* 60 (1991), pp. 570–585.

Snyder, C.R., Cheavans, J., and Sympson, S.C., "Hope: An Individual Motive for Social Commerce," *Dynamics: Theory, Research, and Practice* 1, no. 2 (1997), pp. 107–118.

Snyder, C.R., Cheavans, J. and Michael, S.T., "Hope Theory: History and Elaborated Model," in J.A. Eliott (ed.) *Interdisciplinary Perspectives on Hope* (New York: Nova Science Publishers, 2005), pp. 101–118.

Solomon, A., *The Noonday Demon: An Anatomy of Depression* (London: Vintage, 2002).

Sorajjakool, S., "*Wu Wei* (Non-doing) and the Negativity of Depression," *Journal of Religion and Health* 39, no. 2 (Sum. 2000), pp. 159–166.

Staats, S.R. and Stassen, M.A., "Hope: An Affective Cognition," *Social Indicators Research* 17 (1985), pp. 235–242.

Tangney J.P., Hill-Barlow, P., Wagner, P.E., Marschall, D.E., Borenstein, J.K., Sanftner, J., Mohr, T., and Gramzow, R., "Assessing Individual Differences in Constructive Versus Destructive Responses to Anger Across the Lifespan," *Journal of Personality and Social Psychology* 70, no. 4 (1996), pp. 780–796.

Taylor, H.V., "The General Confession of Sin," *Reformed Liturgy and Music* 26 (1992), pp. 179–183.

Thase, M.E., and Lang, S.S., *Beating the Blues: New Approaches to Overcoming Dysthymia and Chronic Mild Depression* (New York, Oxford: Oxford University Press, 2004).

Thrane, G., "Shame," *Journal for the Theory of Social Behavior* 92 (1979), pp. 139–166.

Thurneysen, E., *A Theology of Pastoral Care* (Richmond: John Knox Press, 1962).

Tillich , P., *Systematic Theology*, vol. 2 (London; Nisbet & Co., 1957).

Tomkins, S., "Shame," in D. Nathanson (ed.) *The Many Faces of Shame* (New York: Guilford Press, 1987), pp. 133–161.

Trafimow, D., Triandis, H.C., and Goto, S.G., "Some Tests of the Distinction Between the Private Self and the Collective Self," *Journal of Personality and Social Psychology* 60, no. 5 (1991), pp. 649–655.

Underwood, R.L., *Pastoral Care and the Means of Grace* (Minneapolis: Fortress Press, 1993).

Van Deusen Hunsinger, D., *Pray without Ceasing: Revitalizing Pastoral Care* (Grand Rapids: Eerdmans, 2006).

Weingarten, K., "Witnessing, Wonder, and Hope," *Family Process* 39, no. 4 (2000), pp. 389–402.

—, "Cancer, Meaning Making, and Hope: The Treatment Dedication Project," *Families, Systems, and Health* 23, no. 2 (2005), pp. 155–160.

—, "Hope in a Time of Global Despair," Unpublished paper delivered at the International Family Therapy Association Conference, Reykjavick, Iceland, October 4–7, 2006.

Westermann, C., *Praise and Lament in the Psalms* (Atlanta: John Knox Press, 1981).

—, "The Complaint against God," in T. Linafelt and T.K. Beal (eds) *God in the Fray* (Minneapolis: Fortress Press, 1998), pp. 233–241.

Whybray, N., *Job* (Sheffield: Sheffield academic Press, 1998).

Williams, R., *The Dwelling of the Light: Praying with Icons of Christ* (Norwich: Canterbury Press, 2003).

Williamson, H.G.M., "Reading the Lament Psalms Backwards," in B.A. Strawn and N.R. Bowen (eds) *A God So Near* (Winona Lake: Eisenbrauns, 2003), pp. 3–15.

Willimon, W.H., *Worship as Pastoral Care* (Nashville: Abingdon Press, 1979).

—, *Pastor: The Theology and Practice of Ordained Ministry* (Nashville: Abingdon Press, 2002).

Wilson, K., and Gallois, C., *Assertion and Its Social Context* (Oxford: Pergamon Press, 1993).

Wilson, P.S., *The Four Pages of the Sermon* (Nashville: Abingdon Press, 1999).

Wimberly, E.P., *Moving from Shame to Self-worth: Preaching and Pastoral Care* (Nashville: Abingdon Press, 1999).

Witvliet, J.D., "The Opening of Worship: Trinity," in L. van Dyk (ed.) *A More Profound Alleluia* (Grand Rapids: Eerdmans, 2005), pp. 1–5.

Wolterstorff, N., "Suffering Love," in T.V. Morris (ed.) *Philosophy and the Christian Faith* (Notre Dame: University of Notre Dame Press, 1988), pp. 196–237.

—, "If God is Good and Sovereign, Why Lament?" *Calvin Theological Journal* 36 (2001), pp. 42–52.

Wurmser, L., *The Mask of Shame* (Baltimore: The John Hopkins University Press, 1981).

—, "Shame: The Veiled Companion of Narcissism," in D. Nathanson (ed.) *The Many Faces of Shame* (New York: Guilford Press, 1987), pp. 64–92.

Yoder, J.H., "Sacrament as Social Process: Christ the Transformer of Culture," *Theology Today* 48, no. 1 (Apr. 1991), pp. 33–44.

Zizioulas, J., *Being as Communion: Studies in Personhood and the Church* (London: Darton, Longman & Todd, 1985).

Index